Mrs. Maria Thompson Daviess

HISTORY

of

MERCER and BOYLE COUNTIES

[KENTUCKY]

By
MRS. MARIA T. DAVIESS

CLEARFIELD

Originally published
Harrodsburg, Kentucky, 1924

Reprinted for
Clearfield Company, Inc. by
Genealogical Publishing Co., Inc.
Baltimore, Maryland
1998

International Standard Book Number: 0-8063-4774-0

Made in the United States of America

The History of Mercer and : : : Boyle Counties : : :
By Mrs. Maria T. Daviess.

T is customary in bringing a work of this kind before the public to state its origin and intentions. Some years ago my brother, James H. Thompson, of Hillsboro, wrote for the county of Hillsboro, Ohio, a valuable and comprehensive history of it, and sent me a copy.

Afterwards, the wife of the Hon. Thos. L. Jones, of Newport, sent me a history written by her of Campbell county, the place of her nativity and residence. It was brief and interesting, and I concluded that if some one in every county would do a like service for it, that in the future there would be, if collected, a full volume of valuable history. I commenced the collection of material for Mercer several years since, but a succession of heavy trouble drove all unselfish work from my mind, until last spring, having leased my farm and home, I assumed this History as diversion from care, and as I journeyed from place to place, wrote these chapters, which should have been called "Rambling Recollections," or "Desultories," rather than by the pretentious name of History, by which I inconsiderately announced it. It comes before you instead of in book form, through our popular and extensively circulated local paper, and will reach many more readers than it would have reached in book form. It will have its interest to those that are curious about past times and manners and customs of those days, and its value as a reference for dates, and names of men who figured in the stirring times of different periods. It will be in some respects like the Better Land. There will be many in it you did not expect to see and many left out you felt sure of meeting. This selection for our pages had to be made by some rule. We have made the holding of official position the standard. Whoever has held civil or military place, from the lowest to the highest, has been enrolled; whoever has been prominent in any order, organization or popular movement, has been listed. We know

"The rank is but the guinea's stamp;
The gold's the gold for a' that,"

and often the most talented as well as the most excellent of our citizens are found in "that post of honor, a private station." The sources that I have drawn from for this history that I compiled years ago as a text book for my first children. The dates I have corrected rigidly by that invaluable historical gazette, Collin's Kentucky. From President Williams of Daughters' College, I have received encouragement and aid in notes for Bacon College, Christian Church, etc., etc.

By Prof. William Marcus Linney of the State Geological Survey, I have been allowed to draw freely from his very complete surveys of Boyle and Mercer for items concerning rocks, minerals,

The sketches of college, churches, etc., etc., I have obtained from the most prominent members of such organizations and shall acknowledge as used.

soils, timbers, fuma and flora.

From Mr. J. H. Grimes, Jr., I received such interesting notes of Burgin that I shall use them with thanks and without change.

From Dr. Cowan, of Danville, I have had privilege of drawing the most reliable data I could obtain of "Royal Mercer."

From the McKees, Dr. McBeatty and Mrs. Young I have received past and expect future favors as well as from the editor of the Advocate and bank officers of Danville in aid of the History of Boyle, so far as I may carry it.

For material I have drawn on all the histories, books, traditions and memories of myself and my neighbors, squaring all doubtful points and dates by Collin's History of Kentucky, the latest, fullest and most valuable of all authorities on such lore.

To any that shall be disappointed that I do not open the closets wherein are hid the skeltons of old scandal and feuds that have scarred our own in common with all other communities, I beg leave to say, if there be any truth in the degrading and humiliating doctrine of evolution, I am thankful I was not developed through the hyena line. I have no taste for the resurrection of past scandals. The poet and dramatist shall have the monopoly of them. Let the'r memories "Requiescat in peace." May the good shine as stars in the firmament for ever and ever.

PART I

CHAPTER 1

Geography and Boundaries of Mercer County—Rocks, Minerals and Prehistoric Remains.

Mercer county is the geographical center of Kentucky. The boundaries which were originally assigned to Mercer, when Boyle was included in her limits, were Anderson and Woodford on the North; Jessamine and Garrard on the East; Lincoln on the South, and Washington and Anderson on the West. Boyle is now the southern boundary of Mercer, and the turnpike bridge that spans Harrod's run, is on, or near the line; originally this line was a little south of Center College, and if still in existence would divide the town into North and South Danville, and situate them in different counties. Of course the counties mentioned above as boundaries took their names long after the formation of Mercer, except Lincoln, which was one of three into which Kentucky was divided in 1780, and out of which Mercer was taken. By virtue the division of the county in 1842, by which Boyle was made, the area of Mercer was greatly diminished; it now contains about 141,992 acres of land, which according to the last census is divided into 1,406 farms, of which 122,475 acres are improved land and valued (including fencing and building) at $4,337,240; average value per acre, $16.20. Much of this lana is rolling but productive. Dr. D. D. Owens, when he made a geological survey of Kentucky, left on record that the lands known as the "Chapline lands" of Mercer county, Kentucky, was the finest grain growing district in the state. The productions of this section bear out Dr. Owen's in his statement, though one might almost think himself in a Swiss canton as he watches the enterprising plowman, winding his circular furrow up the steep sides of the hills. The eye of the traveler as well as the figures of the statistician, assure us that the belt of land in Mercer and Boyle counties through which the great artery of commerce, the Cincinnati, New Orleans & Texas Pacific Railroad makes its way, belongs to the same class as that of Woodford, Fayette, Clark, Bourbon, etc., etc., which have long been designated as the garden region of the United States.

Those are the natural Dairy Lands of America; and their supremacy in this most remunerative of all branches of rural industry, is but a question of time. The cold regions of the north, where close stabling, high and frequent feeding, involve not only an extensive provision of food, but immense expense of labor in the details of business cannot compete with a section where three-fourths of the year, dairy stock require but an open gate to the pasture and brooks; and for the other fourth of the time, simply shelter, and clover hay to supplement the reserved blue grass pastures. What we need to develop these lands is emigrants from our own or Europe's dairy regions, who have the experience, and can prove the desirableness and practicability of coining mony from these, our rural mines. For the present, our lands are used for the staple crops of Central Kentucky—corn, wheat, rye and hemp; and greatly increased attention is now given to tobacco and potatoes, orchards, grapes and garden stuffs have advanced in area little beyond the domestic wants of the people; but railroads, the great educators in political economy, will doubtless suggest these remunerative industries which, for the present, respond to the cultivator, just in proportion to the care given in their cultivation. Mercer has now but few unbroken forests of valuable timber; there is an abundance of cedar on the cliffs of her rivers, and timbers for railroads and cooperage in the hills. When the woodman's axe has felled these trees in answer to the calls of commerce, these lands opened to the breath and sunshine of Heaven, will soon be clothed in their native far-famed perennial blue grass, and will become what nature intended for them to be, viz.: The orchards and vineyards and sheep walks of the west; bringing in a princely revenue and leaving the land in the improved cleanliness and fertility which only sheep husbandry can produce.

It is a pity to see the stalwart young men of our counties, indeed so often well-to-do families, boarding the cars, bound to some El Dorado of their imaginations, to which they have been lured by the highly colored maps and circulars of land speculators; leaving schools and churches and kindred ties behind them; while the same money invested in our wild lands here, with far less of hardships and labor, would bring them returns in fortune fully equal to any venture in the far west and keep them undisturbed in all the precious blessings of their fathers' land.

But as this sweeping geographical description of the surface of these counties will not probably meet the spirit of this investigating age which demands to be carried down to the very root of matter, I must descend below the surface and declare briefly the geology of this section, its rocks and minerals, and the waters that flow through them. According to Indian tradition, "this whole continent (this whole world) stands on a huge mastodon; the mastodon on an immense turtle; and the turtle on what is nobody's business." Accepting this Indian traditional foundation, we find it overlaid with rocks of many ages, growth, naturally divided, and now classified by geologists. According to scientists, in the long, long ago, these rocks were rent by some tremendous convulsive force, and through the many fissures thus produced, and by the water which over-swept these heights, were drained of untold stores of carbon in a decomposed state into the insatiate sea, leaving uncovered Mercer and Boyle and others of the richest counties of the state. All of the rock beds of this county, belonged to the Silurian age, and those left exposed to investigation are about 800 feet in thickness, and are comprised in the Trenton and Canadian epochs. The grand old towers of High Bridge, those indestructible monuments of the enterprise and folly of men who went to work without counting the cost, were built of Chazy limestone, as is the heavy masonry supporting High Bridge, and it is estimated there is enough of it left in the quarries of the cliffs to supply the wants of the world for an indefinite period; and it may be required, for nothing is more common now than to see great trains laden with stone, in transportation from one section of the country to another. In the rocks of the Trenton group is found what is called Kentucky marble. It has been largely used in the construction of High Bridge, and in other work of the Cincinnati, New Orleans & Texas Pacific Railroad. It is, however, well adapted to finer uses and works very smooth, but I have seen none wearing the lustre of foreign marbles. The Clay monument at Lexington, Kentucky, is built of it, as was one of the several State houses we have had in Frankfort, Ky. It was built entirely of this abundant and beautiful stone, and was accounted in its day a marvel of magnificence, and was one of the several costly burnt offerings we have made to the demon of carelessness. In the bird's eye group, are found many beds that work easily and well. The brotherhood of Pleasant Hill have utilized this stone in building, and have made of it tables and other domestic conveniences. It is a beautiful material which like Kentucky marble, abounds in our cliff quarries.

What we commonly call limestone is found all through our counties, and occasionally, but not abundantly, what we term fire rock, which is said to be the stone of which the Capitol at Nashville is built and called Tennessee marble; of this there is a fine quarry on the farm of Mr. Lafon. If Mercer and Boyle have not precious metals or coal, we have material of which kings' palaces might be built and furnished; and of commoner material an abundance to extend and keep up for ages, turnpikes, those indispensible feeders of railroads and the unvalued but invaluable tributaries to social intercourse, the crowning charm of life.

This part of Boyle was never a part of Mercer, but formed a part of Lincoln county. The Ohio Shale and Waverly are the prevailing foundation of the knobby regions of Boyle. These hills are covered with chestnut and pine, and in the lowlands between, with sycamore and maple. These growths might be thinned out, grass sown and thus be profitably devoted to pastoral purposes; but if ever cleared and cultivated they will be irretrievably lost.

Minerals.—Several varieties are found in these counties, such Barytes, Galena, Zinc, Blende, Quartz and Calcite.

But I mark in italics that the geological survey of Dr. Owens and the later and more particular investigations of Mr. Linney, have found no stores of metal, coal, or oil, sufficient to lure the miner or speculator to these regions; nothing to turn the honest tiller of the soil from his ever surety remunerative labor. Part of the county is very cavernous; usually these caves are but reservoirs of water, some of them very valuable for dairy purposes. There is said to be in the neighborhood of Harrodsburg one, not very large, but full of beautiful stalagmites and stalactites. It has never been fully explored nor reliably reported. Mineral springs abound in Mercer and Boyle counties. There is scarcely a neighborhood or large farm that has not some medical spring. The Alum Springs of Boyle have doubtless great virtue and had considerable and rapidly growing reputation and patronage until the building was destroyed by fire. Harrodsburg has a number of springs besides the very celebrated Greenville waters in the grounds of Daughters' College and those opened by Dr. Graham in his palmy days of youth and usefulness.

There are on the adjoining farms of Messrs. Nat Lafon and John C. Thompson, south of Harrodsburg, water that by analysis shows very unusual and valuable medical qualities.

Very lately a well has been bored on the farm of Mr. John Dean, which is of the taste and properties almost identical with the celebrated Blue Lick waters.

There are pure and strong Sulphur waters in several town homesteads and one of fine quality at the Danville tollgate just beyond the handsome home of Mr. Henry Bonta.

Pre-historic Remains.—These are not abundant in our county, doubtless the larger part of them having been lost by the ignorance or carelessness of the finders. Many families have some curious bone, or stone or implement that would make an interesting link in this chain of history.

Some Mastodon bones were found on the land of the Shakers in making an excavation for some farm purpose, and these are now a part of the very interesting collection of natural curiosities in the cabinet of Daughters' College.

The late Capt. Bisset also found some teeth and other remains of this class in some Kentucky river bottom land. On the farm of Hon. J. Kyle, on Salt river, a tumulus was examined in which were found some skeletons of human beings, implements of bone and pottery of domestic utility, showing that in the remote past this country had been inhabited by a race who had commerce with other people somewhat skilled in the uses of metals and other concomitants of a rude civilization. These mounds, Aztec hieroglyphics and Indian traditions, all agree in confirmation of the fact of prehistoric occupancy of this country. The tradition derived from the aborigines is, that in the long, long ago, the Lenni-Lennapes and the Iroquois from the far west, made an almost coincident emigration to the eastward. They finally leagued together and expelled the Allegeni who possessed these fertile lands, almost exterminating them, in proof of which, immense quanties of human remains have been found in the region around Danville; and some islands in the Ohio are said to mark the locality where the final decisive battle was fought between the hostile tribes, the Allegini being exterminated. Whether the allies could not divide the lands or settle the question of supremacy between themselves does not appear. Kentucky was never again inhabited with Indians. It was used as hunting grounds thereafter by northern and southern tribes, and their frequent and sanguinary conflicts gave to it is well known name, "Dark and Bloody Ground," a title confirmed to it, by its being for years the sanguinary battlefield, where the Indians and whites contended for possession. The whites triumphed; they are undoubtedly the sons of Japheth, and if there be any truth in the theory that the Indians are the lost tribe of Israel, then for more than a hundred years has been fulfilling the prophesy uttered thousands of years ago, "that God shall enlarge Japheth and he shall dwell in the tents of Shem, and Ham shall be his servant."

CHAPTER TWO

Soils, Timbers, Flora and Rivers.

SOILS OF MERCER AND BOYLE COUNTIES

The received theory of soils is, that they are the product of the decomposition of rocks, mixed with the humus of decayed vegetable matter that the overshadowing forests have shed upon them for ages.

Perhaps it would be sufficient for the general reader to say, that Salt river is the natural dividing line between the soils that characterize Mercer and Boyle.

To the east of this river, extending nearly to the Kentucky and Dix rivers and into Boyle, around Danville, to where the knobs begin to swell, is found the soil, for which has been coined the new geological term of "Blue Grass beds." It has always been an article of Kentucky's creed concerning herself, that the grass was indignous to Central Kentucky and to Central Kentucky only, and from thence had been carried to congenial soils. Lately there have sprung up many pretenders to this same princely birth-right. Last summer a prominent Ohio journal claimed that some soldier (name forgotten) returning from a northern campaign, found this grass in some border county of Ohio and brought the seed thence to Central Kentucky. Very lately it has been stated, that a few sods were brought from western Virginia, and from these it has spread over our state. This question will do for farmers' clubs to debate and settle; and we will go on to say that the "Blue Grass beds" are based on the lower silurian, and this soil has been named thus because on it this famous and as yet most valuable of all grass grows most luxuriously, and it is on this soil also that hemp delights to revel.

The bold spring known as boiling spring, or better still, as big spring, on the suburban farm of Wm. Payne, has its source in this granular limestone, as has also another, Fountain Blue, on the beautiful farm of James Forsythe, Jr. Any farmer can have a sample of his soil analysed at the State's Agricultural College, and learning in what elements it is deficient, can by the use of proper fertilizers and judicious rotation bring his land to blue grass standard, for the soil of the blue grass region is as nearly perfect for all agricultural uses as earth has ever yet become.

The river bottoms of Mercer are rich, but of course there are deposits left by the streams when high waters bring in their contributions. There is no very large area of river bottom however, the Dix and the Kentucky being fenced in mainly with precipitous cliffs, and what I have denominated the local streams, having their way chiefly among the hills. Salt river flows shallow and almost on the surface of the country, and has more bottom land on its course than all the rest of the country streams.

The lands west of Salt river do not produce blue grass spontaneously, but are what Dr. Owens denominated the finest cereal lands in Kentucky, but from their rolling character they should be put in some congenial grass and be used chiefly for grazing purposes.

Silicous mud stone, is a term applied to the soil which lies west of Dry Creek. This country, if cleared of trees and loosened by cultivation, being of rounded hills, will soon wash ruinously into gullies. These hills should never be shorn entirely of trees, but have the undergrowth cleared out, the trees thinned out and trimmed high, and the ground kept covered with some perrennial grass of matting-root variety. These lands differ from the knobs of

Old Fort Hill Cemetery

Boyle, which are founded on the Waverly shale, and once cleared can never be retrieved, but blast the landscape with a dreariness scarcely surpassed by the most desolate volcano regions.

But all in all, while the abuse of our counties' lands has been shameful, there is no section of the west where intelligent, careful cultivation meets a more abundant and ready response.

I have tried faithfully to get a fair average per acre of the staple crops of these counties but there were such wide distances between the lowest and highest figures returned that I have concluded to set the highest reliable figures that have been given me as the standard to which the farmer should bend his efforts:

Hemp, 2,400 pounds.
Corn, 140 bushels.
Wheat, 45 bushels.
Rye, 35 bushels.
Oats, 60 bushels.
Hay, 4 tons per acre.
Tobacco, 2,000 pounds.

The cultivation of the last staple was very common in this county in the past half century of our county's existence, I cannot fix precisely the time, but think between twenty and forty years. Its cultivation has been too lately revived to give positive figures, but the above I had from good authority and I understand over 2,000 acres were planted in Mercer. But it should be remembered that manuring as yet is confined chiefly to the garden and flower beds. Few fields have had any artificial stimulus. Commercial fertilizers as yet have no place in our county price currents. There is, however, generally practiced a healthy rotation of crops, clover being the almost universal agent of restoration, few having adopted such high farming as the plowing under of green crops, the only fertilizing system the prudent farmer can use.

Timbers of Mercer and Boyle.

Save in the west, beyond the Rocky mountains, there was no country probably more magnificently clad with primeval forests than our own state, and no part of the state was more grandly timbered than Central Kentucky. On the cliffs cedar abounds. On the knobs cedar, pine and chestnut are native. The sycamore, walnut, wild cherry, chinqupin—all trees that love rich, moist ground—were found distributed over this section. Poplar and yellow wood were here; hickory, ash, lordly oaks in all varieties flourished, and sugar maples crowned the hills.

Of these great forests, much was used for building and fencing; a good deal for furniture; and clearing were necessarily made for the farmer. But none can deny, and all should lament the wanton desrtuction that has been made of our timber resources, especially since the investigation of our timber resources show that, beside being drawn on so heavily for use in building, in fencing, and for commerce; drouth, increase of insects, of some undiscovered reason, is causing large classes of our trees to die out, notably the elm and white oak. The least thoughtful person in the community must be grieved at not only the death of the trees, but at the drying up of the springs and many brooks that used to go singing through our woods like merry children. The beneficent clouds that would fain discharge their precious waters on the thirsting fields now follow the line of the woods and leave them to drouth and disappointment. Scientists, who are the wise ones in such matters, say the loss of our springs and the frequency of drouths, are both caused by the destruction of our forests.

The time has therefore come not only to withhold the axe from the tree, but also to plant judiciously seed or young trees on almost every farm. Let there be clumps of trees to shelter the cattle, belts of trees to shield garden, orchard and field from the cold winds that come sweeping across the cleared lands; rows of trees beside the highways for the rest and refreshment of the wayfarer; on every hill which you cannot cultivate, plant trees—plant, and they will grow while you sleep; and in a few years you can begin to thin out for handles and spokes, chair rounds and hoop poles; and in thirty years you will find you have timber for plantation use. There are but three conditions of success in this matter: Plant well and thick, and keep stock from them. Notice what valuable timber grows best on your soil, and remember that the woods which are the most useful for fencing, building and furniture will always bring the best price in the market.

The grape-vine, paw-paw and black haws, sumach, hazel, wild honeysuckle, laurel, red bud, dogwood, spice wood, blackberry and cane, constituted chiefly the original undergrowth of our county, and still hold possession wherever the pruning and clearing hand of man has not been. Occasionally some very handsome shrub is found worthy of transplanting on the lawn; but these are rare now except in the gorges of the cliffs.

Summer and winter grape vines, Virginia creeper, five leaved ivy, poison oak, ulstaria, btter sweet, sarsaparilla, and morning glory, were some of the most noticeable vines.

Flora of Mercer County

The trees, vines and undergrowth of our county, I have given in classes; selecting from the complete list of Mr. Linney, such as I knew to be valuable. I have used, not their botanical, but common names, and shall follow the same rule in a select list of the flowers that were found in our wilds. Of shrubs, there were prickly and common alder, wahoo, hawthorn, dogwood, red bud, tulip tree and bass wood. Of flowers, anemone, crow foot, lark spur, wild flax, violets, pinks, wild roses, sweet briar, snake root, silk weed, clovers, hydrangea, cardinal flowers, phlox, blue flag, lilies of the valley, wild sunflowers, golden rod, ferns in great variety, and ground ivy in verdant masses. Of weeds, were found cockle burrs, burdock in variety, spanich needle, plantians, mullen, horse weed, thistles, iron weed, rag weed and wild buckwheat and nettles. The fibre of the last was substituted for flax in early days, but according to Henry Ward Beecher's matchless definition of a weed, viz.: "Any plant where we do not want it," the nettle now ranks as an undesirable nuisance.

Nuts—Hickory, walnut, chestnut and hazelnut, were found here.

Of fruits, strawberries, raspberries, blackberries, red and black haws, and huckleberries, wild cherries, plums, hackberries. may apples, crab apples, wild gooseberries, summer and winter grapes, and persimmons.

Of vegetables, the indigenous sort were scarce: They were, carrots, lamb's quarter, mustard, pepper grass, parsnips but poisonous, ginseng, angelica, calamus, cumprey, belong to the medical class of roots, as catnip, hoarhound, mints, balm and bergamot, belong to herb medicines; and many valuable plants may yet be masquerading around us in the disguise of weeds.

The Fauna

The animals which were found when the white man first penetrated this wilderness, were the same as found in all the western wilds, except, perhaps, In the mountains, there were some species that did not haunt our lowlands.

The buffalo we know was here, for he was mentioned as coming up tamely with the cattle during the memorable cold winter of 1780-81. to share their provender. The elk was here, for Gen. Scott once said, "They came rushing through the woods where the trees were not two feet apart sprading antlers ten feet wide." The deer was here in variety; the panther, wild cat, bear, fox opossum, hares or rabbits, ground, gray, fox, and flying squirrels, minks, skunks, weasels, mice and rats, but not the improved imported breed from Norway. Our domestic animals were asses, horses, cows, sheep and hogs, all wisely brought out by emigrants, as helps of hardly inferior importance in practical value to our brethren in black, who came as human chattels, as things then stood. All the larger wild animals are gone from our midst, even almost from the mountains of our state, though slanderous people will insinuate that wolves are still raised there for the sake of their scalps. Within my memory there has been a hunting party organized in Harrodsburg for a deer chase in the Chaplin Hills. Two or three reckless specimens having ventured down from their mountain haunts. There is, too, the tradition that my father killed a large bear in his father's woods. It, too, had wandered down from the mountains. This was about the year 1810. Poor bruin's skin made a fine robe on which we young barbarians were wont to play. His flesh was feasted on by the still lingering pioneer epicures. Bear's oil, then greatly prized both for toilet and medicinal uses, I have heard by mother say, was sent for from far and near, and given away by the bottle and vial.

Pelts were currency in pioneer days, but had far less value then than now. One of the most beautiful for capes I have ever seen was made of mole skins; another, handsomer one, I saw some years later, made of the eyes of peacock's feathers. So we see that, as Solomon says, "there is nothing new under the sun:" our foremothers wore as a makeshift what our dames of fashion exult in now as an artistic achevement of modern dress makers.

Birds.

Possibly some of the favorite birds around us now came, like the audacious little English sparrow, following the foot-prints of civilization. I think I have heard the charge laid to the crow and black bird that, courtier like, they follow men of bettering fortunes. The jay, the red bird, the mocking bird, and the thrush are said to have been here with the robbins and the swallows; and owls, hawks, and eagles were here to prey on them, and turkey buzzards to clean up after their betters were served. Wild ducks and geese floated in the cool sequestered water and Selkirked it over the glassy pool and rivers and all the fish therein; pheasants whirred and drummed, and quail piped in the good green wood, and turkeys gobbled, gobbled, before there were any sheep to answer baa.

Rivers of Mercer County

Kentucky river with Dix forms the eastern boundary line of Mercer county. The Kentucky is navigable at seasons of high water, which seasons are lengthened by locks and dams. These improvements so long needed and projected in the early part of this century, and partially carried into execution many years ago, it has been wisely concluded by our beneficent legislators shall be completed, and an appropriation sufficient for the purpose has been made; and this fine stream will soon carry the products of civilization far up into the hitherto obscure mountainous regions and bring thence the immense mineral and forest wealth of that country. Kentucky river is spanned by a fine bridge of stone and iron, linking us to our neighboring county of Jessamine, and is a part of the Lexington turnpike and was made by that company. Over this river hangs the iron pathway of the great Cincinnati, New Oorleans & Texas Pacific Railway. When projected, it was said to be the highest and longest bridge in the known world. But every year science and enterprise outstrip the achievements of the past, and High Bridge yields to lengthier, loftier spans. In close propinquity to the ends of this bridge stand four colossal stone columns, two in Jessamine and two in Mercer. Had these two arched towers supported the structure intended originally to rest on them, they would have been monuments to Kentucky wisdom and enterprise; as it is, they are monuments of the folly that did not count the cost and practicability of the scheme into which they embarked. They were sold at auction, and for $25, became the property of Ben C. Hardin, a young farmer of Mercer county. Kentucky river was used from the earliest date of commerce in this state for flat boat navigation, and still at high tide, fleets of coal and lumber rafts take advantage of the rise and come down from the mountains to cut rates with steamboats and railroads. About fifty years ago, a small steamer first waked the echo of our hills with its shrill whistle. It came up to present Shaker landing, and people flocked by hundreds from thirty and forty miles around on horseback in severe winter, over almost impassable roads, to see it. A circus in the newest possible frontier could not draw a greater crowd; and no animal in the tent could be inspected with greater curiosity and caution than was that little steamer's engine. Kentucky river rises in the Cumberland range, and passing through several counties by our borders, winds its way by our state's capital, and finally at Carrollton, debouches into the Ohio river.

Dix river, a tributary to Kentucky, rises in Lincoln county, and empties into Kentucky not very far from High Bridge. It has no commercial nor not much agricultural value, save the heavy mists which rise from it. It is nearly every where inaccessible by reason of the high, steep cliffs through which it cuts its way. But between the grand ranges of the Rocky and Alleghany mountains, there is no scenery so wild and grand as borders this stream. The deep, rapid waters of the hurrying river sometimes flow on silently and dark, as an evil destiny, and again rushing on like a torrent of broken sunshine, The granite walls chiefly rise perpendicular and look as though in antideluvian ages they had been riven by some mighty volcanic power of which are seen yet the traces of the smoke and white heat of that awful period. From out of unseen footing rise tremendous trees and luxuriant down-trailing vines and flowers of Alpine beauty and hardiness; while far above, navies of white clouds sail like fleets in the blue ether seas; on the everlasting stars shine down, reminding you that this world of beauty and grandeur is but the vestibule of a higher realm to which we may through faith attain.

Salt river has its source in Boyle county. Chiefly it flows quietly through Mercer, with swinging trees and occasional mills varying its monotonous banks. West of Harrodsburg it indulges itself in a playful rush over a ledge of stones that at low water make a convenent foot bridge for the neighborhood, and at high tide suggests the magnificence that cataracts have; this passage is dignified with the name of falls and affords a popular self-teaching swimming school for the juveniles of the neighborhood and village adjacent. After leaving our county, Salt river attains greater importance and winds its way through several counties and finally empties into the Ohio at West Point. It is navigable in high water for some distance, and we presume its course, like that of true love, never does run smooth, as a rowing up Salt river is often threatened as the climax of disaster and disgrace to the candidate for public honors who has failed "to catch the breeze of popular applause."

Shawnee run, Harrod's run, Chapline, Cane run, Lyon's, Trapnal, Thompson's and other creeks are, if the expression may be allowed about running water, our local streams answering all the farm and mill purposes of the country they refresh with their presence, and may be rendered highly valuable as fish-food producing streams.

CHAPTER III

Earliest Days—Harrod and Comrades in A. D., 1773-74—First Dwellers and Their Hardships—First Marriages and Births in the Fort.

Originally what is now Mercer and Boyle counties was a part of the territory over which Sir Walter Raleigh, the English discoverer in A. D. 1584, threw the broad mantle of claim in the name of Elizabeth, then reigning sovereign of Great Britain and in honor of her maiden Majesty, called Virginia. Therefore the first civil existence of Mercer was under the British flag, being a component part of the territory chartered by the English government to Virginia in 1607. This right was also conferred by the aborigines in 1764, when the Iroquois, or five nations placed themselves under British protection and ceded to them, represented by the Governors of New York and Virginia, all the territory south of the lakes and east of the Illinois river, including the state of Kentucky and in which of course Mercer county was enwrapped.

This territory however remained a nominal possession to her Majesty and her representative Virginia, until far into the eighteenth century, not though that the adventurous did not come in from time to time to spy out the richness and beauty of the land.

In 1654, Col. Wood, an Englishman, was said to have explored Kentucky to the Mississippi. In 1730, John Sallings, a Virginian, was captured by Indians and brought to Kentucky by his captors and with them visited the Salt Licks.

As early as 1747, it is said, Dr. Thomas Walker visited Kentucky; but whether then or twenty years later, as some say, he made no claims, not even those of pre-emption.

In 1769 it is said that Daniel Boone wintered in a cave on the land occupied first as Trigg's Station, after which it became the property of Col. John Thompson, and was called Viney Grove, and is now the property of Mr. Thos. Bowman (1). History records that Daniel Boone stayed in Kentucky that winter. The cave was simply a large overhanging rock, and has no protection whatever from wind and rain unless the thick-set cane brake screened it. The letters D. B. were plainly but rudely carved on a large tree above it. This cave was on the paternal acres of the recounter of these incidents, and she would fain cherish all interesting traditions clinging around it, but—she always had too much respect for D .B.'s good judgment to believe for an hour that he wintered in that one when so many more commodious caves and even hollow trees offered their hospitable shelter all around. As to the letters, the average boy is fond enough of climbing and cutting to make that much history. (2).

In 1670, Capt. Bolt, from Virginia, visited Kentucky, but I can not find his report of his impressions. Earlier than this even, Bosquet, a brilliant young Swiss officer in the service of the Colonial government, was sent West with a command to treat with, or subdue the Indians, and passed down the Ohio; and in the elegant translation of his book of this expedition, he speaks of glimpses of the natural beauties of Kentucky almost as rapturously as Telemachus sang of the Isle of Calypso.

It is said that in 1773, James Harrod felled the first tree that took the shape of a human habitation in Mercer county. Be that as it may, it is certain that in 1774, James Harrod, Abram Hite and Jacob and James Sandusky came to the site of the present Harrodsburg in June, and with thirty other men, laid off the town, first calling it Harrodstown, afterward Old Town, and finally by its present time-honored appellation, allowing one-half acre lot in town, and five acres outside, to each claimant; and said party proceeded to erect a number of log cabins. These cabins, as many others built in different parts of the county, were distributed by chance, and known as lottery cabins. The scheme, however, differed from those of the same class today, as there were in it no blanks. But there seems to have been a wonderful tightening of morals by the close of that decade; for Capt. Hugh McGary was put on record as "no gentleman," fined and disfranchised for betting on a horse race. Such a procedure now would sweep gentlemen from the track as a cyclone does the forest.

To reiterate; first, Mercer county lay dormant in the territory of Virginia. Next, the name of Fincastle covered the premises, out of which in December 1776, was cut the county of Kentucky. In 1780, Kentucky was divided into three counties, Jefferson, Fayette and Lincoln, and when these were subsequently subdivided in 1785, Mercer was formed out of Lincoln, and from this point her active civil history begins, her pioneer history antedating this ten or twelve years. The first settlement having been made by Harrod and company in 1774 at Harrodsburg, there were built the following stations, which I mention without regard to the order in which they were made:

Boiling Spring, one of the four settlements represented in the Transylvania legislature at Boonesboro in 1775. (2).

Brown's Station, six miles east of Harrodsburg. (3).

Danville Station, laid off by Walker Daniel.

Laugherty Station, a mile and a half below Danville.

Fontain Bleu, three miles southwest of Harrodsburg on the Bohontown pike. (4).

Gordon's or Harlan's Station, seven miles east of Danville.

William McAfee's Station, one mile west of Harrodsburg, at the mouth of the town creek.

McAfee's Station, a quarter of a mile from the site of the first New Providence Church, settled by the McAfee brothers. (5).

Major Hugh McGary's Station, head waters of Shawnee Run. (6).

Trigg's Station, five miles north east of Harrodsburg, now known as "Viney Grove." (7).

Wilson's Station, three miles southwest of Harrodsburg (8).

Liberty Fort, three-fourths of a mile below New Providence. (9).

Frowman's Station. I remember once while walking through the late Mrs. J. P. McCann's beautiful grounds, the most gorgeous masses of verdure and bloom I have even seen in private gardens, she pointed out some building in the background, and said: "That, I have been told, was the site of Frowman's Station." I have not been able to trace its history or traditions, and regret that I did not then ask facts of my informant, a woman so replete with general information as well as aesthetic culture and taste. The farm is now the property of one of our prominent farmers, Mr. John L. Cassell. (Now William Spilman place).

These Stations were centers in which families were gathered for mutual protection; the men gradually extending out their farming operations as safety allowed. The more daring and restless sometimes made homes prematurely, and frequently had to retire into the Stations, and often the people of the Stations had to crowd into the stronger forts of which Boonesboro, Harrodsburg and Logan's were for many years most secure. The Stations themselves were sometimes small forts; many times only a collection of log huts, around which strong pickets afforded considerable protection. Usually a spring was enclosed in this stockade, or as near by as possible and sometimes had a rough covered way to it, and women are on record who braved Indian arrows to bring water to thirsting men who could not be spared for a moment from the port-hole, while the vigilant Indian besiegers were around.

The life in these Stations was almost inconceivably hard and rough. The first settlers were not as a mass like the half-kilted hardy Scotch clans. Many had been lords of Manors in the Old Dominion, who had hob-nobbed with Lord Fairfax, and whose dames in stay and hoop had been led down the regal halls of the Belvidere "at Richmond on the James," through the stately minuet by Lord Dunsmore, the King's colonial governor. To such as these, to any, even to the poor Dinah's who first came out, this life must have been worse than Hebrew bondage on the green banks of the Nile. The lives of the pioneer mothers as well as of the pioneer fathers, were full of danger and hardships, and required great endurance, and had in them more of the elements of suffering than belonged to the lot of the next generation, that grew up around them who had never known, as they had, a softer life. A sense of lost good often embitters present evil. These women had mainly left comfortable homes in the old states where air and sunshine flowed in with perfect freedom, but in this narrow, crowded quarters of a fort in which they were compelled to live, such existence as they had led was impracticable, absolutely impossible to them. Respectable dress, so dear to the hearts of gentle women, and the luxuries of the table had been their birthright. These foremothers now struggled bravely to gather around them some rude comforts and conveniences of life, and to implant correct moral principles and knowledge of polite usages of society in their children, and they succeeded. But the existence of such furniture and clothes and modes of society as they had known were for a long time only traditional things to their children who lived on in health and happiness all unconscious of their privations.

Dirt floors, or worse, puncheons, which means split logs with all their prickly splinters for little cold bare feet; a log cut out for a glassless window; bear skin curtains to separate into apartments, and stick chimneys in constant danger of burning, is a description of the early homesteads. Into this uncomfortable habitation the whole family, and often the stranger, crowded, barring all possibility of privacy, the most sacred and coveted of all privileges.

There were but few cooking vessels and few were needed. Vegetables were not indigenous to the soil. Orchards were a long time coming to bearing; bread itself for awhile was almost an unknown luxury. The best meat was abundant in the forest, and turkey breast was used for bread; this with venison and the luscious flesh of the bear, made a very satisfactory meal for hungry men and working women. Everything in the way of furniture and clothing was absolutely the product of manual labor in the first stage of pioneer life. One log sawed out made a way for light and air in the house over which rude slats were nailed to bar out the smaller wild animals, and we presume blinds of skins to exclude the cold of winter. In the corner beside the fire place large enough to hold a heap of logs, was usually a window of sufficient size for four panes of glass; but rarely if ever did that substance transmit the light to the inmates of the room; and very proud indeed was the mistress of the lodge if the oiled paper used as a substitute for glass was pure white, or even of paper that was covered with the previous hierogliphics of distant friends and kinfolks. Bedsteads were made by using the cracks between the logs as rests for side pieces and forks cut from trees for posts. Riven boards, served for bottoms to these as well as for chimney boards, as mantels were called and shelves for cupboards which surely might have borne the modern name of "what-not" most appropriately. Floors, stools, tables, etc., were all constructed of split logs called slabs, which were, by the use of the broad axe, considerably reduced in thickness and somewhat smoother. The material for bedding was of forest growth, being simply dry leaves until straw and shucks were produced. All ambitious and careful housekeepers saved whatever kind of feathers the hunters brought with their game. Table ware, such as trays, bowls, etc., were chiefly dug out or carved out of wood. Of course almost every family had tucked in with the necessaries from home some precious article, which if preserved to our day, are treasured heir-looms and certificates of primitive gentility. Forks there were not, but spoons were made of hard, fine grained wood by hand, and sometimes with great nicety. The writer once had some egg and mustard spoons of apple tree wood sent her, the work of an ex-Governor of a neighboring state, who amused himself with this work in memoriam of his pioneer employment when a boy in Kentucky.

The garments for daily use, as also bedding, were literally just pulled out of the earth in the shape of flax, which having been spread, rotted, broken, swingled, and hackled, was then spun on the picturesque little wheel now so sought by lovers of bric-a-brac and were turned by the foot. It was then woven on the clumsy looms that were sometimes built into the wall and the earth floor; and then the web stretched on the grass for weeks and weeks to be bleached by sprinkled water, sunshine and exposure. In time the home manufacture was produced of such textile fineness and finish that one of the stateliest habitues of our street now in his teens, used handkerchiefs of this linen. In those days gentlemen in good circumstances wore only French broadcloth for dress suits, chiefly blue trimmed with brass buttons. These "store clothes" they brought from the old states. The home clothes of all, for winter, were manufactured of sheep, and some times of buffalo's wool which had been washed and dyed with the various colors afforded by barks of different trees. Walnut brown and sheep grey undyed, were chiefly used for men; and peach tree, sumach, hickory, wild touch-me-not and poke berries furnished the gayer colors for the women and children. At the very first, the warp of these cloths were of flax thread of various grades, and sometimes of the fibre of nettles.

Chapter III—Explanatory Notes

Note 1—The initials referred to above, "D. B." are the property of Henry Cleveland Wood, of Harrodsburg. The square of bark and wood, in which they were carved, is framed and hanging in his home. In Collins' History of Kentucky, page 605, is the following: "Colonel Daniel Boone spent the winter of 1769-70 in a cave on the waters of Shawnee, in Mercer county. A tree marked with his name is yet standing near the head of the cave."

This cave is on the farm now owned by Ben Bennett, on the Handy pike. As the century and a half has passed, the timber been cut away and the land plowed for cultivation the earth has gradually washed down and almost filled the entrance to the cave.

Note 2—Boiling Spring is now known as Cove Spring.

Old Greenville or Daughters College

CHAPTER IV.

Clark's and Jones's Mission to Virginia—First Marriages and Births in the Fort—Indian Adventures—Bowman's Expedition.

It is not in proof that Capt. Harrod and company found the fascination of their wilderness lodges strong enough to hold them through these first winters.

Now, the memorable year of 1775 had come and with it the great battle cloud that spread over the eastern slope of this continent, and the dreadful struggle had begun, which eventuated in the Declaration of Independence, that central epoch of the world's history, from which the waves of progress of human freedom have ever flowed outward and upward. It does seem wonderful that any eye could turn from where thunderbolts of this war were falling; or any steps wander, save instinctively toward the fields where our heroic grandsires were making their long and patient warfare for their own independence and the regeneration of the political world. But God's decree for the scattering of the tribes of the earth, given at Babel, seems to have no limit and is still irresistible. There were brave men and true who loved liberty and feared not the battle, and even courted danger, who sought wider freedom west of the Alleghany mountains, and came to the dangers of the wilderness while the war was in progress in the eastern states.

So the next year following 1774 Col. Harrod was again in Harrodsburg, and the McAfees again in the cane brakes on Salt river, where they cleared land, planted orchards, and raised corn preparatory to bringing out their families the next spring. They then returned to Virginia, leaving some one to care for their new homes and warn off intruders, but did not return until they had had a long service in the Revolutionary war.

In this year, 1775, there was a very spirited protest, signed by eighty-four persons, sent to the honorable Convention of Virginia, protesting against their sanctioning the claims that Col. Henderson made for nearly all the lands in Kentucky as a purchase from the Indians. This claim Virginia totally disallowed, but in consideration of the expense and trouble he had incurred, granted him a body of land twelve miles square; Virginia taking his claim and assuming his obligations to the Indians. The first maps of Kentucky had this body of land marked Henderson's grant.

The ensuing year, 1776, George Rogers Clark and Gabriel Jones, by a general meeting at Harrodsburg, were sent to represent this new community in the General Assembly of Virginia, there to manage affairs for the general good of the settlement; and they also accomplished what they regarded as the crowning work of their mission, viz.: the securing of a considerable stock of gun powder. This powder cost poor Jones' life. He and Clark brought it down the river and secreted it near Limestone. Jones afterwards went as guide to Col. Todd and party who were sent from Harrodsburg for it. They were attacked and overpowered by Indians, Jones being killed. Clark subsequently went for and brought the powder to Harrodsburg. Thus, by appointment, if not by election, Mercer in embryo, gave Fincastle, afterwards Kentucky, representatives in a Colonial Assembly, as odd as it may seem, for our independence was not acknowledged until some time after. This year the Poages, who figure conspicuously in our pioneer history, were added to the garrison of Harrodstown fort. It will be remembered that Mrs. Denton, Hogan and McGary (1) had come previously, and I fear me for my foremother's credit, that Mr. Poage was more welcome than the first messenger of the glad tidings of the Gospel that came to the fort, for present necessities do so press, and Mr. Poage, in the plentitude of his ingenuity, constructed bowls, piggins, noggins, and sundry other conveniences (2) long since superseded by lighter wares which in a double sense never had the value of these productions. He also made a loom and some notable woman, Mrs. McGinty (3), I believe, wove cloth of buffalo wool and nettle fiber; her Eden apparel, not the fig leaf pattern, was more in fashion, for dressed skins made into pants and vests were the rage, and not dyed and embroidered either, as you see such work from Worth's and Niagara now. Mr. Poage was killed in an ambush a few years later, and aside from his social worth, was a felt loss in the little community.

Mrs. Thomas, always mentioned in the pioneer sketches, especially about Harrodsburg's early times, was the daughter of Mr. Poage, and I have always heard a little romance connected with her, concerning the land upon which the writer of this resided many years. It was, a part of it, purchased from the heirs of Mrs. Thomas, nee Poage. It was said the land was not her inheritance, but a devise from a stranger who had known and petted her in the fort; whose very name she could not recall. During this year (1777) two marriages took place in the pioneer community; the first a very sad one. The widow of a Mr. Wilson married James Berry, but four and one-half weeks after her husband's death. She had neither protection nor help, and was forced by the need of both and sense of propriety to secure it in this repugnant way, and it is probable the young man married as much from compassion and a rude, chivalrous sense of honor as from tenderer motives (4). The next marriage in the same year is on record as one celebrated with much merriment. The happy young man was Lieut. Linn, which shows then as now the boys with the uniforms carried off the favors (5). Who was the bride elect traditon does not say, and so it cannot be a fact of historic record who are of the very first family in this county.

Tradition assigns to this year also the birth of the first white child in this settlement; it is almost as doubtless as the authorship of "The Beautiful Snow." We were reared in the belief that William Logan was that involuntarily meritorious person, who lived a life of success and honor, closing his career as United States Senator. Some others began life in the same uncomfortable quarters and may have been his peer in worth, but having failed to make their mark in the world, I cannot pass them on to the roll of fame; Mrs. Thomas, who passed her childhood in the fort, says that Harrod Wilson was the first white child born in Kentucky (6). Some one else says Thomas Hinton. If the prosecutor for the last name is a man, we defer to Mrs. Thomas' authority, for whoever knew a woman that did not date everything from the birth of some child, and doubtless all the pioneer women dated from the day the first white child was born in the fort. But this we can intimate, that if the legend is no more accurate than the same items concerning the first colored person born in Kentucky, it is not worth the paper on which it is preserved. Sukey Letcher, this colored person, was born a chattel of my grandfather and died under my own roof far nearer eighty than one hundred years old, as claimed for her in history (7). This very years, the notable 1776, closed with the creation of Kentucky county out of Fincastle, Virginia territory.

The incoming year, 1777, the first of Kentucky's existence, was brief with interesting events. The chronic fear and dread of the Indians was brought to a crisis. Early in March, Blackfish, a famous warrior, with more than two score braves, besieged Harrodsburg, and during the month repeated attacks were made on the fort. Meanwhile the garrison had been considerably strengthened by arrivals from Georgetown, which fort its occupants had been compelled by the Indians to abandon. Amongst these new comers were a number of men of merit and substance, who remained and founded valuable families in the county. George Rogers Clark (8), who figured so sonspicuously and extensively both in state and national history, was one of this number, but did not remain permanently. These repeated attacks upon the stations had weakened their force by the loss of men, and harrassment by Indians was so general that some, disheartened, turned back to their old homes and many went into the stronger forts; in fact, by the close of the year Harrodsburg, Boonesboro and Logan's Stations were the only living nuclei left of the many settlements that had sprung up in Kentucky. The constant apprehension of those attacks and the dread that almost every party that left the fort for work would fall into ambuscade was perhaps as serious and wearing a trial as any endured by these first settlers, and only too often were their fears verified. On one occasion the Rays, step-sons of Capt. McGary, with one Coomes, and several others (9), had gone to work in a clearing for McGary on the Shawnee Run tract. The boys had strayed off to a sugar camp when Coomes saw a number of Indians going in that direction and soon after heard them holding high revelry over their victims. James Ray escaped and gave warning at Harrodsburg (10). High words came up in the fort between Harrod and McGary, who demanded men to go with him to the rescue of the wood choppers. Mrs. McGary stepped fearlessly between the angry men, and the objectors yielded to her mother's plea for rescue for her sons. McGary went out and found the young men dead, buried them (11) and returned to the fort bringing in Coomes alive, who had secreted himself successfully during the battle and butchery of the Indians. This Coomes figures again in an adventure in which a party of thirty men were sent out to Bowman's Station to a general corn shelling for the benefit of the fort at Harrodsburg. The men were, of course, shelling by hand and in pairs. While thus employed a large party of Indians stole upon them and shot Coomes' mate. His blood bespattered face from the wounds of his companion, caused him the double danger of being mistaken for a painted warrior and thus becoming a target for the white and red men. He was not shot, however, by either party. Col. Bowman's messengers to Harrodsburg escaped both pursuers and ambuscade, and succor from there soon arrived; the Indians withdrew, the whites buried their dead, sacked the corn and returned sadly to the fort.

It was during this same season that James Ray and a comrade were target shooting without the stockade, when some Indians stole upon them. His companion was shot, and he, calling again upon his flying feet, reached the gate to find it shut in his face. Think of it! The gates shut in the face of one who had always borne the brunt of battle, and as commissary of the wilderness had never failed of duty from heat or cold, or night or danger. He dropped beside a log and lay while bullets fell like hail around him, until at his own suggestions they made a tunnel under the stockade and drew him in.

Turnips (12) are hardly classical productions, but now and then were the bottom of as serious mischief as was Atalanta's apple of gold. I cannot just recall the particulars, but remember to have heard of a weary, anxious following of tracks of little feet that had strayed from a turnip patch at McAfee's Station 'way down the river miles and miles, and how the terrified little ones thinking their friends were Indians, fled while breath lasted and like to have never been taken alive.

In this very same year, while some men were working in a turnip patch, signs of Indians were seen. Col. Clark, with a little detachment, stole out back of the fort and flanked the ambuscade and killed the Indian prowling around, and following the bed of the creek for only a few hundred yards found a camp large enough for the accommodations of several hundred Indians; so close and yet unknown to the fort, and from whence these savages, singly and in bands, had constantly issued to harass the different stations, killing men and stealing stock, thus rendering the price of bread-winning, blood, as well as the hereditary curse of the "sweat of the brow." Life was in fact an almost unbearable burden, and many who had put their hands to the plow turned back to their old homes. But in this gloomy and disastrous year there had been civil progress.

Kentucky at the close of 1776, had been formed into a county. The next April she elected burgesses to the legislature of Virginia, and henceforth had voice in the direction of her own affairs, but distance rendered this privilege almost nominal. In September the first court was held in Harrodsburg (13) and thus a tribunal of legal right and wrong was established at home. In this same September the census of Harrodsburg was taken, showing a population of 200.

1778 wound its slow length along, and while nothing sensational occurred within our county borders, nor much actual trouble, agricultural operations though uninterrupted progressed slowly, and the tide of emigration was very sluggish, for there was ever a cloud of anxiety overhanging the people. In other parts of Kentucky there was serious and almost continual disturbance from the Indians, and mistrust of the continuance of this seeming security had kept most of the families in the forts, while Mercer men mixed in all the border frays leaving anxious wives and mothers to struggle along in the hardships of fort life.

In 1779, the country or its leaders had conceived the idea of making retaliatory and aggressive invasions of the enemies' country. This policy, as carried out by Gen. Clark in his various raids northwest, had vindicated itself by its substantial and brillant results. So in the spring of 1779 was organized the well remembered and acrimoniously discussed disastrous expedition of Col. Bowman to old Chillicothe of Ohio. Of this command Col. Bowman was chief, Capt. Logan second and Major Bedinger, adjutant.

Harrodsburg furnished a company under Capt. Harlan; and many other men and subordinate officers were from Mercer stations.

The time set was chosen judiciously in favor of the farming interests; the interval being selected between planting and plowing the corn crops. The rendezvous was on the present site of Covington; from this section the companies reporting at Harrodsburg, except those from Louisville, which were to proceed by the river and furnish boats for the troops to cross the Ohio. The men were chiefly volunteers and provisioned themselves, except a ration of parched corn; jerked meat, I suppose making chiefly the other supply, and these provisions were to be supplemented by game taken by the wayside.

This expedition reached its destination, burned the town, captured a considerable number of horses and returned. There has never been a western adventure more bitterly discussed. After the careful and extensive preparations, and long march, it did seem like the ballad account was being re-enacted of "The King of Spain who marched up the hill and then marched down again." The actual exploit was ridiculously small, though the killing of Blackfish and Redhawk, the moving spirits of these continued hostile incursions into Kentucky and the general intimidation of the Indians, were of great value. No doubt there was sore chafing of proud spirits that would never have spoken the word retreat. There were circumstances and recriminations, undoubtedly bad management and worse generalship, but— "panic and cowardice" are words that should never be coupled with the names of those braves by men sitting around their self-feeding anthracites, and enveloped in the smoke of fragrant Havanas.

General James Ray, whose character as a pioneer and soldier, qualified him well to judge, rendered a true verdict, "that Col. Bowman had made the great mistake of going against a brave and well prepared enemy, and had the moral courage to retreat and not sacrifice his men to false pride." Col. Bowman had been commissioned by Thomas Jefferson, Governor of Virginia ,for state services in the west, and had his commission signed by Patrick Henry. He had identified himself fully with us, and followed and led in many a dangerous pass. Spotless, too, were the shields of Harlan, Logan, Redinger and Harrod. The brave men who followed and fought and suffered in the fatigue and shame of that exposition, have long since gone to that land, I trust, where injustice ceases and the weary are at rest.

Again in the fall of this year our peoples' sympathies were roused to the highest pitch by the advent amongst them of the survivors of another smaller, but ill fated enterprise. A keel boat of supplies for western parts, had been attacked on the Ohio and destroyed, and only a few men, like the messengers of Job, escaped and came to Harrodsburg for refuge, bearing the burden of the news of the bloody massacre.

Chapter IV—Explanatory Notes

Note 1—"On the 8th day of September, 1775, Captain Hugh McGary, Thomas Denton and Richard Hogan with their wives, arrived at Harrodsburg, having traveled as far as the Hazel Patch (near the headwaters of Dix river) with Col. Daniel Boone and his family on their way to Boonesboro."—From Collins' History of Kentucky, Page 606.

Note 2—These bowls, piggins, etc., were fashioned of wood. William Poage also made chairs and other articles of furniture. A chair made by him in the fort now belongs to Mrs. Mary E. Sharp.

Note 3—"Willam Poage was remarkably ingenious and while he lived in Harrodsburg from February, 1776, to September, 1778, he made all the buckets, milk pails, churns, tubs and noggins used by people in the Fort, the woodwork of the first plow made or used in Kentucky; the first loom on which weaving was done in Kentucky (by sinking posts into the ground, and piecing the beams and sley to them); while his wife (who in the spring of 1781 was married to Joseph Lindsay, one of the illustrous victims of that terrible slaughter at the Blue Licks, in August, 1782; and several years later to James McGinty) well known to persons still living as Mrs. Ann McGinty, a woman of great energy and self reliance, brought the first spinning wheel to Kentucky, and made the first linen ever made in Kentucky (from the lint of nettles) and the first linsey (from the nettle lint and buffalo wool.")—Collins' History of Kentucky, Page 616.

Note 4—"April 19, 1777, James Berry married the Widow Wilson (probably widow of Hugh Wilson killed by Indians on March 18, four and one-half weeks previous), the first marriage in Harrodsburg and the second in Kentucky county. (The first marriage in Kentucky county was Samuel Henderson to Elizabeth Calloway on August 7, 1776, at Boonesborough.")—From Collins' History of Kentucky, Page 615.

Note 5—"July 9, 1777, at the marriage of Lieut. Linn, at Harrodsburg, there was great merriment."—From Collins' History of Kentucky, Page 616.

Note 6—"The first white child born in Mercer county—so far as it is possible, at this late day, to ascertain — was: 1st, Harrod Wilson; 2nd, William Hinton, who died about 1833, on Fox Run, in Shelby county, Ky.; 3rd, William Logan, afterwards twice a judge in the Court of Appeals, in 1808 and 1810, and also United States Senator in 1819-20, born in the Fort at Harrodsburg, Dec. 8, 1776, died August 8, 1822, when only 45 years old;

4th, Anna Poage, daughter of William Poage, born in the same fort, April 20, 1777, married Gen. John Poage, of Greenup county, Ky., where she died April 24, 1848, aged 71 years."—From Collins' History of Kentucky, Page 614.

Note 7—"The oldest colored person now living (April 16, 1873), who was born in Kentucky, so far as is known, is at Harrodsburg—Sukey Letcher, widow of George Letcher. She was born a slave at the residence of Col. Leonard Thompson, at or near White Oak Spring, on Shawnee Run, in Mercer county, about the year 1781 and is now about 92 years old."—From Collins' History of Kentucky, Page 614.

Note 8—"Gen. George Rogers Clark first came to Kentucky in 1775, and penetrated to Harrodsburg, which had been re-occupied by Col. Harrod. In this visit from his well known and commanding talents, he was voluntarially placed in command of the irregular troops of Kentucky. In the fall he returned to Virginia, and came back to Kentucky in 1776." (This was Gen. Clarks' second visit to Harrod's Fort).—From Collins' History of Kentucky, Page 610.

Note 9—These young men were James and William Ray, Thomas Shores and Williams Coomes.

Note 10—"* * * Ray fled in the direction of the fort. Several of the swiftest Indians followed him in full chase, but such was his fleetness and activity that he distanced them all and reached the fort in safety. The remarkable swiftness of Ray elicited the admiration of the Indians, and Chief Blackfish, himself, remarked to Boone after his capture at the Blue Licks the succeeding year, that some boy at Harrodstown had outrun all his warriors." —Collins' History of Kentucky, Page 611.

Note 11—William Ray, the younger of the Ray Brothers, was killed by the Indians. Collins does not state explicitly the fate of Thomas Shores. The historian says that the party "discovered the mangled remains of William Ray," and says nothing of the body of Thomas Shores, but evidently he was killed or carried off by the Indians, for no mention is made of him returning to the Fort. "The party having buried Ray and rescued Coomes, returned in safety to Harrodstown, which they reached about sunset."—From Collins' History of Kentucky, Page 612.

Note 12—During this year, 1777, the Indians so sorely harrassed the settlers at Harrod's Fort. They destroyed much of the corn and wheat, crops that grew above the ground. So the settlers resorted to turnips, that grew below the ground, and lived largely upon this vegetable through that year.

Note 13—Date of sitting of this first court was September 2, 1777. John Todd was presiding justice, and John Floyd, Benjamin Logan and Richard Calloway, associate justices. Levi Todd was appointed clerk.

CHAPTER V

The Hard Winter of 1780-81—The Conventions Seeking a Separation From Virginia—Kentucky's Admission Into the Union—Items of Harrodsburg's Municipal Affairs Before the Close of the Last Century.

In the year 1780, the County of Kentucky was divided into three—Fayette, Jefferson and Lincoln; and still contained in Lincoln the history of Mercer is continued and the narration as heretofore will be confined as far as possible to the events which transpired within the limits given when Mercer county was afterwards formed out of Lincoln. Benj. Logan was made Colonel, and Steven Trigg Lieutenant Colonel; a kind of board of war, answering in authority, I suppose, to the military commandants created during the late civil war and styled Military Governors.

The winter of 1780-81 figures as memorably in the legends of early times conspicuously as the date of a settlement or an Indian invasion. No wonder the listeners were amused at the graphic description of it by an old man who was a child in those hard days, and whom in his old age people loved to draw out for the vehemency of his descriptions. He said of it: "There were no doors to many houses; no windows; we had no stockings, no shoes and scant linen clothing, and great heavens, sir, how cold it was. Provision was scarce; the wild beasts died in their lairs, or came up dumbly pleading for a share of the husks with the domestic cattle."

The year 1780 is also remembered for the crowds of emigrants that came into all parts of Kentucky, and for the incessant hostilities of the Indiana, backed by unmitigated, unrelenting British hate. Colonel Byrd led them and brought even cannon, which expedition, however, did not penetrate as far into the interior as Mercer. It sounds incredible to those accustomed to all modern facilities for movement that before the idea of the steamboats, railroads, or even turnpikes had entered the inventive head of man, that cannon should have been dragged from the far northern lakes to demolish the log entrenchments in a wilderness of people utterly destitute of spoils to tempt; whole sole wealth as yet was their lands, which the invaders could not hold. It was during this year that an Indian outrage occurred in this county that so far has, I think, never been recorded. A Mrs. Roach, of whose family, many remain in this county to the present day, as she sat at her window one autumn evening, saw her two boys suddenly leap from a haw tree and fly towards the house. One fell breathless almost in the door, the other an Indian brained and scalped leisurely; then stalked off over the hill, leaving no trace that diligent search could find save the body of the murdered boy.

The year of 1781 brought no event of note to our present county. She received her large share of emigrants, participated in all the apprehensions that incessant Indian raids in other parts of Kentucky excited, and her men as usual met promptly every summons to aid the assailed.

The severe reprisals which Gen. Clark had made on the Indians of Ohio and the northwest in payment of Byrd's invasion, seemed to have not intimidated but enraged them, and they had constant aid and comfort from their British allies in shape of counsel, men, arms, ammunition and provisions.

The next year, 1782, the rage of these people maddened by the sight of their favorite hunting grounds gliding from their possession, culminated in a series of invasions far more extensive and formidable than had ever been made since the first settlement of the country. But this most interesting chapter of pioneer history belongs to the annals of the state, not to our county. Our men were there; in defense of Bryan's' station, at Mt. Sterling, and at the bloody Blue Lick. With this disaster our ever brave and rash McGary was charged, and some of our truest and best men were left upon that bootless, bloody field, amongst them the chivalrous Harlan and the lamented Trigg, both cut off in the flower of life.

This fall again Gen. Clark was on the war path of retribution and carried waste and destruction to the Ohio tribes who had so persistently warred on Kentucky. Thenceforth there were no invasions of our borders in force and following the acknowledgment of Independence the halcyon of peace seemed to brood over the land. "But the trace of the serpent was over it all," for mistrust and apprehension were the Lares and Penates of our rude homes. Neither did the British nor Indians keep the treaty in good faith, but the continually threatened incursion of our old foes, and frequent outrages on our borders connived at by their British allies, caused the immediate taking into consideration all over the country of the most effectual measures that could be adopted for protection.

In 1783, Kentucky had been formed into a district and a court had been established, in which John Floyd and Sam McDowell presided and afterwards George Muter came also to the bench. Walker Daniel was prosecuting attorney. This first session was held in Harrodsburg (1), but for centrality Danville was selected, and a hewed log court house and jail were erected, and the long series of conventions through which Kentucky sought and finally obtained separation from Virginia and admission into the Union, were, with one exception, held in this court house. Previous to the meeting of the first convention General Logan had called an informal meeting of the people to discuss their grievances and devise remedies for them. The chief grievance and source of them all was our dependence on a power too far off and too weak to protect us, while we were hampered by waiting for even tardy legislatorial leave to organize and defend and avenge ourselves.

This meeting decided on a convention, and delegates to this convention were elected by the militia of the country, the military being thus made the novel foundation of civil independence and liberty without the force of arms.

Mercer was formed into a county in June, 1785, contemporaneously with Bourbon and Madison; but in May preceding our county's birth, a second convenion had met in Danville, passing strong resolutions in favor of separation from the mother state and sending our addresses to the Assembly of Virginia and the people of Kentucky. And now for a weary time Kentucky was engaged in holding a series of disappointing, but finally successful conventions, through which we worked our way into existence, thus relieving ourselves from the sore evil of living so far from the shield of the power to which we gave tribute and allegiance. In those days of no telegraphs, no newspapers, no daily mails, Danville was the cynosure of all eyes, and living in it was like the privilege of being in the antechamber of a royal palace from whence is momentarily expected the cry of a new born king, so eager, so intense was the desire of the people of these wilds for the privilege of self government.

The years through which these successive conventions lasted, were a period of great interest to the lovers of civil history, and the debates are yet a profitable study for politicians. For in these conventions were assembled the best talent in Kentucky and the ripe experience of the older states. Marshall, Muter, Innis, Crockett, Christian, Sebastian, John Brown, and Wilkerson with all his dash of effontery and real talest. Besides the question of separation from Virginia and independence, there came up a momentous side issue, the navigation of the Mississippi, which the grasping and

Daniel Boone

HISTORY OF MERCER AND BOYLE COUNTIES

domineering East was ready to see bartered, and our own ministers from short sightedness had nearly conceded to Spain for paltry considerations in the interest of the Atlantic side of the mountains. The patience with which our people bore their deferred hopes, which proverbially make the heart sick, has commanded the admiration of posterity of known impatient temperament. The fact was our forefathers had not become fully conscious of the freedom and equality our Declaration of Independence set forth. It is hard to burst the bond of usage.

Petition and remonstrance were the remedies they had been used to seeing applied for the removal of political grievances; and if the doctrine of the divine right of Kings had been exploited, there was still a strong sentiment lingering in them of loyalty to legal power wherever vested. But the spirit of opposition and impatience grew stronger every year, and there were not wanting in the country those who were ripe for speedier revolutionary measures, and that this number was a small minority reflects credit on the spirit of those times. For the temptations were not few or trifling that assailed ambitious western leaders. Indeed the inducements were great to the common people, until the opening of the Mississippi seemed really to leave no tenable ground for discontent; though both Spanish and French emissaries continued to tamper with our leaders until the cession of Louisiana to the United States forever dispelled the dream of French empire in the southwest. Until the opening of the Mississippi by treaty, barred by the Alleghanies from outlet eastward, with Spain, and afterward France holding perpetual ward over this natural and indispensible channel for their commerce, it was no small temptation for Kentucky to accept from Spain the free use of the river, not for the transfer of her allegiance to that power, but simply by erecting herself into an independent state, which her position seemed to suggest, and which the opposition of the eastern states to her admission into the Union seemed to justify.

Conventions in Virginia and conventions in Kentucky continued to petiton Congress until in 1791 our grand old mother joined in our petition to Congress, and Kentucky was formed into a separate commonwealth in June, 1792.

The act of Congress for the admission of Kentucky in the confederation of states was really the first act of that kind after the acknowledgement of her independence, but set the date of admission for June. Vermont, before that date was reached, was admitted; hence we were the second state admitted into the Union, but the first of the numerous offsprings of the Old Dominion. Over all these conventions Samuel McDowell, of Mercer, presided; and beside the men already mentioned as prominent in the proceedings, we find those whose names still linger among up, whom we know were Mercer men: Christopher Greenup, James Speed, Willis Green, William Kennedy, John Jouett and John Brown, who was the first United States Senator sent from Kentucky. He, James Harrod and John Jouett also served in the Virginia legislature from Kentucky and were citzens of Mercer; and Thomas Allin and Alexander Robertson were members of the Virginia convention which ratified the Constitution of the United States. Samuel Taylor, Samuel McDowell, David Rice, George Nicholas, and Jacob Freeman were members of the ninth and last convention which adopted the first constitution of Kentucky in 1792. These represented Mercer.

From the closing of this convention, Mercer had no separate part in the affairs of the commonwealth, but was concerned in them all.

The Indians continued to give a good deal of trouble in the state, until the peace of 1795; but none of these raids extended into the heart of the state.

In all the northwestern campaigns recorded in the state and national history of that period, Mercer doubtless had her quota of soldiers; had her benefit from the peace of 1795 which these campaigns extorted; and I suppose shared in the general discontent that was felt that there should be a treaty of peace with the British, even though it secured immunity from Indian hostilities. By the close of this century, the state was engaged framing its second Constitution, in which Mercer was represented by Thomas Allin, Samuel Taylor, Peter Brunner and John Adair. This constitution was an amendment of the first without any startling alterations, went into operation in A. D., 1800, and was superceded by the third until 1850. After this, regularly recurring state and national elections furnished ample excitement for a people that loved it.

Neither did Mercer escape the French phrensy which infected our country at the close of the last and the beginning of the present century. I, myself, remember a clique of gentlemen who, in the evening of their days, showed still the taint of French free thinking; and I have read letters that were almost Jacobinical in their politics from men enjoying places of honor, trust and profit in those days.

Whether Mercer had any men of the 2,000 citizens that Genet, emissary, or minister of the French Republic, whichever you may choose to class him, boasted that he had ready in Kentucky to descend upon the Spanish possessions, I cannot say. Such muster rolls are not apt to be registered in lawful places. Gratitude has always been accounted a fine virtue. France had come so gallantly to our rescue in our long unequal struggle with the mother country, that an American could hardly feel less than brotherhood for a Frenchman, and hardly humanly speaking, feel else than hatred for the British.

Even after incorporation into the Federal Union, Kentucky was continually tempted by foreign intriguants to secede and secure to herself immense advantages as an independent state, or else become a part of a magnificent southwestern confederacy, or empire. Some of the loftiest of her statesmen were dazzled by these brilliant schemes—Brown had not thought it wrong to consider and correspond about them. Gen. Clark actually accepted a high sounding French commission disconnected from our government, however, and little doubt rests on the facts that for a term of years Sebastian received the red gold of Spain as a retaining fee for his influence for their schemes. The last was an unpardonable offense. But for the others who were ready to canvass it as citizens openly, it may be said, it was hard with the resolutions of '98 before one fresh from the pen of the great American apostle of democracy, to prove either nullifications or secession a political crime. The verdict of the war of the rebellion, however, has construed them differently.

But this discussion belongs to our state and national history, not particularly our local columns.

Previous to the organization of Kentucky as a state, Mercer was represented in the Virginia legislature in 1787, John Jouett and William McDowell being our members; '88 and '89. Alexander Robertson and Samuel Taylor served; '90-'91, John Jouett and Anthony Crockett.

After this we had our own state government, and a complete list of representatives both in the state and national legislature will be given as made out, probably with sketches of the lives of prominent members.

This closes the first period of Mercer and Boyle County History and leaves us under the presidency of John Adams; Thomas Jefferson, vice president; James Garrard, governor of Kentucky; Harry Tailman, lieutenant governor. And to this we will add, what we hope will not be considered irrelevant matter, the life of General Mercer.

CHAPTER VI

Sketches of Eminent Men of the Period—General Mercer, General George Rogers Clark, Col. Harrod, Daniel Boone.

Concluding it best about each period of this history to group all the prominent characters belonging to that time, I give this first chapter to biographies, which must needs be not of men Mercer born, but of such as coming early to this wilderness, had conspicuous places in the affairs civil and military of the county. The sketch of General Mercer is an exception to this rule. He was in the west, but we thought it due to him, for whom the county was named, to give an account of the life and death that won him this lasting honor.

General Hugh Mercer

Was a native of and educated in Scotland; his training included preparations for the profession of medicine. After the disastrous battle of Culloden he, with many others, sought refuge in America, and answered eagerly to the call for rebels to fight against the mother country. He did this less from his passionate love of liberty than for burning thirst for vengeance against a country, on whose throne he held was seated a usurper, and whose soldiers had stained his native heath with Scotland's best blood. He served under General Washington against the Indians with distinguished bravery, and entered the Revolutionary war as a Colonel in Virginia ranks and was appointed a Brigadier General. He fell at the battle of Princeton. Our county could not have been called for a revolutionary hero of fairer fame, nor one who had more bravely fought and bled, and that too for the cause of strangers; and it was a great distinction accorded him, this giving him such an enduring memorial when so many of our own people, struggling daily for the same cause, on the same fields with him, fell and lie in graves unmarked by stone or other monument.

General George Rogers Clark

Of the pioneers, if not the very earliest, there was no man who was more essentially the founder of Kentucky than General George Rogers Clark, nor more useful to Mercer in her earliest days. He was a native Virginian and was educated in that state. Full of courage and adventure, his first exploratoin of this country antedated the first settlement of Mercer county. His coming to the west was in 1775; the first mention of him as a temporary resident to our county was in 1776 (2). He came when the fort dwellers from Georgetown dispersed. Talent, like water, soon finds its level. He had been before this sent to the front of affairs, as mentioned in pioneer history, and soon gave to Virginia her first just appreciation of her brave colony struggling in the western wilds, and induced her at once to extend the wing of protection over it, and establish for it some legal tribunals to justice. But Gen. Clark's genius was essentially military, and too comprehensive to be limited to so circumscribed a sphere as Kentucky. He would have been in a far more congenial field with a Marshal's baton in the camp of Napoleon. He at once saw that the sources of all the western trouble was the alliance of the British and Indians of the Northwest—the Indians backed with an inexhaustible supply of British stores and hatred. He never rested until commissioned to suppress this evil and under circumstances that would have deterred ordinary men, he pressed on until the conquest of the

British posts in Indiana was accomplished under difficulties and hardships that would have made it a brilliant chapter in Bonaparte's Russian campaign. This having been accomplished by his retaliatory policy, he subdued the Indians and forced peace for the white settlers of the west. The heart of the sympathetic must ache as they see soon afterwards the bonds of inexorable circumstances narrowing around to defeat and disappoint the grand program he had marked out for the aggrandizement of the old Dominion; for as yet all Kentucky and the states lying east of the Mississippi were the territory of Virginia. Military glory was the star of his worship, and proved the will o' the wisp that lured him not into fatal, but disappointing delusions when he twice accepted commissions in foreign service. In this there was no soil to his patriotism. The French, in spite of neutrality obligations, were allies of his country to him in heart; and the Spanish provinces were barriers to that country's growth and commerce, and were to be the just guerdon of French valor if won by her arms. But we are drifting far from Mercer. The life of Gen. Clark must ever possess a fascination for every pen that is wielded by a writer of the events of those days and whose words are indicted by a warm heart. He lived to old age; never married; left only collateral heirs to his fortune, and the splendid county that Kentucky has given to perpetuate his name.

Daniel Boone

The life of Daniel Boone belongs so essentially to Boonesboro, that I feel like I am almost feloniously appropriating one of the celebrities of that ancient and honorable hero to our columns (3). But as previously to the settlement of either Harrodsburg or Boonesboro, he did undoubtedly, if not in that historic cave, pass a winter in our present county bounds; I feel bound to record the fact that he did live in Mercer long enough, had elections been the order of the day, to have cast his vote unchallenged as a new comer at the polls. I hope undisturbed use of tent and fishing poles consoled him for the want of the present popular and exciting election day. The story of Daniel Boone is so familiar to every man and school boy, that it seems a work of superogation to write of him at all; but for the coming citizen, who shall live when traditions shall have somewhat died out, we will give a brief sketch of this hero that they may recognize him when they meet as they may, his name in foreign story books, or even on the pages of England's deathless poet, Byron.

Daniel Boone was born in Pennsylvania and after considerable wandering, settled in North Carolina. Incited by the glowing descriptions of Findlay, the first southern explorer of this great unclaimed, unsettled country, he and a few others came with Findlay on his return to Kentucky. His companions were killed, and he was taken prisoner by the Indians, but escaped and made his way back to Carolina, from whence he finally removed to Kentucky with his family, making Boonesboro the base of life. From hence he diverged as spy, hunter, Indian fighter, and not unfrequently messenger of the government to its outposts on the dangerous frontiers. He was fearless, adventurous, and enjoyed passionately the grandeur of nature and solitude. He was not so illiterate as has been represented, but could read and write, and was entrusted with many commissions that required intelligence as well as courage and endurance. He was repeatedly captured, ran the gauntlet, and was threatened with the stake, and once by escape and unheard of exertion saved by warning, Boonesboro, and perhaps all the other stations in detail, from the larger and well armed force of savages that soon after invaded Kentucky. He was robbed in the warming prime of his life of the money for which he had cashed his Carolina home; and had not legal knowledge enough to establish his Kentucky claims. So, landless, disappointed and disheartened, when the country became so thickly settled that he could see the smoke of his neighbor's cabin and could hear the dogs bark and chickens crow, folded his tent and followed the Indian's trail westward, and lived and died at an advanced age in the rugged freedom he loved.

Chester Harding, a very distinguished American painter, whiled away an hour in telling us, as we floated down the Mississippi, of his quest of Boone in the Missouri wilds to paint his portrait. He gave precisely the account given by Governor Morehead through Collin's Kentucky History. He found the old man in a rude cabin, lying on a buffalo robe roasting some meat on the point of his ramrod. Boone received and treated his distinguished visitor with the courtesy that springs naturally from a fine nature. But I cannot close this sketch with this dash of eulogy without overshading it with at least faint censure. Daniel Boone, having assumed the relationship of husband and father, we do not think his long absences from home were quite defensible. There were no daily mails or telegrams to keep Mrs. Boone informed of his welfare and whereabouts, and no post office orders to be transmitted. The canning of fresh meats was unknown and no express to have carried them to her, if prepared, and we sometimes fear Mrs. Boone found as hard times at home as her husband did in his voluntary exile in the wilderness.

For many years his remains rested in the obscurity in which he had lived in Missouri. But in 1845 the state of Kentucky brought them to her cemetery at Frankfort, and he and his wife rest side by side on a very picturesque and appropriate spot on the cliff overhanging the river.

Colonel James Harrod—Pioneer

Of the nativity and life of Colonel Harrod previous to his advent in Kentucky as little is certainly known as of the bloody mystery of his death. There was so little selfishness and egotism in his nature, he probably thought nothing in his past experience worth recounting and became so engrossed in the exciting surroundings of the new wild life he was leading, that the incidents of every passing day afforded more entertainment for evening hours, than the recital of the tame events of bygone days in the old home.

Col. Harrod was of the same type as Boone, only more social in his disposition. Fearless and fond of adventure, whether as the leader of an attack or repulse, or a solitary woodsman hunting game, seeking stock estrayed or ferreting out Indian camps. It is said Harrod was in Kentucky before Boone. Be that as it may he certainly founded the town in June of 1774 that now bears his name, and so secured to himself a memorial of more permanence than stone, albeit the foundation was a rude log cabin. He was of fine personal appearance, tall, erect, and fearless in his bearing and a generous nature beamed through his honest, kindly face. He had not much store of book knowledge, but was intelligent in what a man learns by observation and contact with fellowmen. Having made his home in this new land, he spent his time chiefly in hunting, making himself a free and invaluable commissary for provisioning the fort. For in those days, except his land and the cabin he shared with every new comer, a man scarcely called aught his own, but like the primitive Christians, the pioneers held all things very nigh in common; and to hunt up everybody's lost stock was as commonly expected of Colonel Harrod as to join every excursion made against the Indians. To these red skinned mauraders and rattle snakes, he had mortal aversion, grading however the reptiles as less dangerous than the first named, because they always gave warning before striking. He was at the Point (4) with Col. Lewis where the decisive blow was given to the northwest Indians who had rallied with the hopes of clearing their favorite hunting ground of the hated white man.

He removed from Harrodsburg to Harrod's station, where numbers were drawn around him by that magnetism the strong always exercise over the weak. His home was on the present division line of Boyle and Mercer, where Harrod's run makes its graceful detour through the blue grass of the parklike woodland into the open meadows. He had no ambition for civil distinction, but was prevailed on once to represent his county in Transylvania Assembly; but his heart was in the wild wood chasing the deer. In it he roamed days and weeks, and sometimes these absences lapsed into months, during which time he had many wild adventures with the savages.

On two occasions, it is narrated, that he found himself, when shooting at game, using a common target with the Indians. Each time the rifles of white and red man were instantly turned on each other, and on both occasions Harrod proved victor, slaying his foes and carrying the substantial triumph, the game, with him to the expectant fort families. Once he was discovered reconnoitering a small village of Indian huts, and was pursued from it by a whooping crowd that finally all tired down but three. After swimming the Miami, he stopped on the banks for a breathing spell, when the savages, after a moment's hesitation, plunged in to continue the pursuit. The first sank beneath his shot, the second was wounded and floated down the current out of sight, the third concluded discretion the better part of valor and retreated. A short time after Harrod came upon the wounded Indian lying on a pile of driftwood vainly trying to staunch his wounds. The foes exchanged signs of amity. Harrod bore the chief to a cave that he occupied, and nursed him tenderly and skilfully into health; then provisioning him for his return journey to his tribe, bade him remember when his tribe had white prisoners to remind them how the Lone Long Knife, for so the Indians named Harrod, had treated him and ask them to show like mercy. He never heard from the chief again, but some time after, Boone and other were made prisoners and were treated with very great kindness by the Shawnees.

Not long after this, Harrod went out with a man named Bridges. He never returned, and from circumstantial evidence his wife concluded that he was murdered. He left no inheritor of his name and fame, a single daughter having been born in his house, who married a Captain Fauntleroy. Their descendants are extinct or lost in the confused masses of the present generations. Very recently there has taken breath a strange rumor that furnishes a finale to the tragic story of Col. Harrod's death. It is said that some time within the past quarter of a century, that some citizen of Estill county, in which it was supposed Harrod was murdered, received a letter from Virginia, saying that Bridges had made a dying confession of the murder of Harrod, and had given minute directions for the finding of his body. The story goes that the search was made and the remains of our hero were found as indicated beneath a large rock laid slopingly against a bank. Nearby by were the ruins of a furnace and heaps of ashes containing curious cinders, showing that at this place perservering effort had been made to find metal. The received story of Harrod's departure from home was that Bridges, with whom he was not on friendly terms, came to him and frankly acknowledging himself to be in the wrong, told him he believed he had found treasure in the hills he was willing to share with no one else. Whether Harrod was thus lured to his death, or he and Bridges quarrelled, remains a mystery. However, Bridges' reputed confession was that he and two other men murdered Harrod and concealed his body. We give the rumor for what it is worth, but are sure if it be true his remains were found, there is but one place where they should be laid to rest, and that is among the braves who sleep in the Cemetery of our State's Capitol.

Chapter V—Explanatory Notes

Note 1.—"No house in Harrodsburg could be secured that would accommodate the business of the court, and the remainder of the session was therefore adjourned to a meeting house near "Dutch Station," near the settlement. For its next session the court authorized Daniel May (the clerk) to select some safe place near Crow's Station (afterward Danville.. in which the business could be transacted."—From "Kentucky— a History of the State," by W. H. Perrin, J. H. Battle and G. C. Kniffen.

Note 2.—Collins, in his History of Kentucky, page 610, puts George Rogers Clark's first visit to Harrodsburg a year earlier. See Note 8, Chapter IV. "Col. George Rogers Clark first came to Kentucky in 1775 and penetrated to Harrodsburg which had been re-occupied by Col. Harrod."

Note 3.—"Capt. Harrod and his company encamped at the Big Spring on the east of the place, where it was agreed to lay off a town. * * * On June 16, 1774, they laid off the town, giving each man a half-acre inlot and a ten-acre outlot. While this surveying was going on, Daniel Boone and Michael Stoner—then on their way to or from the Falls of the Ohio (at Louisville)— whither they were sent by Gov. Dunmore, of Virginia, to warn Col. John Floyd and other surveyors sent out by him, of threatened Indian hostilities, reached there and Boone assisted in laying off the lots. A lot was assigned to him adjoining one laid off for (John or Evan) Hinton, upon which was built immediately a double log cabin, which was known indiscriminately as Boone's or Hinton's cabin, until it with the other three or four built nearby at the same time, was burnt by the Indians, March 1, 1777, just after Thomas Wilson and his family had escaped from one of them, into the Fort."—Collin's History of Kentucky, page 517, under Madison county caption.

The location of this double cabin of Boone and Hinton, handed down through generations of Harrodsburg descendants of the first settlers, places it about the site of the present residence of Mrs. J. D. Bryant on the north side of what is now Lexington avenue, about the middle of the second block east from Main street. It is also said that Boone occupied this cabin most of the time on his visits to Harrodstown, and always approached it by walking along a stream that is now walled up as a small canal through Harrodsburg—an instinctive caution that he practiced of going through water to hide his trail from the Indians.

Note 4.—The Battle of Point Pleasant at the mouth of the Kanawha river, in West Virginia, October 10, 1774.

CHAPTER VII

Sketches of Eminent Men of the Period, Continued—Simon Kenton—General Ray—Captain Hugh McGary—Col. Silas Harlan—Capt. William Pogue —Hon. J. Brown, United States Senator.

Simon Kenton

I could not afford to forego chronicling the distinction of having had Daniel Boone pass six months of his solitary existence during his first visit to Kentucky in our county; much less can we pass over the fact that Simon Kenton, the peer of any pioneer in courage and the superior of them all in woodcraft, and who gained more skill and tact in his experience and endured more hardships, was once on garrison duty in our fort, and had a house in our county. Kenton was born in Virginia and fled to this western wilderness, and for years bore on his heart the incubus of having committed a terrible crime in the delirium of a dreadful disappointment in love. He believed he had killed a dear friend, who had won over him the maiden he had loved and wooed. He drifted from point to point seeking forgetfulness or death in the hazards of these Indian haunted wilds, and finally, when the dispersion from the fort of Georgetown took place, came to Harrod's Fort. He played the role of spy, guide, or Indian fighter equally well. He was captured, beaten, tortured and ran the gauntlet repeatedly. Once he was saved from the stake by the renegade who had before been his comrade—Simon Girty—and once he was saved by the compassion of an old Indian chief, and again was released from captivity by the pity and courage of the wife of a white trader in Detroit. Immediately upon his return to Harrod's Fort he led a company from there in Clark's celebrated march to Vincennes. When the Indian incursions finally ceased and peace had been made, he went to Virginia to bring his family to this settlement, and to his infinite relief found the man that he believed he had killed, living and surrounded by a lively progeny of bare foot boys and nut brown girls. Unfortunate in fortune as in war and love, after being foiled and spoiled by the land sharks that infested Kentucky then, he pulled up the stakes of his tent once more and went to Ohio, where he lived in poverty and obscurity to old age. Once he visited Kentucky and was treated with distinguished attention during his stay, and the legislature took some measures to release from embarrassment his poor mountain lands, the last remnant of his Kentucky claims. The populous and prominent county of Kenton is named for him.

Gen. James Ray.

General Ray was of medium height, athletic, powerful, and fleet as a deer. There is not much to tell of him except what has been given under the head of Pioneer Times; yet his name runs like a metalic thread through the crimson web of those days. To scout for Indian signs, hunt the stock missing from the settlements, or men belated or lost, and circumvent Indian ambuscades, or meet them in open field, was his daily occupation, his keen delight and usually his triumph. The reader of the lore of early times remembers he was the first to divide his last morsel with Col. George Rogers Clark on his arrival in Mercer county, and was his faithful aid in all after troubles; also his despatch of the Indian who had spotted the Scotch corn planter for death; his escape with the Shawnee wood choppers and timely

Old Harrodsburg Academy

alarm of Harrod's Fort, thus enabling the dwellers in it successfully to defend themselves. He, for a long while, resided on a fine farm noted for its bold, indeed, reputed fathomless spring, lying a few miles northeast of Harrodsburg, now the property of Phil B. Thompson, Jr. I am not aware that any descendant bearing the name of General Ray is living, but there are several of his offsprings through the female line, living in our county, of whom Major John Duncan, who represented Mercer county in the state legislature a few years since, is one. (The late Mrs. J. P. Steele, of Harrodsburg, was a granddaughter). It has been generally said that Gen. Ray was one of the persons in the "Battle of the Boards," humorously described by Collins, and which has been skilfully woven into an interesting sketch of western adventure. I could not ascertain for what particular campaign he was commissioned as General, but, no matter when acquired, he won it fairly and wore it well.

Gen. McGary.

Gen. McGary was amongst the earliest emigrants to Kentucky, his wife the first white woman who ever trod the soil of Mercer county. Daring, impetuous, rash and overbearing, it is hard to put his deeds, good and bad, into the scales of justice and pronounce upon his character righteously. Much allowance must be made for ignorance was of early training and the spirit of the times in which a man lives. McGary had no elements of everyday usefulness in his character like Pogue, who labored to produce conveniences and comforts, nor of Harrod, who did whatever helpful hands could do, and who as diligently hunted lost stock, or game, for food, as he bravely fought Indians. McGary's bravery was a kind of ferocity that applied the couplet, "Fee, Fa, Fum, I smell the blood of an Englishman," steadily to the Indians, not Englishmen. Fearless he certainly was, and danger seemed to have for him a sort of fascination that he followed heedlessly without the least discretion. We find him fussing and fuming and raging in the fort, while Harrod takes a moment to consider before sending out for the wood choppers, in the adventure in Ray's life of early times. But in this there was a redeeming circumstance; the Rays were the children of his wife and her distress naturally impelled him to haste and hazard. He built the first cabin ever erected on the site of Cincinnati, it is said, which to shelter some wounded men who had followed him in some of his hair brain expeditions to the northern side of the Ohio river. He led the disastrous passage of the Blue Licks, challenging brave men against their judgments to follow him to their deaths. His remains lie on the old fort hill and a mossy grey stone used in times past to mark his grave. He was not without civil honors, being a member of the first court ever held in Kentucky and one of the first men ever indicted before its bar for what would be adjudged trifling peccadilloes these degenerate days, viz: swearing and betting.

Colonel Silas Harlan

Col. Silas Harlan was a native of Berkley county, Virginia, and after coming to our state was made a commander under Col. George Rogers Clark. He came to Mercer in 1774. He died a bachelor and like many of his comrades has his name perpetuated by the name of a county. But folklore, that loves to link love and war, says he was betrothed to a Miss Caldwell, and that after telling her farewell as he dashed off from the lorn maiden sitting on the stile, a clod of turf flung from his charger's hoof struck her and she took it as did Napoleon the stumbling of his horse on the morn of a battle, as a sad omen soon and sadly realized in the death news from the fatal Blue Licks. But God in time healed even wounds of the heart, and I must spoil my little romance with a hard historical fact. My heroine married a kinsman of the gallant Colonel, and was, I believe, the progentress of our Col. Wellington Harlan, and the several Harlans, fathers and sons, who gild the legal rolls of the day. Col. Silas Harlan left extensive landed estates, some of which remain in the family to the present day, though the farm on which his station was has passed into other hands. Col. Harlan was brave and generous, and no victm that fell in McGary's vast and fatal move at Blue Lick was more lamented than Harlan. With him, too, fell Trigg, another native Virginian, who had cast in his lot with us and had made a station on Cane Run. He was bold, true, active and indefatigable, and had won that popularity that would have insured him fame and wealth had he lived. Trigg county was named for him.

Captain William Pogue

Capt. William Pogue lived in Harrodsburg, and raised crops as early as 1776. He was an ingenious and useful man, manufacturing with what rude tools he had or could construct, the pails, buckets and first loom used in the fort, perhaps the first in Kentucky. His wife, afterward Mrs. McGinty, made the first linen produced in the state, though possibly cloth had been made previous to this of the fibrous bark of the nettle and buffalo's wool. Capt. Pogue's life was not long spared to the community in which he had been useful, obliging and esteemed. On his way up to Lincoln on business, he was shot by an Indian, and brought back to Harrodsburg to die.

Very near Harrodsburg, Mrs. Thomas, a daughter of Capt. Pogue, lived to extreme old age. Her memory was a perfect store house of traditions, and it is to be much regretted that we did not realize the value of such lore while she lived amongst us. She was the lassie of whom I wrote, in "Pioneer Times," that received a large devise of land from some habitue of the fort whose very name she could not remember. Since writing that I have had an interview with one of her descendants, who told me the true version of her great-grandmother's romance. She says when the Harrodsburg troops were summoned to the aid of the beseiged Bryan's Station, five young sportsmen went out of Capt Pogue's homestead. Amongst these was a handsome and gallant young man named Overton, to whom her great-grandmother was betrothed. Not one of the five soldiers returned—all were victims at the fatal Blue Lick, and Overton's will was found devising his large land claims to the lady of his love. "And alas for the constancy of women," said the recounterer, laughingly, "grandmother comforted herself with a new lover;" but added soberly, that after a while she could talk calmly of her lost husband, but to her last days would weep over the fate of Overton. I know that a son of hers, as handsome a lad as e'er I saw, bore the name of the lost lover and that Overton runs through all the genealogical records of her descendants. Mr. Harvey McFatridge now owns the romantic inheritance and lives in the very house in which she passed her long and useful life; but it has been modernized and improved and is now one of the most convenient and tasteful of our country homes.

Hon. John Brown

Hon. John Brown was a native of Virginia, and though his mother was of Irish descent, his father was a Presbyterian clergyman, and naturally sent him to Princeton, the then educational mecca of these religionists. During his term there the army of the republic swept in its retreat from New Jersey through this locality and our student fell into ranks and remained some time among the volunteers, adn subsequently served under General Lafayette. He returned after hostilities ceased and finished his course in

William & Mary College. Reading law was always done in those days in the office of some practitioner. Mr. Brown took his course under Mr. Jefferson. They were ever after fast friends. In 1782 he came to Kentucky and was for many years the most conspicuous politician of the state. He was one of what I have termed elsewhere the military board, who with Scott, Innis, Shelby and Logan, exercised large trusts, such as enlisting men, commissioning officers, in fact had an influencing voice in the decisions for war or peace. He had considerable executive ability in war matters as well as in councils of peace, which he exercised in planning some of the Indian campaigns of that period. He seemed not ambitious for office, but steadily declined positions pressed on him in Washington City by Jefferson and his successors. He ranked peer of the many lawyers that filled the bar of Kentucky in that day of abundant and intricate litigation. He was the first senator elected to the congress of the United States from Kentucky, and served three consecutive terms. That he lived in Harrodsburg and was one of its trustees, is a morsel of honor for our old town too precious to be lost. What he did as councilman went to record in our first municipal books which have, except one volume, been lost. This volume states that he was succeeded on the board of trustees by John Waggoner. The somewhat Jeffersonian tincture of his politics acquired in pupilage and after intimate association with Mr. Jefferson, subjected Mr. Brown to unjust and acrimonious aspersions from the Federal party. He was a Chevalier Bayard, "Sans peur, sans reproche."

CHAPTER VIII

The McAfee Family.

The McAfee family were too prominent in the pioneerage of Kentucky not to have a chapter given them in a History of Mercer county, the home of their election and the field of their adventures. Having had the generous loan of Gen. Robert B. McAfee's MS., an eminent member of this clan, as we used to call them, I have made from it such notes as I thought pertinent to my history; and I sincerely regret that so interesting and valuable an exponent of early times should not have been put in book form for the use of the general public and made part of the archives of the State Historical Society. The McAfee family can be easily traced back to the wars of Cromwell when they lived between Glasgow and Edinburg, Scotland. They were driven thence at the time of the persecution under James II, of the Covenanters, and settled in the north of Ireland, to which place they were followed by numerous connections including the McCoun's of this history, and many others in this county under various martially acquired names. The father of the McAfees who came to this country was in the Revolution that brought William of Orange to the throne of England. James McAfee and Jane McAfee Michael, ancestors of the McAfee brothers that emigrated to Mercer county, Kentucky, came to America and bought land in Lancaster, Pennsylvania, where these pioneer brothers of Mercer county were all born. Finding themselves straitened in land, they made several changes and finally settled in Virginia; from which state his sons, impelled by the same restless desire for change and acquisition, finally came to Kentucky. This progenitor of the McAfees was a brave, hardy, upright man, of so rigid a cast of "Seceder Presbyterianism" that he could hardly tolerate his more emotional wife in hearing Whitefield, who seems to have evangelized in that part of Virginia; and to his descendants to this day he seems to have transmitted the bluest blood of Presbyterianism, every member of the family under whatever name, so far as known being, if in any church, of that communion. The report of the hunters, 1770, Walker, Boone, etc., having been circulated through Virginia, and the governor of that state having made what was called his proclamation—grant of 400 acres to all soldiers in the French and Indian wars—these McAfees, who had all participated, determined to explore and take claims, if they proved worth having, in these new Kentucky lands. Accordingly, James, George, Robert and Samuel McAfee, with ––––––– Adams and James McCoun, all neighbors and kinsmen, came in 1773 to the head waters of new Kenawha, sent their horses back home from that place, and meeting Capt. Bullett, Hancock Taylor and company, who had been sent out to survey the proclamation grants, remained with them. During their explorations they came upon a village of hewed logs and clapboards, which seemed to have been deserted for 18 or 20 years, and which they concluded from signs, had been built by the French previous to the surrender of Fort Duquesne, now Pittsburg. This party continued its exploration southward, tarrying awhile at Bigbone Lick, and speculating over the relics found there. An old Delaware chief they met there assured them that these remains were just as they had been since he was a child. They halted a day or two on the site of the present capital of Kentucky, and Robert McAfee had a survey made there, but failed to have it entered, and it was afterward entered as vacant land. From this point they made their way still southward to our section, and we may properly date the beginning of Mercer from the day when James McAfee stuck the surveyor's staff into the bluff heading at New Providence spring, saying: "Men, you may hunt as much more land as you please; as for me, I intend to live my days out here by the blessing of Providence." They proceeded then to survey from the mouth of the creek at Harrodsburg to Salvisa, plotted and possessed it by using marks and forms ;then Hancock Taylor and party wended their way to meet Capt. Bullett at the falls of the Ohio; and the McAfees struck southeast for Powell's valley for their homes in Virginia. After enduring almost as great privations and hardships as detailed in Riley's narrative of his journey across Sahara, they reached their homes in the late summer of 1773, expecting to return the next year and open their lands. But serious hostilities having broken out with the Mingoes, Delawares and Shawnees, they joined the troops that hastened to strengthen Gen. Lewis, and had part in the battle of the Points, Sandusky Junction and consequently did not return to Mercer until the spring of 1775. They spent the seasons respectively in making small clearings for corn, and in planting peaches, apples and other fruits. They then departed for their homes leaving men to continue clearing and to warn off intruders; but meeting Col. Henderson on his way to Kentucky, James McAfee only resisted his tempting and plausible offers, and the others turned back to take up claims under Henderson's Wanga treaty made the year before with the Cherokees. The reader will remember, as formerly stated, that Virginia repudiated all of Henderson's Indian treaties, thus crushing his magnificent land speculations. But a grant of a large body of land in that state fully reimbursed him for all expenditure of personal service, time and money he had made. Robert McAfee was sergeant at arms in Henderson's memorable convention at Boonesboro. The McAfees remained long enough with Henderson to see that the bubble must burst, and then went on to Virginia to their homes expecting to remove their families to the newly selected lands in Mercer county. But they were again called into the Indian wars. However, before these Indian hostilities interrupted emigration they had moved their household effects by water so far as Greenbriar, but from a prospect of many insurmountable obstacles, they had concluded to build a cabin and secrete their goods, but to their dismay, when the Indian campaign was over, and they came to transport their goods on packhorses to their new Mercer homes for use when their families should come, they found their cache rifled of all its priceless stores; for neither love nor money could at that day, in Kentucky, replace these things. A maurading white runaway bound servant from Virginia, had plundered and destroyed their goods in the most wanton manner, and thus they were stripped of all the comforts and luxuries that untiring industry and forethought had gathered for their wilderness homes. It seems almost strange that so religious a people and so watchful of all indications of Providence, should persevere in this emigration after being so frequently baffled and imperiled in their efforts to make the change. But having delayed two years longer, 1777 and 1778, to fight in the ranks of all the Revolutionary war, the early fall of 1779 found them in the cane brakes on Salt river, their families with them. This fall the commission appointed by Virginia to examine and decide on land claims and pre-emption rights were to meet, and the McAfees felt bound as were all Kentucky land claimants, to be in place at the session of this all important court. The families went to their several cabins and some strangers to the station of James McAfee, in which from time to time they all had to take refuge from Indian harrassment.

 This first winter, 1779-80, was a severe trial of their faith and courage. It was the memorably severe winter of the history. This year, 1780, General Clark determined to make a retaliatory raid on the Indians north of the Ohio river. William McAfee went as Captain of a company on this raid and was shot by an Indian in the shifting evolutions of a battle. The wound was hoped not to be mortal, but the long exposure in the travel on a litter, produced inflammation and finally mortification. He came as far as the Ohio river, and his wife having been apprised by a special messenger, started on horseback and reached him before he passed away. He was buried where he died; and Maj. W. Daviess obtained the relinquishment of the rights of inheritance to his lands from his heirs in Indiana not many years since for Joseph Morgan, whose descendants now live on them.

The 9th of May, 1781, McAfee Station suffered the severest attack in its history. The families of the brothers then had all gathered in to the station. The women themselves employed in making nettle cloth, the men cautiously extending the clearings and hunting sufficiently to provision the fort. The attack commenced with lively skirmishing out in the over-hazardous fields of work—the turnip patches—one man having been shot, and Samuel McAfee having killed one highly decorated savage, supposed to be a chief, the men retreated into the station. The fight continued many hours, the little band of defenders administering their fire whenever an Indian showed himself. The munitions of war were scarce, which the women remedied as well as they could by rendering their pewter spoons and basins into bullets while the men fought. But it was a clear, still day and the sound of firing was conveyed by the water of the river to William McAfee's Station at the mouth of our town creek, whence runners were sent to Harrodsburg and to McGary's Station. Pioneers all were minute men, and rode like centaurs, and in an incredibly short time, the thunderous sound of a troop of horses came to the besieged little fort, more welcome than even that which heralds coming rains in drouth. The white troops came with a yell, the Indian troops retreated with a whoop and were pursued until their dispersion rendered any longer concentrated action against them useless.

Gen. McAfee tells a story of how Jerry Tilford, father of the long time president of the Lexington bank, was thrown over his horse's head, the horse bounding over him, he rolled on in the dust, then vaulted into the saddle not waiting to pick up his his hat, and fought and pursued all day with only his handkerchief tied on his head. This hero was the great-grandfather of our townsman, Mr. James Matheny. McAfee Station was never seriously attacked again, but the families remained in the station a long time, tilling their fields for some distance away, but never going to them without their guns.

This year a mill of hand-stones was built on the river—one having been set up in Harrodsburg the previous year.

This year (1781) the mother of the McAfees, who had come with them to Kentucky, died, and was buried on a high knoll on Salt river in the neighborhood best known as "Mud Meeting House," so called from the material largely used in its construction. The present building is a neat frame structure, and in it there is regular preaching by the pastors of the two Presbyterian churches of Harrodsburg. The same year Mrs. McCoun, mother-in-law of Robert McAfee, died, and David Rice preached the funeral sermon, probably the first discourse of that kind ever preached in Kentucky, certainly the first ever delivered in Mercer county

The Indians, even after they ceased open hostilities, continued pilfering raids—horses and cattle their usual plunder—thus continually harrassing and keeping alive an uneasy dread in the minds of wives and mothers. But the McAfees now moved out of the station and kept on their lands during the rest of their lives. They were a very distinctly marked family of people. Some had the light complexion, hair and eyes of their farback Teutonic ancestors; and occasionally there occurred a clear cut profile with the black hair and piercing black eyes, showing the traditionary crop of the Italian. They were, as the Scotch, clannish, and used to move pretty much together in politics, and for a long while almost holding the balance of power in their hands in the county. They were brave, enterprising but ambitious people. The captaincy of William McAfee in Clark's expedition in which he fell, and the magistry and sheriffalty of Sam McAfee, showing the only record of office holding in this numerous family until the second generation, when Robert B. McAfee took some civic as well as military honors, which will be shown in his biography as Lieutenant Governor, and occasionally one of their descendants named will be found on the Legislative roll which will be found in this series. The McAfees were devoted to Gen. Washington, their old military chief. He was to them pre-eminently the father of his country. They utterly scorned and abhorred the treasonable practices of Sebastian and Burr, and falling into Jefferson's doctrines all of the blood, rank and file, of whatever name, in every state, are found in the Democratic party. They were as thoroughly Presbyterian as democratic. Cold Sunday dinner and catechism being the distinctive marks of each household, and I was not a little surprised to find in Gen. McAfee's reminiscences, that dancing was their habitual holiday and evening amusement. (Gen. McAfee states that dancing was indulged in to keep up the spirits of the young people—Editorial Note).

So soon as these brothers were sheltered in their own log cabins they proceeded to erect a like house for religious worship, and continued to extend and improve their farms proper with their own homes. They called this church New Providence, not as has been supposed as an acknowledgement of the over-ruling influence that led them to this land or protected them through the perils of the wilderness and pioneerage, but in memory of the one in which they had worshipped in the mother state.

Of the McAfee brothers who came to this state, James seems to have been counsellor and leader. He married Miss Clark; George, a Miss Curry; Robert, Miss McCoun, and Samuel, Miss McCormic, of Rockbridge, Va. There is a tradition that there was one brother who turned back from the mountain pass and finding himself lonely in his old haunts, drifted off to South Carolina, named and was the progenitor of the McAfees whose names are occasionally seen on the legislature rolls of the western states. Very few of the name remain amongst us. The pretty little village of McAfee was named for this pioneer family.

CHAPTER IX

Mode of Living in Early Days—Customs, Fashions and Manners.

As we have noted, no invasions by bands of Indians had harrassed Kentucky after the peace treaty of 1795; nor indeed as far central as our county for several years previous to this date. But long ere this the fort-dwellers has begun gradually to disperse; some of the more restless and daring to even newer fields of enterprise and risk; many more had located on the rich and unappropriated lands within our own county borders.

A. D. 1800, found our county busy opening farms, building houses, home making and gathering comforts generally; and it suits better here than elsewhere in these columns to trace the progress of this phase of its life before commencing the history of this period.

Curiously enough, neither the memory of their homes, nor the bitter experiences of their block house life seemed to have suggested much architectural wisdom to the home makers of the first periods, and there was a notable absence of fire places from all their plans. In the midst of such immense forests where yearly almost enough wood was burned simply to clear the ground, to furnish our people with fuel now, only the family room and a few others were arranged for fires at all, and stoves were not yet introduced, and only the living room was habitually kept well warmed. Hence it was the common sitting room for all the family, children and nurse included. Thus reading and thought were much circumscribed by force of circumstances, and self culture almost placed on the list of impossibilities. Log cabins were built for homes as a rule, and not as an exception. They were of round logs with the bark left on, though sometimes beautifully hewed. Some of the most comfortable and respectable looking houses m the county and town now are these same log cabins weather boarded without and finished as nicely within as their more pretentious brick and frame neighbors. Plaster houses were also common, that is, frames which were finished inside with lath and plaster and outside with a rude preparation of mortar which was often held together with straw instead of hair. Paint and whitewash were rarely used, and soon the weather-stained wood work made the general aspect of these dwellings very old and dreary looking.

Soon after the inauguration of this second period of log house homes, the extremely coarse furniture was moved out gradually to the negro cabins or the wood piles, and plain, substantial conveniences were made of hard woods, often of cherry and walnut, that would take polish from waxing, followed by persistent rubbing. Chests and three cornered cupboards held the office of bureau and sideboard, and they were mostly of heavy, clumsy contrivance. Low post bedsteads now came in use. The posts were shaved down to rather a small point on which they stood free of castors. They had narrow foot and head boards and holes bored opposite on the sides and head and foot so that a lattice work of home-made rope run through these holes supported a coarse tick stuffed with straw, or mat such as Peter Henderson directs us to make now for covers for our flower pits. Tables and even in some ambitious houses, mantles were made of walnut, and to the keeping of these bright, the honor of the whole family seemed committed, and maid servants and children spent every interval of leisure increasing efforts to keep the polish of these chef d'ouvres immaculate. I think the turning lath and cabinet maker were hardly fairly established in this county before the war of 1812. Chairs with split bottom and oak were the first advance from fort furniture, and would they had proved heirlooms, but the

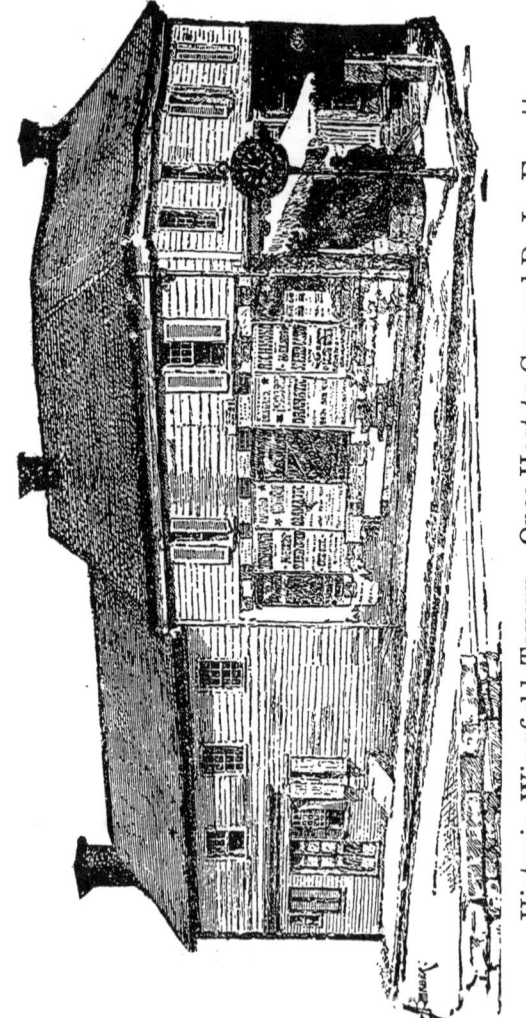

Historic Wingfield Tavern—Once Host to General De La Fayette, Aaron Burr, Harmon Blannerhassett, and other Celebreties.

Windsor superseded the hard and uncomfortable chairs, albeit supposedly from the name, the style descended from her Majesty's royal castle; and sets, including settee of the structure that filled the niches, now filled by luxurious velvet clothed sofas. I believe I know of the first sofa ever made in Harrodsburg. It is still in use. It is very low, stands on lion feet and is ornamented with some very well executed carving. The original haircloth had been superceded by oil cloth, and occupies an exposed position; the upholstering was fastened on with wide brass-headed tacks, in uniform with coffin trimmings of the same era. The springs had entered into its arrangement. I know of no modern sofa of more graceful style. It cost $800, I have heard.

Before the close of this second period of which I now write, cabinet work became of pretty common use and the purchase of clocks, homemade, and of the style of "My Grandfather's Clock" prevailed almost epidemically, and in the cabin house will be found a niche built especially in which to have this timepiece enclosed. I was once present at an interview between a thoughtless purchaser of one of them in our village and the executor who had the sale. The purchaser found himself in possession of a piece of furniture as unmanageable as the Vicar of Wakefield's family picture, could not set it up in the house anywhere. The merry executor suggested letting the base down in the cellar, or giving the face way through the ceiling, so the upstairs folks could see, or building an addition to the house for it. However, he bought it back himself, finally and expressed it to where it was joyfully received as an heirloom and it is now said to preside on the first landing of a mahogany stairway, as valued a piece of furniture as any in the handsome home. Another of the same make was expressed to Washington City and in one of the government's fine mansions notes the passing hours. So thanks to the craze of antiquity, Harrodsburg tells the time and seasons still in high places. Sideboards put in their appearance during this period, large enough for the use of a regiment's commissary, and there were sets of dining tables. Looking glasses were set on chests of drawers and could be and were carried from room to room. Mainly this furniture was heavy and clumsy, but there are extant one or more bedsteads of such good and elaborate carving that they would be counted firstclass treasures in the eastern store of bric-a-brac.

Early in this period of our county's' history geese must have been very numerous, for new feather beds soon ceased to be luxurious and were classed as necessities for every household's comfort, and were made of such ambitious height that steps were necessary to ascend to the realms of balmy sleep. However, this was due to the use of trundle beds, which the upper bedsteads had to be tall enough to allow to be hid away under it in the day time. These trundle beds were very convenient and unhealthy abominations, the hot beds in which all our men of mark grew and which have been happily superceded by our luxurious lounges and more modern deceptive folding bedsteads. Bed clothes were chiefly homemade, at least through the greater part of the period. About the middle of it notable housekeepers sometimes used factory spun cotton for sheets, the main and finer ones still being homemade linen; and the rich in this world's goods stretched a point and had for use on state occasions Irish linen bolsters and pillow cases, but with none of the dainty adornings of the present day.

In the first of this century cotton fabrics were still too scarce for many quilts to be constructed of new calico, but all mother's dresses were cut down for the girl's, or made into quilts for everyday use, or as substitutes for blankets. These quilts were individually sometimes almost a load for a horse in weight, being heavily stuffed with tow; but the better class of these covers had a wadding of cotton of wool. White counterpanes were woven of many pretty figures with beautiful fringes. These fringes were sometimes made nearly a yard wide and served as valence, and window and mantel lambrequins, which name, however, was not in use then.

Bureaus and little tables had covers of the counterpane fabric. The clean, white-washed walls, window blinds of gay paper, and hearths filled with evergreens and pots of wood flowers, made altogether quite sweet, attractive sitting rooms. But the aspect in winter was cold; few carpets had come into use; there were no pictures on the walls; no center tables covered with books; no pianos suggestive of sentiment; conversation had to come up of the mind's own fertility; however song without instrument accompaniment, and cards in the non-religious community were common resources for social enjoyment. But to revert to household affairs. The pride of every woman was to outdo her neighbor in the quantity and beauty of her textile fabrics; and the quantities produced by the slow means used were marvelous. Every house had its store chests, and I remember with distinctness two houses, the homes of several spinsters (and in one of these homes were many maid servants), where large rooms were shelved like stores and there arranged on them were dozens of pairs of sheets and blankets and quilts and counterpanes and curiously wrought coverlids of colored woolen yarns. There were shevles of huck-a-back and birdeye toweling, and webs of linsey, flannel, jeans, and bunches of socks, gloves and stockings, laid up for what possibly rainy day no one could guess, as there were no heirs apparent, or missionary boxes to fill. Every woman and child knit their own stockings then, and a girl worth having had usually two or three dozen pairs of stockings rivaling the fineness and whiteness of the genuine costly English that were brought cautiously into the store. Some of these were exquisitely clocked, and when at length knitting was displaced, measurably at least, cotton knitting, by imported hosiery, hand embroidery took its place in homes of refinement; and marvelous flowers grew under fairy fingers that had been released from cards and wheels and shuttles and knitting pins. Will it not be a pity that this precious nervine knitting for the young, this solace for the old, should ever perish from the land? I have known ladies spend three months industriously on a band of inserting for a dress inferior when done in beauty to one of hamburg that three dollars would purchase readily now.

The appointments of the culinary department, including the dining room, did not advance faster than other departments of home life. In almost every house one would find some relic of the olden homes that women had brought to the wilderness as devout Catholics carried their beads or crucifixes in crusader times; a plate or pitcher, or a few silver spoons, kind of vouchers for their ancient gentility. But a coarse, yellowish, blue edged delf was in common use. Iron knives and forks with thick horn or wooden handles and iron or wooden spoons completed the outfit, and for the table, blessed was that housewife who owned a set of pewter milk basins. After a while a little better style of china succeeded the blue edged delf. It was of less heaviness and strength than our granite, and covered with red, blue or brown flowers. In those days, too, castors and common glass tumblers were concomitants of the better china. I suppose it must have been near 1820 when Captain Jacob Keller, then a popular and tasteful merchant, brought out half a dozen sets of real French tea china containing about 60 pieces of beautifully gilt, and some hand-painted in colored landscapes. The quality was expuisite, the shape beautiful, and they were appropriated with frenzied eagerness, and some pieces of these sets linger yet in the community and are held as priceless treasures.

CHAPTER X

Mode of Living in Early Times—Customs, Fashions and Manners.

With these innnovations the croakers say, have passed away the charm of the hearty, unceremonious hospitality of good old times. This sounds better in theory than it proves in practice. In pioneer days it was needful that the string of the latch should hang outside the door, and that men should run out like Abraham and Lot and fetch in strangers. There were Indians without and no inns for the wayfaring man, but no housewife that has gone through the charming unceremonious period would vote for its restoration, and thereby relinquish the reserve privilege of today, of inviting her own guests and naming the time most convenient to receive them. I have very vivid recollections of the current of one of those winters of the "Good Old Times." A heavy snow lay for weeks, affording splendid sleighing. The young people were in a furore of fun all these weeks and the days were a series of surprise parties. The jingling of bells, the pawing of horses, the stamping of feet and clatter of many tongues became to us poor children the sounds of doom. It was doubtless to our pretty aunties and their gay gallants, who dashed to and fro from Danville to Providence, from Cane Run to Harrodsburg, very exhilirating dissipation; but to us, scarce weanlings, it meant exile to the kitchen, weary waitng for second tables and nodding in the corner while the lads and lasses danced into the "wee sma' hours," and a little one could hardly get a chance for a single cry on the mother bosom. The sleighing turnouts of these festivities were nondescript, there were no robes of fur or gay afghans. Hot rocks and hay were their foot warmers. The girls wore cloaks of gay Scotch plaids lined with biaze, a course woolen material. Several widths of these were gathered into a collar; a hood of inelegant pattern finished this singularly ungraceful garment.

About this time leghorn flats came into use; very costly, and in some styles, which varied in the many years they were used, very pretty. The girls used coarse knit over-socks instead of rubbers as now, and mittens of yarn; and it was a poor improvident father who did not keep a good riding horse and side-saddle for his daughter, and afford her a handsome broadcloth riding habit, and this, except lack of length, not differing essentially from the riding habits of present day. One young lady wore a habit trimmed with dozens of buttons, said buttons being May peas covered with green silk. The gallants wore surtouts, or well fitting overcoats, generally drab colored, with large double cape with a simulation of many more and bell-crown hats of fur; for tasteful caps and comfortable soft hats had not been invented. I remember hearing a gentleman asked, as he settled himself in his fine boots en route to the ball room: "What did your coat cost you, Archie?" "I stand from top to toe," he replied, "in just $100." Whether than was in the days of Commonwealth Bank depreciation I do not remember, but the gentleman wore a fine linen shirt with broad double pleated frill of finest linen cambric, a black broadcloth suit which cost $10 per yard; white Marseilles vest, fine calfskin boots ,and held a $10 fur hat in his hand. This must have been part of A. D. '20. It was a summer eve, and I remember how our well dressed gallant and we filed down the street to the present Morgan House about with the setting sun, en regle for the ball room where I as a child, played looker-on from an aside situation.

Waxed floors, numerous clipped candles, negro fiddlers and long rows of blooming girls in white muslin and sashes, going through the mazes of simple cotillions and reels, is the gay picture that "hangs on memory's wall." But yet, in bolder relief, the long, narrow table, decked not with flowers, or glass, or silver, save spoons, makes poor comparison when spread after such a lapse of memory's hall, with the bountiful and beautiful tables of today, for which levy has been made from the tropics to the arctic for fruits, wine, ices, and flowers. Salt fish, chip beef, homemade cheese, coffee and biscuit were the basis of the refreshment; and sweet cakes of various shapes, iced snow balls, sliced cake, custard and floats crowned the feast.

The time of assembling was worthy of admiration and imitation; they recognized the fact that girls are just as fresh and fair when the candles are just lighted, as when they lay in bed sleepy and fagged at nine or ten p. m. The time of dispersion was somewhat faulty, after the fashion of the present day. I do not remember who kept that then leading hotel of that day.

Perhaps in this connection it will be as relevant as elsewhere to speak of the dress of women and children. We have seen that in pioneer days, except relics brought from old homes, the style and material of pioneering was extremely rough. In the first quarter of this century, up to the War of 1812, there was for home use only a refining of the first materials, though for Sunday wear the increasing number of stores afforded a superior material. During the war, goods and groceries were at famine prices. Sugar and coffee, $1 per pound, and but little to be had at these figures; and I remember a child's calico wrapper preserved as a memento of war times, of indigo blue, sprinkled with white crescents, the quality of the calico answering to four cents goods of today, price one dollar per yard. A single nutmeg in a grater that could be had on any nickle counter now, cost the same money—one dollar.

After the war, by modifications of treaties, I suppose, or by invention of superior machinery, imported goods were more plentiful and cheaper, but enormously dear compared with present prices of linen and cotton goods. But there were none of the exquisite fabrics of those materials, now so common and cheap, to be had. In fact, bleached cottons were not introduced until about the close of this period, and the first painted muslins and French lawns were not on the market until midway of the third period. Silk goods and canton crepe seem to have been cheaper, our great commoner not having introduced the lauded policy of protection; and a dress could then be constructed of so few yards that at any price the aggregate amount did not come up to the cost of the trimming of the fine dress of today. The first style of dress I remember, was narrow skirted and conveniently short, straight sleeves and the waist draw string coming just below the shoulder blade, this line continued around the waist. This fashion is well preserved in numbers of coarsely painted family portraits by an itinerant artist who sometimes made marvelous hits of likeness, mainly, however, caricaturing the unfortunate subjects of his art. All dresses were worn low in the neck of evenings and for day wear were finished at the throat with wonderful wide quiltings, called collarettes very Elizabethan in proportion, and the girls wore capes of thin figured muslin or leno edged with narrow crimpled ruffles. These capes, while half concealing, half revealing the charms of beautiful busts and throats, were hardly improved by the snowy fronts that came in with high necked dresses, with revers (like gentlemen's lapels) turned back to display them.

The dresses of the old ladies were very distinctive; ample skirts, long waisted dresses, and white handkerchiefs folded across, entirely covering the bosom; close fitting muslin caps with quilted borders of plain muslin, much prettier than the high crowded, clear starched muffs which could be seen through and through, which were ceremoniously adopted immediately after marriage, as a badge of the blessed estate. But to finish the old lady's picture before the canvas dries; she wore a white lawn apron at home, and when she went out a close fitting black satin band, with narrow skirt to it, and trimmed with narrow black lace. All the saints in my calendar wear those hoods, the saintliest of them all of quaker colored satin. When the conflict of life waxes sore, I always feel like immuring myself in one of those hoods, taking an armchair in some quiet corner with folded hands, like a child sheltered in its mother's arms, and say, "who dare molest me here?" so restful, so revered are all the grandames who sit in the chambers of my memory of the old, old time. Extremes will meet. On no principle of association of ideas can I account for old ladies suggesting babies, unless cap borders prove the connecting link, but being beguiled from one fabric and style to another, I have wandered on in the labyrinth of this recital without once having glimpsed at a class ever to the front in modern days, viz: babies and children. We have never heard what was the gear of babies in pioneer days; but poor dears, we opine after the slender stock of garments brought from the old states was exhausted, that the much enquired for first born children were not clothed in soft raiment as those who dwell in kings' houses. The first baby trousseaus that I remember, were of calico and ginghams, and were most likely of mother's and sister's dresses cut down. A narrow and shortish dress with genuine infant waist, short sleeves and low neck, without regard to season, was their visible garniture; and when I record no sacks, no aprons, and that often the little blue feet kicking out were bare, we think the doctrine of the survival of the fittest was severely tested, and as no great mortality is recorded of that period, the fittest must show up handsomely in the census of A. D. '10-'20 of this m:: exalted century; but I rather think the close cap with its soft frill about the little red wrinkled face was prettier than the shining bald head of the present fashion. I remember when the bachelor favorite of a whole village brought a green young country girl to preside in his domicile, and when the "living image of its father" was unfolded, the admiration of all the neighborhood, with dress up to its throat and down to its wrists, that an audible titter ran 'round the room—in fact round the neighborhood. The sensible woman. We all appreciate and have followed in her footsteps since. The progress of comfort and luxury in other departments of home life were not much, if any, in advance of wearing apparel. Almost every housekeeper had some bowl or dish she had brought from the old states, that was kept carefully along with perhaps, a few silver spoons, as proof of her primitive gentility; but blue edged dishes and plates of coarse delf were in common use. After a while a better quality, but hardly equal to ironstone, ornamented with red or blue or parti colored flowers, superceded the blue edged, and I think it must have been somewhere about '20 that Capt. Keller, a popular merchant, brought a half dozen sets of pure china, gilt, and some of them hand painted. This importation made a memorable sensation. These sets were taken up with great eagerness, and some remnants are left that are treasured as priceless heirlooms now.

From thence forward the possession of such a set of china was the end and object of every housekeeper's life, and no importation of goods was complete without fine china; and some cut glass, such as tumblers, decanters and wine glasses came along to complete the outfit. Nothing was more common then than to send silver money to the cities to be converted into spoons. Glass and precious spoons never ran the gauntlet of kitchen chances for keeping whole. A housewife would have been as thoroughly ashamed of not washing her own china as of her husband's wearing an unbrushed hat or buttonless shirt. As to what filled those dishes, we think their bill of fare was scarcely less plain than their wares. They were scanted in vegetables, and the few they had were of coarse quality. Pumpkins, cabbage, beans and corn had possession of the earth. Potatoes had not the indispensability of today, nor had they the perfectly shaped and flavored tubers we have now. Sweet potatoes were an after addition; they were not commonly cultivated; and salsify, celery and summer cabbage came a long time after; and tomatoes and egg plants ranked as vegetable curiosities; the last has hardly left that list yet; but the universal favorite of today, the tomato, was then kept as a mantel ornament. Peaches were abundant almost from the first settlement of the county, and orchards of apples w' planted at every new home from the beginning, and were as fine and plentiful as was possible. Hens and hogs fattened on them; they were baked and fried and pied and stored in earthen pits for winter. Cider and vinegar flowed like water, and apple and peach brandy were manufactured without stint, and do doubt did their part in making us the nation of drunkards we are accused of being. Some attention was given to melons; but grapes were rarely found until our fathers had been gathered to their rest, not indeed in abundance until within the last twenty-five years.

Cooking stoves were not; and strange to say, did not find favor for a decade or two after their introduction. People naturally did not study common sense in ante bellum days as they do now, when subject in emergencies to get into the kitchen themselves. On the plantations, the kitchen fireplace was ample enough for a log heap, and the cook, or the nondescript "chillen," who infested the rear of the premises, often packed the wood from the forest to cook with; and the spring was usually more than a Sabbath day's journey from the kitchen, and that indispensible office itself was frequently absolutely outside of the yard. Central in the great cavern of a fire place, hung a large iron pot, in which the meat (bacon commonly) and all the vegetables for the hands were cooked—cabbage, corn, turnips and beans together. Wheat bread was scarce but commonly only used for breakfast; and coffee and tea were not usually on the tea table. A large oven of dodgers or batch of bread very sweet and wholesome, was baked in the ashes, sometimes wrapped in wet paper or cabbage leaves, or spread on a board like hoe cakes and set like roast before the fire, and this was called "Johnnie Cake." On the same rack with the dinner pot, hung all winter, one for hominy which was prepared by beating the husk off the corn in a mortar with small maul or scalding them off with lye. Gathered around these large kettles, like chickens around the mother hen, were all sizes of cooking vessels, in which more delicate preparations of the same ingredients the larger boilers contained, were preparing for the white folks' table. The unfailing ham and game, or chicken and squab, or oftener shoats were the meats most used. Eggs were plentiful, and homely pie abounded. An old ham at the head and roast turkey or chicken at the foot, a few vegetables for side dishes, with plain pickles, bread, butter and jelly was about the bill of fare of the best dinners. Pancakes or fritters with tree molasses were the dessert. On high days and holidays mince pie, with custard or rich milk, crowned the feast. Ice cream and loaf cake did not come into use before '30. Sliced cake, however, had been served for years before on that waiter, which it had been as gross an omission not to hand to lady visitors as it was not to invite gentlemen to a stand on which set the inevitable bottle and sugar dish! I have seen a table into which these had worn their trace as plain as foot prints on the snow. Gentlemen sometimes used mint and sugar or honey with whisky or brandy, ladies cordial or domestic wine. Peach liquor was a favorite of both parties. Then, too, the regulations were for every man to put himself at the back door with the bottle at the blowing of the dinner horn and give the men and out working women an antifogmatic every morning; and sometimes a pack of hounds roused by the blast, would give a chorus of stirring music. Some painter will distinguish himself yet by coloring for the world this characteristic scene of Old Bargo times, as the negroes called them.

CHAPTER XI

Burr's Conspiracy—General James Wilkinson.

Had Kentucky, like Israel, been given to raising memorial stores, she might have gathered around the last mile mark of the eighteenth century quite a pyramid.

Imprimis. She had possessed herself of a vast tract of country which is still called, and the title rarely questioned, the Eden of America. She had buried the hatchet of war and smoked the calumet of peace with her aboriginal foes. She sat now by rights in the county chambers of a confederation of states that had wrested their independence from the mistress of the world. The executive seats of the nation and the state were satisfactorily filled and her own amended and renewed constitution was just going into operation. The navigation of the Mississippi, the most coveted of all privileges, had been secured for the outlet of the product of her virgin soil that was just opening to the plough shares of her thronging emigrants. But ere she had set up her Ebenezer and counted the pioneer troubles over which she had tided and the blessings now enjoyed, many perplexities of a civil nature arose to disturb the public mind. In the first place, the emigration to Kentucky was not merely of the adventure-seeking class, such as Boone, Girty, Kenton, etc., etc., but owners of wornout lands from the old thirteen colonies, chiefly Virginia, with admixture of Carolinians and some Pennsylvanians, flooded the country expecting to have for the price of the old home a farm for every living child. This was a financial stroke or policy easily then made. There came also many men of the Sir Walter Raliegh order who saw in this western wilderness an Eldorado; and before Kentucky had been settled a quarter of a century while she was yet a territory, she had been divded into counties, counties were dotted with incipient villages; her choicest lands were shingled with conflicting claims, and lawyers and politicans were as plenty as Indian fighters had been in the first decade of her pioneer existence. There was consequently a harvest of litgation soon, such as no legal field of the country had ever produced; and few were the landlords who did not find themselves the unhappy parties to as many lawsuits as claims, and to persons curious about the issue of these suits, I refer them to their own family record, or Dicken's matchless illustration of the course of law in "Great Expectations."

The series of conventions held in Danville had been not only assemblies where statesmen had discussed and devised measures for our independence and plans for successful home government, but they had also been schools in which the people gained a thorough knowledge of their rights and wrongs. This knowledge, backed by the intense desire which human heart has to always get at least its own, if not other people's rights, kept our county, in common with the rest of Kentucky, almost at ebullition points. This excitement was now, too, fed by the mails which, though their coming was "like angel's visits, few and far between," still bore the burden of Indian harrassments in the northwest, and from the east the story of British outrage and insult to our navy, which causes were heading surely and not slowly to the war of 1812. The newspaper, too, had become by this time, a factor in the creation of public sentiment, and while it had neither the size, type, frequency or variety of the present journal, still it let off steam enough to

Old Mud Meeting House

start and keep hot the hearts of a people always on the qui vive for a sensation; and the mental giants of those days fought their battles in these columns as well as sometimes on the miscalled field of honor. Early in this period, however, in 1803, the public mind had a perfect and final quietus on one of their supreme anxieties, viz: the navigation of the Mississippi which, even after the treaty with Spain, had been faithlessly and capriciously interrupted. In consequence of his conquest of Spain, Napoleon had acquired Louisiana; but far too wise to undertake to hold these distant colonial possessions against the great maritime power of the foe with which he was grappling for the mastery of Europe, he, willing to strengthen a rival rising power of his adversary, ceded to the United States for the paltry sum of $15,000,000 this first magnificent annexation to her territory. Thus Mr. Monroe, as our negotiating minister, laid the first substantial foundation of what is termed his American policy. Thus also was barred the further overtures of these governments of our people for secession from the Federal Union. But the cancerous growth had left its germs in the hot bed soil of western mind, and so when not longing after the baleful star, Aaron Burr rose on the eastern horizon and took his course westward, withering in his passage the Blannerhasset paradise, he landed even in Harrodsburg, scarcely then the nucleus of the town it is now. His headquarters were in the old frame hotel lately demolished and its site now occupied by the Mercer National Bank. He seems to have exercised as much fascination in the little society of Harrodsburg as in the wider metropolitan circles. Neither his misfortunes nor indictment for treason could ever wholly extinguish the pride with which men spoke of the time when "my old friend, Col. Burr, was here;" nor did women cease to keep, bright as their hereditary silver, the charming nothings that gallant knight of the carpet as well as of the field, had lavished on them. What was precisely the nature and scope of Burr's scheme, has never been clearly eliminated from the confused mass of traditional assertion, denial, slander, and vindication of which it was composed; and in that day there were no reporters of the genus moles and beavers to work under and work up this case for them or posterity. He was supposed to aim at the conquest of Mexico and its consolidation with the south and west. This would have a magnificent empire, and he, its emperor or dictator, might have almost claimed peership with Bonaparte, and have scattered crowns and principalities as largely as did that banker in thrones.

I will not undertake the invidious task of saying who was individually concerned in that scheme. History gives some names, tradition more; but who would not rather let scores escape, unwhipped of justice, than affix the stigma of treason on one innocent character?

Of course, Mercer, having been during the convention period the arena of debate on the State's Right theory, and the canvassing of this right and the grand results to Kentucky that would follow her incorporation into this southwestern empire, was stirred to the core by Col. Burr's presence and the breath of suspicions that arose that he was here to revive this scheme. But the people of Mercer took no taint of this treason and the revelation of the fact that our own town was the actual plot ground of this grand scheme and the speedy bursting of the bubble thereafter, so completely dazed the county that it took no action in meetings of repudiation or denunciation; and the people pondered over it as some wild dream that had swept over their diseased imagination.

The doubt, like a brooding cloud that for a while was left over General Adair, was soon all over after Burr's trial that lingered in their mind. But when Adair had demanded a trial and been acquitted, and had, as though exempt by years, so readily responded to the tap of the drum for volunteers for the war of 1812, the wave of popular enthusiasm lifted him above the lingering mists of suspicion, to the pinnacle of public favor, and the Burr conspiracy was passed to the archives of the oblivious past, and will only, in this little memorial, be revived as connected with the life of Col. Joe Daviess, United States prosecuting attorney, who was reared in this county on the Daviess farm, now a part of the landed domain of Peter Gentry, of Boyle. Col. Daviess likewise resided in Danville a term of years and belonged to that bar, and as one of the chief dramatic personae of the Burr play, we follow with a sketch of his life, upon which the curtain fell before the opening act of 1812 in the next chapter, finishing this with a brief memoir of Wilkinson, who also had a prominent part in this memorable episode of western national history.

Gen. James Wilkinson.

In this connection, there is space for one whom those conversant with the revolution of 1776, and the exciting period of our county's history over which we are now passing, might naturally expect to meet General James Wilkinson, a native of Maryland, who possessed a versatility of talent and unflaggging energy rarely equaled, and an ambition that brought him up to heights seldom attained by one, who after all, was not a man of firstrate ability. He was born for a division general, never for Generalissimo. He was a Captain in the Revolutionary army at eighteen, and a brave General at twenty, and a prime favorite of some of the leading spirits of that time.

After the acknowledgement of American Independence he came west and was a leader in merchantile enterprise and politics, and while never a citizen of Mercer, had more to do, perhaps in moulding public sentiment than any man in the bounds, certainly more in fermenting the discontent of the people, and developing the unholy desire to become a separate western power, than even Aaron Burr. He was one of the delegates from Lexington to several of the state conventions in Danville. He was a man of fine personal appearance, suave manners, and was a brilliant debator, having the tact to bring out the full support of his side in debate as well as vote on roll call; and to his views of Mississippi policy he brought the weight of having actually negotiated for himself commercial arrangements in New Orleans with the Spanish authorities, that set the people wild to participate in. He made a contract to supply any quantity of tobacco for a term of years at 10 cents per pound, which was really like opening a mine of gold.

The question of his life was doubtless "whether or not he should embark in Burr's enterprise?" The question posterity asks concerning him is "Did he?" After a careful reading of the history of his tmes, and of wading through what of his memoirs of 1816 I could have access to, I am bound to render the verdict of guilty. Could the prosecuting attorney have compelled the attendance of the witnesses he demanded in that celebrated trial, some of them doubtless could have been indicted for misprison of treason, but Wilkinson for the high misdemeanor itself.

Burr's plot was probably unrolled as a panorama before the different classes of dupes into whose minds and tempers his keen knowledge of human nature gave him deep insight. To the mere seekers of commercial advantages he was only going to widen the channels of commerce; to more adventurous but still loyal, he was going to be the entering wedge into Spanish territory that the country would gladly follow; to the yet more reckless and less scrupulous, empire and wealth were to be the guerdon of their swords.

To Wilkinson was most probably unfolded the whole scheme; and when the news of the disaster and failure of it reached him, he adroitly shifted his preparation to the defensive side, denounced Burr, seized and sent around suspects to the government at Washington for trial.

Hon. Ben Hardin took me to the Vicksburg heights and showed the plateau on which Wilkinson's guns were to have been planted to force the surrender of Burr's flotilla in its descent to New Orleans.

However I will not mark the execution of so distinguished a man with a politcal bar sinister without giving the grounds of his protest against this desecration of his shield.

Judge Wilkinson denied these charges by word and pen. He continued in correspondence with Mr. Jefferson, then President, posting him with whatever information he could get of the rise, progress and aims of this conspiracy. He demanded an investigation of his conduct, was acquitted, and was subsequently appointed commander-in-chief of the northwestern army, but proved so inefficient that in the re-organization of that branch of the service he was silently dropped. He then retired to Mexico, after publishing his voluminous memoirs in 1816, lived on his magnificent estates in that country until his death, which occurred in 1828.

PART II

CHAPTER XII

Colonel Joseph Hamilton Daviess was the son of Joseph and Jean Daviess, and was born in Bedford county, Virginia, on the 4th of March, 1774. The parents of Mr. Daviess were both natives of Virginia; but his father was of Irish, and his mother of Scotch descent, and the marked peculiarities of each of those races were strongly developed in the character of their son. The hardy self-reliance, the indomitable energy, and imperturbable coolness, which have from the earliest time distinguished the Scotch, were his; while the warm heart, free and open hand, and ready springing tear of sensibility told in the language plainer than words, that the blood of Erin flowed fresh in his veins. When young Daviess was five years old, his parents removed to Kentucky, then an almost unbroken wilderness, and settled in the then county of Lincoln, in the immediate vicinity of the present town of Danville. An accident which attended their journey to Kentucky, although trifling in itself, may be related, as exhibiting in a very striking light the character of the mother, to whose forming influence was committed the subject of this notice.

In crossing the Cumberland river, Mrs. Daviess was thrown from her horse, and had her arm broken. The party only halted long enough to have the limb bound up, with what rude skill the men of the company possessed; and pursued their route, she riding a spirited horse and carrying her child, and never ceasing her exertions to promote the comfort of her companions when they stopped for rest and refreshment. The parents of young Daviess, in common with the very early settlers of Kentucky, had many difficulties to encounter in raising their youthful family, especially in the want of schools to which children could be sent to obtain the rudiments of an English education. It was several years after their settlement in Kentucky, before the subject of this sketch enjoyed even the advantages of a common country school. Previous to this time however, his mother bestowed considerable attention on the education of her sons by communicating such information as she herself possessed. At the age of eleven or twelve he was sent to a grammar school taught by a Mr. Worley, where he continued for about two years, learned the Latin language, and made considerable progress in his English education. He subsequently attended grammar school taught by a Dr. Brooks at which he remained a year, making considerable advances in a knowledge of the Greek language. At school he evinced unusual capacity, being always at the head of his class. He was particularly remarkable for his talent for declamation and public speaking, and his parents felt natural anxiety to give him as many advantages as their limited resources would permit. There being at that time no college in the country, he was placed under the charge of Dr. Culbertson, where he completed his knowledge of the Greek tongue. At this time, the sudden death of a brother and sister occasioned his being recalled from school, and he returned home to assist his father in the labors of the farm. There is a tradition that young Daviess was not particularly distinguished by his devotion to agricultural pursuits, frequently permitting the horses of his plow to graze at leisure, in most unfarmerlike way, while he stretched supinely on his back on some luxurious log, indulged in those delicious dreams and reveries so sweet to young and aspiring ambition.

In the autumn of 1792, Maj. Adair, under Government order, raised some companies of mounted men, to guard the transportation of provisions to the forts north of the Ohio river, and Daviess, then in the 18th year, volunteered in the service, which it was understood would be from three to six months duration. Nothing of particular interest occurred in the course of the service, except on one occasion when Maj Adair had encamped near Fort St. Clair. Here he was surprised, early in the morning, by a large body of Indians, who, rushing into camp just after the sentinels had been withdrawn from the posts, killed and wounded fourteen or fifteen of the men, and captured and carried away about two hundred head of horses. These were taken within the Indian lines and tied. After the whites had sought shelter in the neighborhood of the fort, young Daviess, discovering his horse at some distance hitched to a tree, resolved to have him at all hazards. He accordingly ran and cut him loose and led him back to his companions amid a shower of balls. The exploit nearly cost him his life, a ball passing through his coat, waistcoat, and cutting off a small piece of his shirt. He, however, saved his horse, which was the only one retaken out of the two hundred.

When his term of service expired, he returned home, and spent some time in reviewing his classical studies. He ultimately concluded to study law, and accordingly entered the office of the celebrated George Nicholas, then the first lawyer in Kentucky. Daviess entered a class of students consisting of Isham Talbott, Jesse Bledsoe, William Garrard, Felix Grundy, William Blackbourne, John Pope, William Stuart and Thomas Dye Owings, all of whom were subsequently distinguished at the bar and in the public history of the country. Nicholas was very profoundly impressed with the striking indications of genius of a high order, manifested by Daviess while under his roof; and so high an opinion did he form of the power of his character and the firmness of his principle, that at his death, which occurred but a few years after, he appointed him one of his executors. He was a most laborious and indefatigable student; he accustomed himself to take his repose upon a hard bed, was fond of exercise in the open air, habituating himself to walking several hours in each day; he was accustomed in the days when he was a student, to retire to the woods with his books and pursue his studies in some remote spot, secure from the annoyance and interruption of society. In connection with his legal studies, he read history and miscellaneous literature, so that when he came to the bar his mind was richly stored with various and profound knowledge, imparting a fertility and affuence to his resources, from which his powerful and well trained intellect drew inexhaustible supplies. He commenced the practice of law in June, 1795; in August he was qualified as an attorney in the court of appeals, and in his first case had for an antagonist his old preceptor, over whom he enjoyed the singular gratification of obtaining a signal triumph.

At the session of 1795-6, the legislature passed a law establishing district courts. One of these courts was located at Danville, one at Lexington, and one at Bardstown. Daviess settled at Danville, situated some ten miles from Harrodsburg, and soon commanded a splendid business, not only in that, but in all the courts in which he practiced. He continued to reside in Danville until the abolition of the district courts, and the substitution of circuit courts in their place. He then removed to Frankfort to be enabled more conveniently to attend the court of appeals and the federal court, having been appointed United States attorney for the State of Kentucky. In the year 1801-'2 he went to Washington City, being the first western lawyer who ever appeared in the supreme court of the United States. He here argued the celebrated case of Wilson vs. Mason. His speech is said to have excited the highest admiration of the bench and bar, and placed him at once in the foremost ranks of the profession.

That he appeared before the august tribunal in spattered leggins and rough surtout has gone to history as an illustration of his eccentricity and contempt of the conventionalities of society, dress, etc. This was untrue; his habit was doubtless in strict conformity to the regime of that day as to dress, as all of the several pictures of him show. His fine portrait, by Jouett, is in full military costume, lace, sash, eqaulettes, as well as pistols and sword. His appearance before the court at the capital was a necessity. He knew his case was set for that day; he rode directly to the court room in Washington, found his case had just been called and went into it in his traveling costume, without one thought of his own personnel, leaving his horse and colored valet in the street. Neither was his habit of walking chiefly on his circuit from point to point while his attendant rode and led his horse, affectation; it was his habit to study thus at home pacing to and fro in the solitudes of the mighty forests.

During this trip he visited the principal cities of the north and east and formed an acquaintance with many of the most distinguished men of these times, with whom he continued in correspondence during his life.

He returned by invitation from Chief Justice Marshall to visit him in Virginia. He there met his fate in the person of Miss Ann, sister of the Chief Justice, to whom he was united in marriage in 1803. There was no issue from this marriage. Mrs. Daviess was married twice again, but I have heard, lies under a tombstone marked in compliance with her own direction, the "wife of Jos. H. Daviess."

He lived for a while after his marriage, in Frankfort, and it was during his residence there, that came up, if not the most brilliant, the most noted passage in his profession and career, certainly the most exciting and interesting. He differed wholly from Burr in political faith; he was Federal almost to the defense of centralization for the sake of a state and strong government and loathed Burr's treachery as leprosy; and being thoroughly convinced of his guilt, Kentucky's infatuation for this unprincipled adventurer humiliated and stung him almost to madness. Her worship for one that he knew, like Lucifer, that "son of the morning," must so soon fall from these heights to the lowest depth of infamy. Probably there was never seen in the west such mental gladiatorial strife as on that occasion was fought between Col. Daviess, the United States prosecuting attorney, and Henry Clay, the defender of Burr, in the fullest faith of his innocence, in the plausible vindication of himself, was only less eloquent than these transcendent orators.

The last time I ever saw Mr. Clay, was the afternoon after his address, by invitation, to the enthusiastic masses in the Legislative Hall on the state of the union. We stood together at the door of the new Capital Hotel waiting steamboat signals for departurue. "You wear," he said, "the likeness of Col. Daviess." I unfastened by brooch, an exquisite painting on ivory, and handed it to him. He gazed on it intensely and sadly. There had always been reported jealously and rivalry from him toward Col. Daviess. He handed back the miniature saying, with kindly eyes: "Madam, you have heard otherwise, but in all this broad land there was no one admired that magnificent man more than I." Could I recall verbatim the words of eulogy he pronounced on the subject of my sketch, I should have weakened them with no phrase of mine. We walked slowly on to the landing, I going aboard the little craft that plied between the capital and our county landing, and he en route for Washington on a fine river packet. As he stepped aboard the brass band struck up, "Hail to the Chief," the Stars and Stripes floated above him, and again and again he answered with his own gracious majesty the salutes, (do I exaggerate) the idolatrous crowd from Kentucky shore. Thus he passed from my sight forever, and if Indian mythology were true, he and the chief of my story wander today under the palms or the heroes' hereafter.

From Frankfort, Col. Daviess removed to Owensboro, the county seat of the county named for him, to attend to a large estate he had acquired in that region. But soon tiring of so tame a life, he went to Lexington, Ky., in 1809, and for the two years that he practiced there he had one side of every cause of importance. It is said, on one occasion as he journeyed across the woods and wilds for a point in his circuit, while his groom carried his horse by the highway, that he came upon a crowd in a country school house eager to hang a horse thief. He stopped; his sympathies were aroused for the cowering criminal so he went into the trial and by an impromptu effort, saved the man from his peril, and great was the surprise of the crowd when they learned this volunteer attorney was Joe Daviess.

In the early fall of 1811, Col. Daviess joined the army of Gen. Harrison in the campaign against the Indians on the Wabash. He received the command of Major, the duties of which office he discharged promptly and to the entire satisfaction of his superior officer. On the 7th of November, 1811, in the celebrated battle of Tippecanoe, he fell at dawn, in a charge against the Indians, made at his own request; and thus sacrificed in war with savages a life replete with all the elements of usefulness to his country and kind. Col. Allin, his bosom friend and comrade in arms, came to tell his kindred the sorrowful tidings. "All day long," he said, "he lay under the shade of a giant sycamore tree, his life ebbing slowly away, and awaiting his last enemy, death, with unquailing eye. His spirit passed out with the setting sun, and by the starlight his soldiers laid him in his rude grave, wrapped only in his soldier's branket, and as the thud of the falling earth fell on their ears they wept like children."

Col. Daviess was tall, with a vigorous, athletic frame, which combined with the fine intellectual expression of his face, gave him a remarkably commanding and impressive appearance. The light of his eyes was softened by a melancholy tenderness, the firm mouth sweetened by a smile of ineffable tenderness. His bearing was grave and dignified, his manner courteous, even affectionate to those he loved. He was a charming colloquest—the life of every circle in which he entered. As an orator he had no superior and few equals, was the opinion expressed by Boyle, McKee, Pope and others. Kentucky, Missouri and Indiana have perpetuated his name by counties. Indiana has erected a monument, which rests on the spot where he fell.

A few interesting relics of Col. Daviess remain. Some jewelry woven of his hair, his watch, the property of the heirs of Gen. Camillus Daviess, of Missouri, a beautiful miniature of him in youth, a gift to Mrs. H. D. Pittman, of St. Louis, Mo., from her grandfather, Col. Daviess' brother, and a splendid portrait of him in maturer years, from the studio of Jouett; also the pistols he wore when he fell, and with which it is said Clay and Marshall fought their duel. His sword was presented some years ago to the Grand Masonic Lodge of Kentucky, of which Col. Daviess was Grand Master when he died, by his legal disciple and friend, Judge Levi Todd. It was offered in a box made of sycamore under the friendly shade of which he died. There is also left the table on which the indictment of Aaron Burr was penned and the press in which his fabulous mass of papers were kept in faultless alphabetical order. There were masses of letters to him, some from the most distinguished men of his time. Of his own, he preserved no copies. There was also one printed work extant; it is an address to the Congress of the United Stattes elaborating a system of defense for the country by organized and trained militia. His strong tincture of Federalism, however, so prejudiced the then supreme democratic party, that they did not entertain his comprehensive and possibly, also, very wise views. The most interesting relic remaining of Col. Daviess as most characteristic of his energy and untiring industry, is a large, heavy leather-bound volume of several hundred pages. It is a digest of law in his own clear hand without one blot or erasure.

Scene at the Preliminary Meeting on June 16, 1923, for the 150th Anniversary Celebration, June 16, 1924.

CHAPTER XIII

War of 1812—Men of That Period—General John Adair—General Robert McAfee—Colonel Gabriel Slaughter.

Until the breaking out of the War of 1812, Mercer county moved on with only the ordinary ripple that private and local affairs give to public events. But this war followed quickly on the current of time that had borne to the past the conspiracy of Burr. The history of the War of 1812 belongs to the records of the nation; the part which our troops had in it belongs to the history of Kentucky. But it can not be amiss to heighten the interest of our county's limited share in these campaigns by reminding in brief the general reader, and especially the young, of the causes which led to the declaration of war with England; and of the reasons that this declaration was received with such boundless enthusiasm in the West—in our state and, of course, in our county.

Firstly: Oppression and wrongs from the mother country, which had led to the rebellion of 1776, still festered in the memory of our grandsires; they had been handed down from father to son, and were aggravated each year by repeated insults and injuries.

Secondly: The constantly exercised right, which Great Britain claimed, of search of ships and seizure of every sailor found aboard of them in whom could be found a tinge of Irish, Scotch, or English blood, and the cruel treatment of these sailors, had roused, not only national but human, resentment against these flagrant outrages. England was then warring with France, who had come with almost Quixotic chivalry to us in our unequal fight with "the old bruiser," as one of our public men has branded our unnatural mother; and though France had trailed her fleur de lis in blood, and had gilded our republic flag with Imperial Eagles, the sympathies of the warm hearted south were still with her; and indeed the glamour of Napoleon's beneficent tyranny, to this day blinded the masses to his enormous oppression.

These causes of war affected the country paradoxically. New England, whose goods were borne under every sail that swept the ocean, and whose sailors were impressed from every barque to rot in holds, or to perish in unhealthy climates, opposed the war almost to the verge of secession; while the west, where these high handed measures scarcely trenched upon the morale or material of a living being, was phrensied with indignation and answered the call for troops by pouring out her thousands. For a long while, the ill-managed but finally successful campaigns lingered on the border states of the lakes, and closed out triumphantly on the Thames. Whether the Kentucky troops floundered through the marshes of the Indian territory, or marched over the frozen fields of Ohio and Michigan, Mercer men were there.

I do not know that the ill-kept muster rolls are extant that a complete list of the soldiers of these campaigns might be given. I know that General McAfee and Major T. P. Moore were o fthe number.

Few leaders of Kentucky history will forget that from our old burg, the faithful pig started out that went and returned with our boys and lived to old age at "Traveler's Rest," the residence of Governor Isaac Shelby. That model farmer, as well as Governor, should have founded a race from that patriotic source and scattered them wide to point a moral with that sterling lesson of fidelity and devotion to country that was so well illustrated in her weary march from the lakes. Indeed, that historic pig was less like the Israelites than some of our men, for truth compels me, as a faithful historian, to record the fact, that while our troops were rash in volunteering, and brave in battle, it was hard, during the long marches to keep them from turning back to the flesh pots and firesides they had left behind them. In extenuation we must add that the commission stores were insufficient and miserably managed. Whatever may be said by metaphysicians, it will always be found that courage is not purely a mental quality, but depends very much for life and energy on that material basis—a well fed body.

But to revert from the digression about the partiotic pig, given for the benefit of our juvenile readers. Before the returned soldiers had rested from their weariness and suffering in the service on the lakes and in the northwest, Governor Shelby made a call for volunteers, which elicited a hearty and prompt response. "The bugle had sung truce" over the waters, but its lulling notes had not swept across the seas and penetrated to our wilderness homes and ere it did reach· them our county men were again in the ranks of the country's defenders in the swamps of the menaced Crescent City.

General Jackson was in command at New Orleans. The city was totally unfortified; there was no maritime defense, but a few boats, too contemptible in size and numbers to be counted. He had but two regiments of soldiers; these and the militia of the city being his whole dependence for defense. Two thousand Kentucky volunteers, under General Thomas, were hastening to his aid; but there were not enough arms when they reached the camp to equip them, and it is said that several hundred men, panting for the fray, were left out of the battle of New Orleans for the want of equipment. Meanwhile the American troops were confronted by the finest British army that had ever trod our continent. This splendid body of veterans had been released, by the downfall of Napoleon, from European service, having served under the Duke of Wellington in his last triumphant campaign against imperial France. They were sent under General Packenham, a connection of Wellington's, and a distinguished officer, to America, to seize and hold New Orleans, the most important military post in the south. But the discipline and strategy of this accomplished commander of these veterans, trained in the severe school of experience, were unable to cope with the activity, energy and readiness for emergencies habitual to American generalship, and our proud old mother was again humbled before her comparatively undisciplined wilderness children. Our Mercer men were amongst the half-equipped forces that bore the brunt of the British attack below the city; and half armed and half naked as they were, constituted a part of the famous reserve which Adair held ready and with which it is said he turned the tide of battle on that memorable day. General Jackson, in his exultation over a success, which it was thought by many that Adair planned and which certainly his troops conquered, made some inconsiderate charges of misconduct on the part of the Kentucky troops, of which Mercer men were a part. These charges were substquently retracted, as narrated in the life of General Adair.

The war being closed by treaty before the battle of New Orleans, so soon as the news reached the government, peace was proclaimed and our troops disbanded. For many years soldiers of 1812 were familiar to us all, but they have passed away one by one.

Maj. John G. Meur, of Boyle, was on the staff of General Adair that day. Mr. James Curry, the founder of the family of successful and well known business men of our town, who all remember, was one of that volunteer band of Mercer men. So was George Davis, whose tall, spare figure we but lately miss from our court yard. George Myers has just died in the Christian armor that he put on perhaps, before he wore his country's uniform at memorable New Orleans; and just outside our town limits still lingers the venerable James Hardin. If there be any more amongst us I regret that I do not know their names to include in this feeble effort to do "honor to whom honor is due."

Governor Gabriel Slaughter.

Col. Gabriel Slaughter was born in Virginia and married there his first wife, Miss Hord. He did not come to Kentucky in time to participate in its pioneer struggles, but identified himself fully with his adopted state, and went out leading Mercer troops in the second British War of 1812, and showed himself a faithful soldier and competent commander, not to be swerved from his conviction of duty even by the despotic chief, Gen. Jackson, himself. The self-willed Generalissimo informed Col. Slaughter that the verdict of a court martial, in which Col. Slaughter had presided, was not in accordance with his, General Jackson's wishes. "I know my duty, and have done it," briefly replied our Mercer militia Colonel.

Col. Slaughter was elected in 1816, Lieutenant Governor of Kentucky. George Madison had been elected Governor and died not long after his inauguaration. Col. Slaughter took the reins of government into his hands and proceeded to administer without fear or favor, though the storm raised in the state over this proceeding might have decided many a more sensitive and yielding nature to throw up and submit to the new election for which the people vociferously clamored. John Pope, secretary of state, resigned hoping thus to modify public sentiment; for he was conscious that his opposition to the War of 1812 with Great Britain had rendered him very unpopular, nay, odious, to the state which had gone into it with most unselfish enthusiasm. This resignation failed of its intentions and the discontent was so general and violent, that Col. Slaughter could not very readily find a successor to Mr. Pope. But he persisted, in the discharge of his executive duties, and thus forever practically settled the principle of succession to office; that constitutionally in case of the resignation or death of the Governor elect, the Lieutenant Governor succeeds to the vacancy. Death has several times occurred in the executive mansion of the United States, and the accession, without demur from the people, of the Vice President to the President's chair, has endorsed the legality of Col. Slaughter's action though in point of time his proceeding had priority.

The home of Governor Slaughter was modest frame house embosomed in orchards and locust groves in the center of a farm lying on the east of the Lexington and Harrodsburg turnpike, midway between Harrodsburg and Pleasant Hill. The house has long since been superceded by a more extensive and tasteful structure, erected by Maj. John Handy, who came to Mercer county to superintend the building of Bacon College, and was by him devised to his daughter, Mrs. Hugh McElroy, but has in the past years passed into the hands of strangers. Across the turnpike, in the middle of a large field owned by the friends of Pleasant Hill, in a small enclosure in a thicket of evergreens and weeping willows, rest the mortal remains of this sturdy, old patriot. He left a considerable family of children, whose descendants are scattered under various names from the lakes to Texas, his only son living in the latter state, and I believe without an heir to his name.

General Robert B. McAfee

The only descendant of these pioneer McAfees who, bearing the name, reached the standard of office in Mercer county, to which I have limited these sketches, was the son of Robert McAfee, whose home was on the banks of Salt river, occupying the site of an aboriginal Indian village. General McAfee inherited this homestead and built upon it a spacious brick house, in which he collected many prehistoric relics and souvenirs of Indian times found on the farm. The house is now the property of Mr. Mat Curry, of Harrodsburg.

Robert B. McAfee, by the untimely death of his father, was left an orphan at eleven years of age, and by will of his father was left in guardianship of his cousin, John McCoun, and the Hon. John Breckinridge, who allowed him every opportunity for education that his native state then afforded. He graduated at Transylvania University and afterward studied law under his guardian, Mr. Breckinridge. He then returned to his paternal home and practiced law under the great disadvantage of living in the country miles from the county seat. He was greatly harrassed by law suits—the most fruitful crops of every land inheritance by reason of carelessness and ignorance of the early surveyors. He had a natural proclivity for politics, to which he gave his attention, with one digression to the tented field. He volunteered immediately upon the declaration of war in 1812, and with a company of mounted riflemen, joined the northwestern army and returned as second lieutenant. In this campaign he did considerable services and in 1813, being commissioned by Governor Shelby, he raised a company again and participated in the battle of the Thames. Returning from the war, he made his home on his farm, spending much time however in the capital of the State, serving several sessions in the legislature and being four years there as Lieutenant Governor. He was appointed by General Jackson minister to Bogota, and had the rare distinction of being made member of the Royal Antiquarian Society of Denmark. He took to himself in the beginning of his manhood an almost childish wife, and had numerous children, but the most of them died ere they reached the meridian of life.

General McAfee was reared in the strictest of Presbyterian tenets, and seems never to have passed entirely from under the influence of his home training. He passed through all the demoralization of camp and hustings, and the influence of the skeptics of that day so plentifully generated by Paine's "Age of Reason," and the savants of the French revolution, and settled down by mid-life in the professed conviction of the truth and value of the Christian religion. He was a long time an elder of the church of New Providence and the bosom friend of his revered pastor, Rev. Thomas Cleland, side by side with whom he stood during the stormy ecclesiastical passage of 183-, which rent the Presbyterian churches into New and Old School.

General McAfee wrote a great deal at this time, as well as for the papers during his political life; but the only durable work of his pen remaining is a history of the war of 1812, now hard to be obtained. It is an excellent record of that interesting period. He died in the bosom of his family, and now sleeps in the rural cemetery of New Providence, the churchyard where his forefathers lie.

CHAPTER XIV

General John Adair

Alphabetically first, and meritoriously not second to any on the list of Mercer's military men, stands the name of Gen. John Adair. He was born in Chester county, Carolina, of honest, honorable, plain Scotch parentage. He and his brother were sent to Charlotte, North Carolina, for college education, but were soon recalled to the protection of their father's family from the teign of terror instituted by Tarlton, of the British army, and his lawless Tories. At seventeen years of age he formed one of the nucleus of Marion's and Sumpter's famous bands, who were found sometimes swooping down on the cruel and insolent foe, sometimes fleeing like the wind, and sometimes chained for months to a cheerless dungeon floor, or in charnal prison shops.

He fought in the Revolutionary war to the sunset hour, coming out as Major Adair, having served lastly on the staff of General Sumpter. He fought at Rock Mountain, Hanging Rock, and in many minor battles. He lived almost in the saddle, as did the men of deathless fame of Marion's band, whose tent, like that of Allen-a-Dale.

"Was the blue vault of heaven,
With its crescent so pale,
And all its bright spangles."

When the bugles sang truce, Quixotic in love as in war, without one thought for the morrow he buckled down with "Miss Katherine," we ought to call her from her queenly looks—Katie Palmer, as he ever called her. In the twilight hours of life as she would sit with hands clasped on the arm of the oaken chair in which he always sat by the window, smoking his pipe and looking silently and tenderly down at her as she chatted and chatted to "Johnnie O'Dear," I thought it the finest, prettiest tableau I had ever seen of "John Anderson, my Joe John."

In 1786, General Adair moved to Kentucky, whether for the betterment of his future or from an instinct that led him wherever adventure or danger beckoned him, it were hard to tell. He never seemed to care to accumulate wealth and while he answered at every appeal of his country, he never apparently sought the camp for mere pleasurable excitement in the hazards of war. He never seemed to seek civil or military promotion; and yet the records of peace and of war, wherever he lived, are marked with his name in shining characters.

In 1781, he went with Wilkinson's expedition against the Wea and Miami Indians on the Wabash. He was then Brigade Major, and signally honored himself by his fearless attack on a large party of Indians gathered at the ruins of Tippecanoe, who had hovered invisibly and unknown in close proximity to Wilkinson's quarters. His horseback dash across the river upon the Indians was so sudden that they fled in dismay; and General Wilkinson made to the Military Department at Washington, most just and complimentary mention of General Adair's military efficiency—a record that in after years, General Wilkinson could fain have expunged.

In 1792, he was again in the field of Indian warfare, and was sent to reconnoitre and to escort provisions from Cincinnati and neighboring points to Fort St. Clair. It was in this campaign that he was attacked by Little Turtle unexpectedly, and fought desperately in sight of the fort without succor, and was finally made to retire with small loss of men, but with considerable loss of horses and supplies. General Adair exhibited great prowess and heroism, and was ably supported by his officers and men. Governor Madison, then second in command, was wont to speak of the blazing eye and heroic bearing of Adair in the engagement, as the old Greeks did of the heroes of Troy. It was in an after meeting in the piping days of peace, when General Adair and Little Turtle were exchanging memories of this brush of war, that the Indian warrior enunciated to the white brave a good maxim, viz.: "That a good general is never surprised." General Adair had led too many successful surprise parties to resent this insinuation.

In 1794, he was again in the northwest building forts and gathering supplies for a campaign that was never inaugurated. General Adair's services were now called for in the councils of the nation; and from that period on to old age, the annals of the state and of the United States, show that he was very frequently representative of his country's interests—serving from the Legislative hall of Kentucky up to the Senate of the United States, having ascended by every ring of the political ladder. It was during his first term in Congress that the scheme of Burr and Wilkinson came upon the country with terrible excitement. That Col. Burr placed every inducement before General Adair to join in his brilliant, bewildering and treasonable enterprise is certain. Burr lingered around Harrodsburg for a while and at various western points, everywhere exercising that fatal magnetism which he possessed so preeminently. Burr passed on his oblique orbit; and Adair went south to meet him, as afterwards supposed, but where undoubtedly he had large land interests and other business. There Wilkinson had him arrested and sent round in a prison ship to Baltimore. Wilkinson's was an undoubted act of treachery to Burr against whom and his confederates actual or suspected, he thus turned practically state's evidence; and to Burr, doubtless, he was treasonably committed. Adair was finally acquitted, and apologized to in open court, and had the paltry sum of $2,500 damages awarded him by the United States Government under whose authority Wilkinson was acting when he had Adair arrested. This was a contemptible sum to compensate for absence from his family, personal suffering, inextricable conclusion in his southern affairs and hardest of all to bear, suspicion of treason to his country, a stain on the fame he had won in hard fought fields from Carolina to Canada.

General Adair was in every sense a peculiar man. Tall and erect as an Indian, he sat his horse like a Centaur, and rode through the crowd with stately recognition of its salutations, attended by his valet, the indispensible adjunct of every gentleman of the olden school. In this case the valet was a little weazen gentleman of pure African descent, who carried the portmanteau and cared for the holdster, and answered to the high sounding cognomen, Philander.

General Adair was not only reticent, but impressively silent. He conversed with you without speaking, his eyes giving you assurance that he heard and heeded, and with a simple nod, he assured you of his intelligible assent or dissent, rarely removing his pipe to give full expression to his opinions. His self-control was immovable, and rendered him impenetrable. My own impression is that Burr either never fully revealed his schemes to Adair, or else the latter heard, and while he scorned the scheme, also scorned to betray what he thought had been rashly committed to his keeping in the presumption of his entering into this wild plot for dominion. What were the facts of the Burr conspiracy as involving Kentuckians, can never be known. The late Capt. Samuel Daviess, brother of Col. Joseph H. Daviess, had as his executor all of his papers which it was known were prepared fully and accurately enough to have convicted Col. Burr, had not the insane cry of persecution of a favorite of the people changed a legal trial into a bitter partisan strife.

The writer of this sketch spent a winter looking over a mass of papers which had accumulated in the hands of three men of exact business habits. The object of this sifting was not to find matter of general interest, but particularly to collect the private correspondence of Col. Daviess with various heads of the public departments; to get also some autograph letters of Gen. Washington, and the Burr papers. The first were secured; the second had been sent to Jared Sparks, the historian, whom we know returned them, but they were intercepted on the way by some lover of relics, whose vague ideas of property did not include letters. As to the third, the envelope of the Burr papers, marked and dated in Col. Daviess' handwriting was found. It seemed to have been left in his desk in its alphabetical place to assure us of the uselessness of further search. William Daviess, only child of Capt. Samuel Daviess, said he had heard his father say that he had been often and strongly appealed to to destroy these papers, and though they might easily have been surreptitiously abstracted from a lockless desk in the attic, he never had a doubt but, that from a tender regard to the descendants of those men who had been implicated in Burr's conspiracy, his father had destroyed them. A well and kindly meant deed, but a wrong one nevertheless. It had been better that the obloquy should have settled rightfully on a few guilty than thus have left the tarnish of suspicion on the names of many. But our people are not prone to visit the sins of the fathers upon their children, and the fierce struggle that has since been made to sever the Union, while altogether from different motives, has softened feeling somewhat against Burr and his confederates.

These trials over, General Adair returned to Kentucky to find himself financially wrecked. Men of ordinary mould would have found in neglected homestead and a brave wife, with the care of ten daughters and two young sons, sufficient excuse for his retiring from active military life, exempt as he was by age from further calls to service. He soon, however, went south to gather up the remnants of his Attakaps estates, and while there received tempting offers to wealth, position and power from the Mexican government just beginning its series of long protracted, fruitless revolutions. General Adair had the qualities they needed, experience and ability to command; but he turned contemptuously from the position of mercenary chieftainship, and no sooner heard of the declaration of war against England, than he offered his services to Governor Shelby, of Kentucky; but before his letter reached its destination he had received from Governor Shelby an entreaty for his aid and counsel. He reported at once at New Orleans and General Thomas, being unfitted by ill health for the field, General Jackson appointed General Adair to the command of the Kentucky troops, which he assumed with rank of Brigadier General. Some have contended that the brilliant success of the 8th of January was attributable to his very simple, but effective, suggestion to hold about the center of the American lines, a reserve corps, which could at once be thrown to the brunt of the British attach, both divisions being held in perplexing uncertainty by the impenetrable for which completely veiled the movements of the enemy whose approach could be known only by sound. General Jackson, General Claiborne of Louisiana, and the Legislature of Kentucky, all passed resolutions of thanks to General Adair.

Strangely after this; when
"Gentle peace returning"
had restored him to his Mercer home, news came that General Jackson

had thrown some unmerited slur at the Kentucky troops. The next day after the arrival of this news, the still stately figure of General Adair, followed by his well known valet, of scarcely more than dwarfish dimensions, was seen riding calmly through the streets of Harrodsburg, bearing southward. He conferred with no one, but somehow it took breath that General Adair had gone to call General Jackson to account for his slanderous charge of the Kentucky troops. There were no railroads, no telegraphs then, and but few mails. Public curiosity and feeling rose to fever heat which was not appeased; for General Adair after not many days, rode back through the village as silently and grandly as he had passed out. And whether at tongue or pistol point the remonstrance was made, it matters not—General Jackson made the amende honorable, and public enthusiasm knew no bounds.

A chatty granddaughter of his, once telling me of this incident, said, "I asked grandpa, 'suppose General Jackson had not backed down?'" "Then I should have backed him into the Cumberland river," he answered, and he never alluded to the occurrence again."

Mercer county was in those days entitled to three members of the Legislature. Three quite locally eminent young men were on the track, each one steering very clear of any allusion to General Adair, who up to this time was under the shadow of the Burr conspiracy. One of these men who had an irrestible humor that would not suppress facts, if funny, used to give some very ludicrous accounts of the hot haste that he and his fellow candidates made to declare themselves rampant for the election of General Adair to the United States Senate after the tide of admiration rose so high in his favor.

General Adair after this supported General Jackson for the presidency. He had received no personal wrong, the indignity to his state had been fully atoned for, and their sentiments were identical.

In 1820 he was elected Governor of Kentucky. His administration was through a stormy and distressing period. The perplexities and trouble arising from the making of conflicting land laws were acting as they were bount to act, disastrously either on the occupant or on those who, holding to a different construction of the laws bought these occupied lands and sought to evict the prior claimants. The Commonwealth Bank, a frantic effort of relief, was established. Its palliative influence was brief. Its issue soon depreciated. General Adair was of a tender, sympathetic nature. He felt for the multitude rioting for relief, and he signed the bill establishing the Bank and supported relief measures generally. But showed his sincerity by receiving his own salary in its money for the last two years of his incumbency.

From his retirement from the executive mansion till his death, he resided on his farm in Mercer county, as fine a piece of land as is found in the Blue Grass region. The entrance to his home was through a gate between two of the beautiful elms extant in the country. The woodlands were chiefly of magnificent beeches, for which many an Englishman would almost have given his earldom. Whether the axe-man has spared those trees, I do not know. His home was neither stately nor ornate—a plain white two-story frame—a mecca for his kindred and friends. Often as many as half a hundred of his descendants would string here with him in the summer. This place is now owned and occupied by Mr. George Handy, who is in every way able to make manifest the value of his fertile acres, and who has made him a home meet for a lord of such a soil.

The descendants of General Adair, under various names, are scattered over our broad land. He died in ripe old age and was laid in the private

A View of Old Shakertown.

burial ground of his home, where not many years after was placed by his side the patient companion of many adversities, the beloved Katie Palmer of his youth. For a term of years, when strangers passed that way, along the Lexington and Harrodsburg turnpike, there was pointed out to them, plainly in view on each side of the road, the graves of two Governors of Kentucky—Adair and Slaughter. Their homes in death, as in life, had been only divided by the highway, though their political tenets had led their loves as far as possible. But when our state had made her beautiful cemetery at the Capital on the picturesque cliffs of Kentucky river, the Legislature asked to have the remains of General Adair honor the place; and there the old warrior and statesman rests, with many more of our commonwealth's illustrious dead.

CHAPTER XV

Civil Commotions After the War of 1812—Eminent Mercer Men of That Period—Boyle, Robertson and Owsley, of the Old Court Party; Haggin of the New Court.

Kentuckians seem constitutionally organized for excitement and Mercer from some cause, has been always, if not productive of, then the center of the trouble.

Peace was scarcely restored after 1812 when, by the death of Governor Madison, the question of the constitutionality of the succession of the Lieutenant Governor, Col. Gabriel Slaughter, to the vacancy, agitated fiercely the whole country.

Col. Slaughter was not a man to elicit enthusiastic partisanship; so doubtless a strong element of prejudice entered into the dissatisfaction. Many regarded it as a grave constitutional question, and earnestly contended according to their conviction of right. But Col. Slaughter was deaf to insinuations or remonstrance, and silently ignoring the bitter discussion, resolutely administered the Government to the close of the term for which Governor Madison had been elected; the Senate electing his successor to the Senatorial Speaker's chair.

The agitation of this purely constitutional question, however, soon faded before the white heated excitement generated by the conflicting elements of the Relief and Anti Relief parties, which every one almost, as debtor and creditor, had a personal interest. During the long protracted war period of Europe the credit of the contending powers had been sustained by all the means known to reckless pilots of state, especially in war's fearful emergencies; and when, upon returning peace, a solid monetary base was sought and the inflated war currency had collapsed, its disastrous effect was felt from center to circumference of the financial world. We too, had our wars, those of 1776 and 1812, and had our own monetary expansion and contraction. The issue of the paper of forty banks without requiring specie redemption had created a wild spirit of speculation, brief, brilliant, and disastrous in results. To control or remedy these troubles, the Legislature had begun its unwise tamperings with the laws, passing even ex post facto measures.

The right of replevy was extended to twice its usual limits. Law was passed requiring the creditors to take the paper of the banks at par with silver, or wait three years for the collection of their dues. Appeals against this rank injustice went up from every part of the state to the Superior Courts. Meanwhile General Adair had been elected Governor in 1820, and he sustained the legislature fully in their mad measures for relief. They had chartered a Commonwealth's Bank which was not required to redeem its issues with specie, and if the creditor objected to this currency he could replevy for two years. Incensed with the people who contended, and the courts that decided against the validity of these laws, the legislature proceeded to revolutionary measures. It turned out and replaced the bank directors with a more compliant board, who received the Commonwealth Bank notes at par with silver. These measures were initiated by the chartering of forty-six independent banks in 1818; they culminated in the acts of 1824, repealing the establishment of the Court of Appeals and the excitement and confusion of all legal processes, beginning in Slaughter's administration lasted through that of Adair and into Desha's term, when the returned sense of right and loyalty to the constitution constrained the legislature, over Governor Desha's veto, to repeal all the illegal relief measures and restore the records and jurisdiction of the original court. This repeal and restitution of right and order took place in December, 1826. The legislature recognized Judge Boyle, Chief Justice, and Wm. Owsley, afterward Governor, his associate. Judge William T. Barry had been Chief Justice, John Trimble, James Haggin and Rezin Davidge, Associate Judges of the new Relief Court.

Thus for several years was seen the extraordinary spectacle of two supreme Courts holding session in one commonwealth. The reasonable loyalty and justice of the people compelled the restitution of the old order of things through the polls. A legislature was elected which was committed to this end; the pledge was kept; the New Court was abolished; and all its proceedings pronounced null and void; the Old Court's jurisdiction was, and all its proceedings during the time that the usurping tribunal had claimed its powers, sustained. During this long protracted struggle, of course our county was stirred to her lowest depths. It began while Governor Slaughter, a Mercer man, was in the chair of State. General Adair was also a Mercer man, and Chief Justice Boyle was one of her most honored civilians; James Haggin, too, had been to the manor born; so that county partisanship was complicated with many private ties, but the ferment worked not as actively here as it did in other parts of the state. The most important elections that took place during this period were those of the members of the legislature. The candidates for the standard bearers of their respective parties, Capt. Samuel Daviess, of the Relief or new court party, and John B. Thompson, of the Anti-Relief or old court party. The county went decisively for the new court. The antagonistic leaders had been friends from childhood and fellow-barristers for years, and whether "coming events cast their shadows before" in the approaching marriage of the son of the former with the daughter of the latter, which afterward bound the two families together, I do not know, but the bonds of friendship between the families of the two leaders of the opposing parties in Mercer were never broken; and this, perhaps, was influential in keeping party spirit from becoming more exasperated. However, fiercely political controversy raged, there was no disruption of social ties in Mercer as in many other communities; as far instance, in the localities where the parties of the celebrated Beauchamp-Sharp tragedy had lived. The influence of this horrible deed, which had its origin in no political cause, was so strong, that it seemed to need but the ascension of a signal rocket to set the state aflame in a civil war. This was not only the cause in the native places of Beauchamp and Sharp and the unfortunate fair, frail woman, the occasion of the trouble, but also in the capital where the foul deed was perpetrated, and where the second startling act of the tragedy eventuated in the attempted suicide of both Beauchamp and his wife, and the execution of Beauchamp in a dying condition.

Peace and finally prosperity having been restored, Mercer, with her sisterhood of counties, sank to normal rest, only disturbed by the periodical convulsions attending the Presidential elections; in other words, that ever recurring struggle between the ins and outs. The contests of these parties that ever divide republics, and Jackson and Clay who were supposed to represent these parties, occupied and divided the attention of civil Mercer along with the rest of the nation, until the Mexican war marked another epoch. Mercer has usually on the main mustered under the Democratic banner, but, perhaps, could the spirits of our grandsires be evoked from the shadowy realms, nothing would give them a stronger sensation than the sight of the political tents in which their descendants bivouac today.

John Boyle

Judge Boyle was one of the four eminent actors that Mercer furnished to the great political drama that was enacted in Kentucky just at the second period of this history, which convulsed the commonwealth to its center, and held spellbound the attention of statesmen, as scene succeeded scene on the stage. The events of this period we chronicled in the chapter on civil commotions after 1812.

Boyle, Robertson, Owsley and Haggin were four of the prominent dramatic personae of that play, and Judge Boyle the central figure of every scene. Indeed, to the courage, vigilance, firmness and forbearance of these old court Judges, Kentucky owes her present peace, prosperity and more, the preservation of her honor from the stigma of repudiation and possibly from civil war.

Judge Boyle was born in Botetout county, Virginia, but was reared in Garrard county, Ky., and educated chiefly in Finley's classical school, and while a citizen of Garrard received his first political promotion.

He married early Miss Tilford, built that historic Buckeye cabin, and from that humble, honored structure went three times to Congress. He was appointed by President Madison to the Governorship of Illinois, but finally declined, and I grieve that I cannot record that this mantle which fell on the shoulders of one of the most deserving men, Ninian Edwards, at that time crowded with men of ability, can in no way be claimed by our counties.

Following the decided bent of his genius, Judge Boyle thereafter devoted himself almost wholly to legal pursuits, finding his recreation in the management of his farm, on which sometimes he resided, and to the pleasure of which he always retreated in his vacations. This farm is now the property .... Boyle, which wears his name with such appreciative pride.

After declining this territorial governorship, he accepted the place of Chief Justice of the State Court of Appeals, and remained there during the bitter and violent contest between relief and anti-relief, old and new court. When the storm was over, he resigned the helm; but afterwards exercised the office of Federal Judge in the district of Kentucky. During some of these intervals between public employments, he presided in the law school of Transylvania University, Lexington, Ky. A large class of students followed him to his Mercer home, and what with these young men, several of whom rose to eminence, and the months that the elite of the south and west spent at Harrodsburg, our town had a society hardly equalled in the west.

Judge Boyle was mentally, morally, officially a diamond of the first water and largest size; but a diamond does not attract and dazzle like a towering white column in the cemetery; but the lawyer and politician, as they look over tomb after tomb of his consecrated wisdom know that they shall rarely ever look upon his like again.

General Jerry T. Boyle was his son, who has earned a separate column for himself, which will fill its space in loyal Mercer.

Hon. George Robertson

George Robertson was the son of Margaret Robinson and Alexander Robertson, both of whom were of Scotch-Irish descent. His father, as has been shown was a man of usefulness and importance. He lived at Gordon's Station and built there what has gone into history as the finest home in Central Kentucky of that period.

Judge Robertson was educated in the very good classic schools of that time, and continued a student through life, and supplemented by that reading and reflection which even with the best advantages is necessary to make the mind of man like the sun,

"Full orbed with all its round of rays complete."

He married the daughter of Dr. Bainbridge, of Lancaster, before he attained his majority, and took her to that historic buckeye cabin from which Judge Boyle, Hon. Samuel McKee, and Governor Letcher successively passed up to Congress, and Boyle and Robertson to the chief justice's seat, and Letcher to the gubernatorial chair.

Judge Robertson served with great efficiency and credit in Congress. He originated the land bill which has made the possession of the homestead possible to every citizen, and from his speeches and writings naturally followed the Missouri compromise, which certainly put off the evil day of war; but possibly had the irrepressible conflict come then, the struggle would have been shorter if fiercer, but the consequent evils could not have been so extensive and long protracted. But Judge Robertson's forte was law, and his fairest theatre for display was the bench; upon the last he sat for many years as chief justice. He wrote with great force, and in various emergencies, but his mind and will power held his wearying and wavering party together. He had a strong, clear and logical mind, with extensive general knowledge of science and belle lettres, was refined in his taste and passionately fond of music, and perhaps it is worth while to make an N. B. for the consideration of those who scout all male accomplishments as effeminate, that George Robertson delighted in song, and John Boyle to draw from the violin its sweetest melodies.

Judge Robertson died almost literally in the harness of legal work, and it gives pleasure to note that he, as nearly all the master minds of that day, were firm believers in the Christian religion. He died in the full faith and communion of the Presbyterian church.

He wrote an autobiography which is very interesting. It is a simple record of his genealogy, his loves, his early struggles through poverty up to affuence and fame. It could not be that a man of such mind should be unconscious of his superiority, but he wrote and moved on as if all unaware of the aureole on his brow at which the passer-by gazed.

He was paralyzed on the bench in the discharge of his duties, but his resignation was so resisted that he held on silently for a few months; but when after administering the inauguration oath to Gov. Preston H. Leslie, he turned, as if satisfied with having placed the guardianship of his beloved state in competent hands, and unexpectedly resigned him own high place. Silence fell upon the cheerful crowd and they went out in tears, for they felt "that they should see him free no more." The remnant of his days he passed in the bosom of his loving and his beloved family, and died May 16, 1874. He left numerous descendants; the only ones remaining in Mercer being the family of Mr. James Prather, who married his granddaughter, Miss Bell, of Lexington, Ky.

Governor William Owsley

William Owsley was born in Virginia, but was brought to Kentucky in infancy and was reared in Lincoln county. He passed up the common path of that day for impecunious, ambitious young men, seeking means and qualifications for a profession. First carrying his education through the stereotyping process of teaching, then through that best of all training schools for law, the sheriffalty. Thence he went to the office of Judge Boyle to learn the theory of that science whose details he had already mastered in practice, and not many years afterward sat beside his preceptor on the appellate bench of Kentucky, in those days that tried men's souls when Greek met Greek in the contest of the old and new courts. Retiring from this high position, he finally came to Mercer to reside on the farm now owned by the

McLean family. That baronial looking mansion was, I think, built under his own supervision. Soon after he came to this property, our enterprising daughter, Boyle, demanded "her portion," drew the line which cut off this noble Roman from our citizen's roll; indeed I am not sure the excision did not take place before Governor Owsley was domiciled in our midst. In a short time after he was elected to the governorship of the state over General W. O. Butler, a knight worthy of any man's steel, but over whom Owsley was elected by a very heavy majority. A county of the state and a handsome shaft in the beautiful shades of the Danville cemetery commemorate his name and fame. Governor Owsley was tall, thin but stately; very reserved in manner and reticent in speech; clear in his convictions of right and duty springing from it and inexorable in will.

James Haggin

Was one of the four men of Mercer who were in front of the struggle between the relief and anti-relief parties; was one of the marshals that led the attack on the constitution of the state so it did not stand. Shoulder to shoulder was Boyle, Robertson and Owsley in its defense.

He was one of the judges of the new court, whose creation, brief existence and legal extinction is found in the chapter on civil commotions.

At an early day Capt. John Haggin came to this county and made a Station on the farm now occupied by Bijou Moore. He left of sons two respectable farmers; Judge James, of whom we write, Terah T. Haggin, a successful lawyer, of the Harrodsburg and Louisville bar, and several daughters, who maintained their beauty and belleship almost as long as the celebrated Ninon l' Enclos. One of them married Harvey Daviess, of Georgetown, father of Theodore Daviess.

The subject of this sketch I have understood, had his legal training under Judge Samuel McDowell, whose name starts every court and convention of that conspicuous period of Mercer county. James Haggin resided in Harrodsburg and he built the house now owned by D. J. Curry. He subsequently, I suppose, lived in Lexington, Ky., as I remember a handsome surburban home there was pointed out to me as his. He was doubtless a man of talents and legal fame, or he would not have been selected by his party in such an emergency as the organizing of the new court. The decisions of that court were digested into a printed volume, but I understand are not accepted as precedents. But a note which James Haggin gave has survived his legal decisions; in it he stipulated that "Said Haggin was not to be hastened in payment therefor." "Said Haggin" attached to him as a sobriquet as long as he lived, and a large class of debtors had the force wherewith to stay the often inconvenient collecting process. This saying was picked out of the "Jaw bone songs" which were as current in those days as "Tip & Ty" in the log cabin and hard cider campaigns. Solomon was right, "there is nothing new under the sun," and nonsense as well as sense has its line of succession.

CHAPTER XVI

PART III

Restoration of the Old Court by Legislature—La Fayette's Visit to Kentucky As the Nation's Guest—Emancipation—Colonization and Temperance—Cholera 1933.

A. D. 1825, closed the second period of Mercer county history, but left it still seething in the heat of Old and New Court troubles; but as intimated in "Civil Commotions after 1812," the stormy waters finally subsided and our ship of state was at last anchored on its old constitutional mooring. The New Court was repealed out of existence; all its acts were made null and void; and strong resolutions were passed towards having made to the state restitution of salaries, etc., that had been paid to the New Court. But after much legislative maneuvering, the contest was closed by Preston Blair delivering on requisition all the books and records of which the New Court had violently possessed themselves early in the contest. The restoration of the Old Court by legislative act occurred in December, 1826. The only civil event, in the double sense of that word had occurred in the closing year of the period, 1825, which had been the visit of La Fayette to our nation. It was in fact a triumphant progress he made over the country, everywhere being received by masses of people with every enthusiastic demonstration to be conceived of. Processions, triumphal arches, fetes, songs, etc., etc. He passed through Kentucky, only delaying for the ovations of Louisville, Frankfort, Lexington and Maysville, so only the spent waves of excitement reached us, though there be those living still who went to some of those points to see the nation's guest, our gallant French defender. This nation of national gratitude ought to have a sky reaching memorial stone to testify everlastingly against the slanderous charges the world makes against republics of ingratitude. Congress also made an appropriation in the shape of a large section of land, which I think, General La Fayette chose in Florida. General La Fayette's invited visit to and reception in the United States, was an event worthy of such record.

The agitation of Old and New Court had hardly subsided before the calm seas before us had a fresh ripple in the shape of a new topic of general interest. Gradual emancipation had taken hold on some minds, and colonization on many more. On these subjects, Mercer had her full share of agitation. Centre College, in Danville, belonging to the Presbyterian Church, was the favorite and frequent meeting place of the Synod of Kentucky. This subject came up naturally, and some scheme of gradual emancipation had many and powerful advocates. James G. Birney, a native of Danville, and for some time a professor in Centre College, began with the advocacy of gradual emancipation, but became an abolitionist; and who sealed his faith not with his blood, but by the manumission of his slaves, which to some seemed more of martyrdom than bloodshed. A number of prominent citizens of Kentucky, including Judge John Green, of Boyle, and his younger brother, Lewis, afterward President of Centre College, went practically into the gradual emancipation scheme. Then Rev. John C.

Young, ever earnest, dispassionate and powerful, bore steadily on the advancement of the colonization cause to the day of his death.

About this time the first breath of temperance stirred in the air. It did not come as an aggressive force as it moves now; but rather exercising in negative influence. It was conceived in the spirit of gentleness; touched gently on the festal levity of society, and struck rude blows only at strong drink and actual drunkenness, and only proposed we should deny ourselves for example's sake, and put no stumbling block in the way of our brother. But this was but an entering wedge, and we have had all manner of temperance organizations since then. The Washingtonians, the Sons of Temperance, the blue and red, great knots of various societies have been worn by our old people and their lads and ladies. The Knights Templar have possessed us; we have had banners, processions, speeches and songs. For some time we had by local option, closed the bars. The waves of reform have ebbed and flowed, and like the overflow of the Nile, each time these floods have left some richness, and sponged somewhat the surface of society. Long ago the bottle has been displaced from the side board and the counter; the ladies' waiter from the parlor, and the jug from the harvest field, and how many have been upheld that would have fallen, the Merciful only knows.

We have not learned yet, that parades and badges, nor even crusades will take the place of religious principles. So intemperance, the monster, still fluctuates. There is still drinking in the land, but it is solitary or in saloons; not in social circles. There is still a long procession tending surely to drunkards' graves every year, but society does not bear the crime of making or destroying these unfortunate victims. None of these causes stirring in the public sentiment of Mercer, in common with the rest of the state, we may say even in the country, were recognized as religious movements, but doubtless all had their root in the soil of the churches. It is only amongst those who recognize the obligation to do justice, love mercy and walk humbly, and to deny themselves to accomplish their ends, that such grand schemes arise; and surely the conception of lifting four million of bondsmen out of their degredation, setting them in freedom in their native climate was a grand scheme, even if a failure.

Between the years of 1826 and 1830, there had been extensive revivals of religion, and there had been many additions to the churches of people eager for the Master's service, wheresoever He should lead, and many thought He called into active service in emancipation and temperance. The history of emancipation was written in fire and blood some two score years later. That of temperance is being chronicled by the daily prints, and I hope ere the fugitive papers shall take permanent form, I shall be able to get what I have so far failed to obtain, any connected history of the rise, progress. and shall I add, downfall of temperance in our counties. No; we know religion shall finally prevail, and will hold drunkenness, as every other evil, in check.

The next event of any interest in our county was the appearance of Asiatic cholera amongst us. The warning note had been given in 1832 by a few sporadic cases, but in 1833 it fell like a thunderbolt from a clear sky. All sanitary measures had been taken, the most rigid abstinance from all kinds of usual food had been prescribed and observed almost universally, though there were many vegetables and an unusual profusion of fruit loaded the trees all around. The sky was clear, the air seemed pure, and we humbled ourselves in sackcloth of fear if not of penitence before the Lord. But nothing availed. There was victim after victim at noon-day or midnight. Week after week it progressed, slaughtering indiscriminately the young and the old, the slave and the master. Sometimes the subject lasted a day or two, but generally succumbed in a few hours. The physicians began by temporizing with the remedies that usually control milder diseases of the same type apparently; adopted a heavy calomel prescription that sometimes saved, but often left the constitution wrecked. But terror neutralized the effect of almost any remedy, in fact seemed to dehumanize some hearts. I knew of a lady who left her dead husband and dying child, and after a fearful ride by herself twenty miles, died of exhaustion and fear that night, and I believe fills a forgotten grave somewhere in the Old Fort Hill Cemetery. I knew another and braver one, lately laid in her grave, that it was said, closed the eyes of all her household, then locking up her home, now a charnel house, came twenty miles with a faithful woman servanut in the night to her father's house to send help to bury her dead.

People fled in every direction; some to escape and often to meet the fell plague. Many went to their friends in the country, and so lost the chance of medical aid they might have had, my father's family amongst the last class. But he went incessantly from house to house of such as had abandoned their homes, and poor dependents. One evening late he stood beside me awaiting to mail a letter I was writing to communicate to a friend, her mother's death; before the next dawn I was summoned to his bedside, where he lay already collapsed; before that sunset he was borne off on a slide to his grave, in which one true friend and a servant laid him.

One family in which I had refuge, the largest in the county—there were at least with their large number of servants a hundred people—had not a single case; two miles further on, a whole family was wiped out save two negroes, and the next neighbor, a patriarchal man and eight stalwart negro men went to the grave in a few days.

This dread visitant came almost like the angel of death over the land of Egypt when He smote the first born; from every house there went up a wail and though the grave closed so quickly on the dead, there were many years before the faintest whisper of coming cholera would not make the stoutest heart stand still. It lasted about six weeks in Mercer, and about sixty persons died in Harrodsburg. I know not whether fewer in Danville. nor how many in the whole county.

Its periods of visitation have shown no regularity, its course has been erratic, and for it no reliable remedy has yet been found. It is emphatically the fearful messenger that we know not of—when it shall come, in the day, in the night, or at cock crowing.

This terrible visitation brought out some fine characters. There was an apparently timid, harmless old man, a kind of steward in a Methodist boarding school of Rev. Mr. Spruill, a man of lovely character. With the breaking out of cholera, he took up the role of good Samaritan and went with tireless feet and willing hands to wherever he could trace the plague, and without distinction of classes, nursed the sick, consoled the dying and buried the dead. At last he succumbed to the fatal disease himself, and going into a vacant house, he locked all the doors behind him and was found dead in the harness of work for his Master.

I knew another man whose peculiar emotional and impulsive nature had rendered him the butt of all the dreary jokes reckless people could make of the terror of cholera which haunted this old man; but when it came many of these people fled their own homes in a panic, and the old man's courage rose in the emergency. He took the physician's family to his house and kept them that the doctor might go wherever called, free from anxiety; he brought the friendless to his table daily and went around like a pastor visiting the sick and caring for the poor whose rightful protectors had deserted them.

And now for a term of years our county men went on in the way of the rest of the world, improving their farms and stock, and building finer homes and wearing finer clothes, which will be hereafter described. Our men never lack excitement while elections and their concurrent barbecues, conventions and mass meetings remain institutions in the land. The canvas of '40 was of white heat compared to that of the past November. Albeit it displaced the regnant power of the past twenty-five years and replaced the party that has been clamoring for restoration for the same period.

CHAPTER XVII

Elections—Celebration of First Settlement of Kentucky, at Harrodsburg—Advance of Comfort in Living, Dress, Etc., to Present Time.

There were in those days mass meetings in variety; frequent and interminable processions, with log cabins and cider on it on floats like those used in city trade celebrations. A coon was looking out of the window from which cider was ladled with untiring prodigality, and flags were flaunting the candidates' names in your face at every corner. This of course closed out with illuminations, balloon ascensions, fire crackers, and all the extravagances of today; in fact the boys may well fling back to the censorious multitude: "Our father's did so before us." Then the excitement had a grand eruption in Washington City, as has just been enacted, and the office hunters lingered there in uneasy expectation for a while; and then people subsided to work for a spell; and the newspapers kept up their usual running fire of personal squibs and wholesale party vituperation, until guns of larger calibre were ordered out in '44 for the next campaign. I have made no mention of speech making in these canvasses, that is always understood to be in Mercer as well as everywhere in Kentucky, the end and crown of all these demonstrations, and speeches flowed as free as air and liquor.

I do not now remember who were the local orators, or whether others were called in from abroad; but I guarantee the American bird was tossed fearlessly aloft and brought down with the lone star, or the thirteen stars, or a whole constellation of stars as needed for the adornment of our flags and speeches.

It was during these years lapsing peacefully by, that our people in 1841 threw away all distinction of politics and religion, and for two days held high revelry in Harrodsburg. Boonesboro had had a celebration of its settlement, and incited by rivalry or example, we decided to have a celebration too—that our pioneer fathers should no longer rest in the oblivious graves on which time was every year heaping higher the dust of forgetfulness. So committees went to work in earnest. Everybody agreed to open their houses and improvise beds and lengthen their tables, for the exercise of free home hospitality and to send of their larders bountiful stores to the free barbecue dinner on the grounds; and everybody kept their word. A heap of flour, high almost as Cumberland mountains, was baked into bread, pies and goodies generally; and holocausts of beeves and sheep were slain, not to mention the wild waste of poultry life. The clean, green forest, then opposite Mr. O. Redwitz's home was selected ground, and in its shades an ample stand and seats and tables commensurate with the crowd were prepared. The day dawned auspiciously, and with flying banners and rolling drum and pealing horns, under many stately and badged marshals the long, long procession took up its line of march. Among the officers and orators of the day on the stand were many Pioneers lingering in the county, and conspicuously amongst these, Mrs. Wilson and Mrs. James Harrod, relics of Fort dwellers both, were included. "God hath not dealth so with many people," was the theme, if not the text, of the

Rev. Joseph C. Stiles,

one of the most remarkable pulpit orators of that day. He was as fluent as he was graceful, and the most elegant man I have ever seen on secular or ecclesiastical stand. He was a thorough soldier of the cross, counting its labors and self denial naught, but his air impressed you with feeling that he had had his first training in worldly warfare; so calm, so fearless, so gallant was the expression of his whole personnel. The next day was a duplicate of the first in ceremonies and abundant hospitality, and Ben Hardin, of Bardstown, second to none in intellect and oratory of his own scathing kind, had the stand and tuned his lyre to the softer strains of praise to Heaven and the courteous men and women who had made the wilderness blossom as a rose.

For these two days the people had fraternized as though whigs and democrats existed in unknown quantities and had no significance any way.

Mrs. Harrod and Mrs. Wilson had been guests of the town and were located at the Harrodsburg Springs, to which place steady streams of callers tended. But the ridiculous often borders the skirts of the sublime, so our grand pageant did not pass without its foil. Mrs. Harrod had in attendance a great black amazon who did feloniously filch the purse from Mrs. Wilson's pocket, whereupon there came up a police trial. The town, or some of its proud citizens, stayed the trial, bought off the criminal and mollified the feelings of Mrs. Wilson by the restitution of her money, but that falcon hearted dove, Mrs. Harrod, was greatly angered at this impeachment of her frail and faithful maid's honesty; and these two old fort dwellers, sisters in hardship, I have heard, thenceforth kept separate ways.

Another incident connected with this celebration always amused me because so characteristic of a pair that must have been drawn together by the affinity of opposites—they were so unlike. Capt. Daviess was so emotional, impetus and prompt; his wife cool, imperturable but decisive. He was wholly engrossed in the approaching celebration.

"Hannah Daviess," he said, his eyes snapping like revolvers, "you are the most impracticable woman I have ever seen; here you may say the whole country is astir getting up a great celebration of our forefathers, and yes, of your forefathers, the McAfees, madam, and you are sitting dead still." She folded her hands quietly and answered: "Capt. Daviess, the celebration is still a month off; when it comes, your house shall be open and your table spread; as to our forefathers, I think the people are making more ado about them than is needed. My forefathers had small farms and large families in Virginia, and they determined to sell out and come out here where land was cheap and rich. I do not think they had any spite at the Indians, nor particular intention of helping anybody but themselves." I have often thought our good mother's tongue was an incisive blade of good sense, that day dry cut to the marrow of all our pioneer ancestors' motives for coming to the wilderness .

As it would be unfair to make no resume of the progress in home making and furnishing and style of dress, equipage, etc., etc., I will avail myself of this broken chapter to bring up that breach of our county's growth briefly. The improvement in homes and their tasteful surroundings will be shown in notes on Harrodsburg. In equipage the advance was slow for many years. Some gigs and dearborns were used, family carriages were rare as diamonds, and for children's funerals were used as hearses. Spring wagons are modern conveniences, and the first buggy, that universal conveyance now, first crossed the Ohio river in '37, bringing the daughter of Governor Trimble, of Ohio, a bride, to Harrodsburg. From the homemade yarn carpet and cherry wood furniture period, there has been a steady advance in style and luxury up to the present very general use of marbletops, mirrors, velvet carpets, lace curtains, and velvet and brocade upholstery.

From the close of the wars in Europe, the nations made haste to a rennaisance of civilization, luxury and art. Our country was the market then competed for by the merchantile world, but from the close of the second war with England, bleached and printed American muslins rapidly superseded family domestic and foreign cotton goods. The soft woolen goods, so dear now to the heart of every woman of sense and correct taste, did not come into our market until past '30. Merino and its imitations had been used, but serge and muslin de laine, now came into pretty general use. Bombazine was used strictly for mourning and had been introduced years before, and so far as I know, trimmed with crepe, has been the regulation dress for the sorrowful from time immemorial, and has always been, as now, expensive. Thibets, cashmeres, henriettas, etc., are all modern improvements, and have come to give blessed propriety to ordinary dress, holding a place between cotton and silk, fit for home, street, church or fete. The next transition of styles of dress after that depicted in the Turner portraits, was ample skirts worn over stiff underskirts which gave the effect of hoops, but not so graceful as the yielding cage, since contrived by obliging caterers to women's wishes. Long pointed waists belonged to this style, also the "mutton legged sleeve"—the shape before gathered into the arm hole truly suggesting the name. The wide top was supported in its fulness by various devices, generally pillows of feathers, so the figure presented, when in full dress, a balloonish base, shoulders of extraordinary breadth, and waists exceedingly waspish through corset power. All this, when the head was bare, was crowned with marvelous construction of hair, rising in mighty tiers until it formed a perfect coronet from which behind the ear fell one or two ringlets. The ladies often attended night meetings bareheaded. When on the streets bonnets were worn with large upstanding fronts affording a needed background to the pinnacle of hair. Numerous knots of ribbons and some artificial flowers were the trimmings. A pretty contrast was at one time afforded by the use of an equisite little English straw cottage bonnet simply tied "under the chin, and many a young man's heart within," with the silken ribbon. But fashion loves exaggeration, and soon the Dunstable, with its long poking front and ugly skirt spread like an angered turkey's feathers travestied the sweet cottage bonnet, and from that period to this, individual taste has reigned measurably, and we see the sensible sundown, the daring, brimless turban, the coquettish half-drooping Gainsborough and many fantastic structures of lace and ribbons, that wise millions make of odds and ends, and simple one's buy to be in fashion.

Between the thirties and forties, before the panic, there was a very rapid increase in luxuries, and consequqent extravagance. Not many pleasure vehicles as yet, were used, but fine furniture and carpets were getting into general use, and French goods began to supply our markets with fabrics of rare richness and beauty. Satin of dazzling lustre, ribbons, laces and flowers, and toward '40 those exquisite linen and cotton goods, more resembling woven air than textile, and blond laces and gauzes as thin and silvery as a mist were introduced.

Somewhere in the thirties, there was a notable wedding in our county. The trousseau and bridal cake were brought from Lexington by private express. The important robe was of creamy white satin, several other dresses were of changeable silks; "peacock's breast," and "setting sun" were two of the colors. The bridal cake was a solid fluted pyramid, exquisitely iced, and was served after the regular sumptuous supper, in the parlor on a circular table of inlaid woods, with cordials and wine, and many a dainty bit was enveloped in paper to be placed under the pillow to give prophetic tone to dreams that night.

About the year '39, Mr. Hocke, a confectioner, who had catered to the luxury and style of Washington City, came to Harrodsburg. He was an unsurpassed artist, and from then to now the bridal feasts have had

"Their gorgeous palaces and cloud capped towers"

of confectionary, as pure and as white as the snowy traces of the Mammoth Cave and wrapped in mists as pure as the bride's veil of illusion.

I will describe as illustrative of the style of fine dressing of that period prevailing in Frankfort as well as in Mercer, the walking costume of the wife of the then Speaker of the House of Representatives. En passant, she and her husband were the handsomest pair of people I have ever seen, and for many years afterwards she reigned supreme in the world of fashion, the leader of fashion in Kentucky, nay, in the west. It was a bright, crisp afternoon in January; about an inch of snow was on the ground and she was going out to return calls, walking with another lady. As she stood framed in the doorway, she was a rare picture of mortal beauty. She wore silver kid slippers and silk stockings of flesh color; her dress was of white grounded chaille (a fine silk and woolen goods), plentifully sprinkled with green and wood colored figures; a trippet of white fur spotted with black such as children wore some years ago (muffs had not obtained or were not yet used), lined with rose colored silk; her white velvet bonnet was also lined with rose color and also trimmed with plumes; and her whole figure was enveloped in a white blond veil that floated like a silver mist about her. Are any curious to know what her lady companion wore on that memorable occasion? A changeable blue silk, slippers to match, a white fur cape and an abominable white satin Dunstable bonnet trimmed with a profusion of satin ribbon, and both ladies carried lace edged handkerchiefs and mother of pearl cases in hands enveloped in delicate colored kid gloves. Then the beau monde glided on through several stages of silk and velvet mantillas and the lace and silk net shawl period, the graceful scarf, every now and then coming in to redeem from the utter ugliness of other modes. The blanket shawl for traveling and common use for ladies and sometimes for gentlemen has held its own for the last forty years; but for the last twenty, gentlemen have pretty much subsided into staid business suits for common wear; cloth for dress occasions in sack or frock coats; swallow tails for festal uses, and the snug overcoats of qualities to suit the season, leaving shawls and cloaks to the traditional period.

This brings us to within the present decade in which close fitting skirts, polonaises, over dresses and basques have prevailed, with much puffing and draping, and many combinations of color and material which were first received by said people with violent protest, until the possible economy of utilizing by this mode all remnants and scraps became apparent; since when popular sentiment seems to demand a stereotyping of this style to secure it for all future use.

For many years past ladies' wraps have been various, but chiefly cloaks. Furs have been used for fifty years, and should be, like bonnets and shoes, kept for comfort, without regard to fashion or quality. But pride would rather shiver with cold than live comfortably in seal skin, and so except used as for trimming, or by old fogies, these beautiful and comfortable appendages to outdoor comfort, are generally discarded.

There has been no mention of jewelry. There has never been a time some family ring, or locket, or brooch has not been seen. In old, old times our great-great-granddames would as soon have had their husbands make counterfeit money as to have adorned themselves with "pinch back" jewelry.

Real gold and precious stones were too rare and costly for common use; a cornelian or coral set was the utmost bounds of extravagance, until now when almost all people of wealth have invested in diamonds. Of course the habit of using the thousand beautiful trinkets that skill has manufactured out of metricious material in these last days has become here as elsewhere a universal custom, and few stop to consider whether watches and other jewelry are genuine or electro plated. The effect in dress is the same, and surely it is more pleasant to wear imitation baubles than to have a hired policeman dogging your steps to protect your finery from theft. So endeth this history of dress.

CHAPTER XVIII

Mexican War—Its Origin—Annexation of Texas Immediate Cause—Enthusiastic Volunterage of Kentuckians—Capt. Phil B. Thompson's Mercer Company Accepted—Its Service and Return—Sketch of Its Officers.

It was in 1844, and again Mr. Clay was a candidate for President, to whom, as individuals, the devotion of Kentucky, as a state, was unparalleled, unless we perhaps, except the devotion of Carolina to Mr. Calhoun. The last was sectional; and it is but just to Mr. Clay to say this feeling towards him largely overflowed Kentucky's bounds and filled the National Whig party with quenchless enthusiasm.

The question on which this election hinged was the annexation of Texas; Mr. Polk for it, and Mr. Clay opposing it, on the ground that it would inevitably involve us in war.

It may with truth be said that Presidential elections are the great disorganizers of American finances; and if these political storms carried in them the power of purification supposed to exist in the agitation of the natural elements, this would certainly be the purest government in the world. But it simply keeps us in a state of unprofitable unrest. The approaching election, with its uncertainty about the coming man and his policy, and the great revulsive ebb when the contest is over, keep us like the disturbed sea, morally "casting up mire and dirt continually."

This was peculiarly the condition of the country at the close of Tyler's administration who, it will be remembered, filled all but a few months of General Harrison's term. To annex or not to annex to the United States a territory almost as large as the original states, was the real final question, though written on the programme and the banners of the day, was only Texas and her emblem, the Lone Star. For Texas had thrown the gauntlet some years before to Mexico and been conquered, though for a time her's was, so far as Mexico was concerned, an unacknowledged independence. As it had been a successful rebellion, of course it had been written "Revolution" in letters of glistening gold on the column of fame, where is ever promptly inscribed the names of successful men or nations; and now the question was whether this new state should be added to the galaxy of stars that already adorned our national banner.

The last act of Mr. Tyler's administration was to sign the resolution of Congress admitting Texas as a state, and July, 1845, Texas became one of us, and the event was celebrated with the wild rejoicings due the birth of this grandly dowered young child of the republic; a state of larger area than all New England, and having every variety of climate and production.

As the Whigs had predicted, and Democrats had expected, a rupture with Mexico immediately ensued, and April 3, '46, Congress declared a state of war existing between Mexico and the United States. This war could not have in it the elements of self-denial and suffering that our soldiers had borne in the two contests with Great Britain. Abundant means, men, and war material, manipulated by trained and experienced leaders, made it more like one of Napoleon's brilliant dashes over southern Europe; and nothing could be more interesting than to follow the lines of these two great military divisions; one that swooped down and planted its eagles on the palace of the Montezumas in the city of Mexico, the other in its sweep over California and New Mexico, hoisting its standards in the very surf of

First State House of Kentucky at Danville.

the Pacific. But this belongs to the annals of the United States, not even to Kentucky, except as an integer of the Union, and I must reluctantly draw in, even to the county lines of Mercer.

The Announcement of War

with Mexico, a nation of semi-civilized brigands, that had harrassed us for years by land and sea, came to our people like the sound of the trumpet of the war horse. General Gaines, commander in chief of the United States armies, made a requisition on Kentucky for 2,500 men; but before this was answered, Governor Owsley had called for two regiments of volunteers, which call was responded to by our 7,000 men. Of these a company of infantry from Mercer was accepted, and a company of cavalry raised by John B. Thompson, was declined. A second call was made on Kentucky the next year, and as freely responded to, but none of the companies were from Mercer. A second company, however, after Capt. Phil B. Thompson's was received, failed to get in, and was incorporated in Col. McKee's regiment. For a while our Mercer county men tented in the woods lying back of the now nice row of houses that border the Cane Run pike, known then as Cunningham's wood. For a while there was a good deal of straggling to and from the town and a good deal of marching and countermarching to the sound of the fife and drum; some patriotic hurrahing for our military boys, and a good deal of censure of the young captain who was leaving his girlish Mississippi bride with three boys scrambling at her feet, the oldest scarce three years old. There were a good many stories of the camp going around as how funny Ensy looked when, after the Captain's elaborate heading of a will for him, he could not remember a single devise except a tombstone on which his own name was engraved and under which some malicious person suggested, an ambitious man might not covet to lie. And there were some who laughed when the boys declared they would "do or die," and old man Christman curtly responded that Uncle Sam's officers would see to that. And there was a solemn meeting Sunday evening when the company filed into the Presbyterian church of Rev. John Montgomery—young and fervent then—who gave them solemn farewell words and benedictions, and for their motto,

"We Will Die at Our Post."

But brief time was given to drilling, briefer to adieus to wives and sweethearts, and then the company went aboard the Alexander Scott, and for awhile tarried in the rendezvous in the suburbs of Louisville. There they were incorporated in Col. M. R. McKee's command, drifted down the river with some delay; then across the Gulf, and finally joined General Taylor's army of occupation at Point Isabel. He had just had the hard duty to perform of sending a heavy re-inforcement of his veterans to the support of General Scott, then beseiging Vera Cruz, while Santa Anna was advancing on him with a quadruple force. He had fortified Fort Brown and gone to Point Isabel, but hearing signal guns from the fort, started to its relief, but ere he reached it had to fight his series of victorious battle, Palo Alto and Resacca de la Palma. These battles had been fought during the absence of our soldiers. They had been detailed as guards for commissary trains going to and fro between the divisions of General Taylor's army. They made a forced march to Monterey and then were stationed awhile at Lone Oak. They had just rejoined General Taylor's immediate command when Santa Anna advanced to Buena Vista. It was a hard fought field between most unequal forces. They fought from dawn to the setting sun, the Americans remaining masters of the situation, with 267 dead comrades around them, mingled with 2,000 of the tawny enemy.

In July, 1848, the President announced that the war with Mexico was ended, and our men were mustered out of service at New Orleans.

The officers of this Mercer company of volunteers for Mexico, were Phil B. Thompson, Captain; George Cardwell, 1st Lieutenant; Joseph Ewing, 2nd Lieutenant, and Temp Withers, 3rd Lieutenant.

Capt. Phil Thompson

Captain Phil B. Thompson was the youngest son of Hon. John B. Thompson, who died of cholera in '33. He was educated in Alleghany College, Penn., and was the youngest brother, and a partner-in-law of the late Hon. J. B. Thompson, and though born and bred in the atmosphere of politics, has never betrayed any ambition for himself in that line, until his recent departure into a candidacy for the House of Representatives of Kentucky. It is said his special aim is to make some by-paths through the tortuous ways of litigation, and by stripping law of some of its technical verbiage, reduce it to the comprehension of the common people. If so, in the language of the popular old ballad of Lord Lovell, we surely may wish him

"Good speed, speed, speed."

Capt. Thompson, with his boys scarce in their teens, went early into the rebellion, and was appointed representative of Kentucky in the Provisional Council of Kentucky and after Bragg's invasion of Kentucky, was commissioned to raise a legion in Kentucky, but before accomplishing that patriotic purpose took part in that inexplicable retreat. With peace, he returned to Harrodsburg, Ky., was in time relieved of his political disabilities and resumed extensive and successful practice of his profession in criminal law, ranking second to no one in the state.

George N. Cardwell

was the brother and for a long time commercial partner of Capt. John W. Cardwell. He went to California after his return from Mexico and died there. His remains have been removed by the state and lie now among the soldiers Kentucky has gathered into her memorial grounds at Frankfort, Kentucky.

Joseph Ewing

Second Lieutenant, still moves amongst us on the even tenor of his way, making as good a citizen as doubtless he did a soldier in the Mexican war.

General Temp. Withers,

Third Lieutenant, was from Cynthiana, Ky. He was a student at Bacon College in Harrodsburg when he entered. He volunteered again promptly at the breaking out of the rebellion, and to follow him through the chances and changes of that war through which he rose rapidly to his present rank, would make a story which does not belong to the history of our county, but will possibly adorn the pages of another work.

These men are all yet in the prime of life and are making their histories every day. May they win many honors and wear them all.

They were but a handful amongst the thousands that won for us the magnificent domains of New Mexico and California with their inexhaustible mines and that great frontage of sea coast that looks to the orient. While the heirs of the sons of 1776 have scarcely ceased to draw pensions, and while that same mantle of charity still covers the heirs of 1812, while every soldier of the rebellion, from the generalissimo to our lowliest brother in black has been bountied, paid and pensioned, to these men has never been offered so much as the warrant to an acre of land of all the many thousands they conquered.

CHAPTER XIX

From A. D., 1850, to A. D., 1860—Formation of Boyle County Out of Mercer and Lincoln in 1842—Political Condition of the County and State from '50 to '60—Abolition, Its Origin, Spread and Influence on the War—Election and Inauguration of Governor Magoffin in 1859.

As a matter of historical fact, the erection of Boyle into a county ought to have been recorded as an early event in the last chapter, as early as February, 1842. But as the bearer of evil tidings always lags by the way; as the patient doomed to the surgeon's table, with averted face, walks shrinkingly around it before taking the desperate upward step; so I have, except in the incidental mention of this excision in the life of Governor Owsley, ignored this, the severest passage in the civil existence of Mercer county.

Wherefore? Because it was the loss of a fair and fruitful domain, the finest land of her birthright; peopled with substantial yoemanry; with chiefs of high degree, and fair and noble women, the wives and daughters of these men, and many flocks and herds, and much merchandise, followed in this movement, and prestige if the possession of the first college and benevolent institution of the State.

Danville early threw the gauntlet for supremacy to Harrodsburg, and after near a half century's struggle, was successful under the legislatorial supervision of Renfro and Sweeney in the house of representatives and Tomlinson in the senate, in securing a county made of the south lands of Mercer and north of Lincoln county, which was called for the distinguished Chief Justice Boyle, whose home was in its limits. From that date, the civil existence of the two counties has been separate, though they are occasionally in the same judicial and political districts. Hence, Boyle had no column in the chapter on the Mexican war, though she had her soldiers and record there as will appear in the future columns of this serial, should circumstances indicate the propriety of following up the history of Boyle to the present day.

The struggle for the establishment of this county was long, arduous, and obstinate; not limited in the expenditure of money or services of the best citizens in local canvass, in lobbying in the legislative hall, even to the parlors of the state capital's hotel, where the daughters of the counties essayed the rhetoric and logic of their personal influence over the young solons gathered in the state legislature. Ah! these were "the merrie days" and memory brings up a gallant cavalcade of youthful knights just coming into the tournament to tilt for the honors of the world; but who have dropped out of the lists one by one, until enough are not left for pall bearers when a comrade falls.

But the controlling influence in that decision was not seen in journals or in the halls or lobbies. I have been told, and believe it, the legislature was full of the alumni of Centre College, educated by the life-long president, John C. Young. They heard his voice in the roll call, and as loyally as the Scots followed when the heart of Bruce was thrown forward into the battle, these young men rose, and for the creation of the county of Boyle, for his sake, answered, "yea."

I now take up the fourth period of the history of Mercer county, extending from '50 to '85, which makes this term ten years longer than either of the three previous divisions, which covered twenty-five years each.

The beginning of this era found us under the national administration of General Taylor, who soon by death, left Millard Filmore to the occupancy of the presidential chair; who in turn gave way to James Buchanan who came in by election, in which we were interested to the extent that John C. Breckinridge was elected to the vice presidency, of which we were justly proud, not only that he was a Kentuckian, but had had his training and education under John C. Young, the president of Centre College, the leading literary institution of the west, located in Danville, Mercer county.

Mr. Crittenden was our state gubernatorial chief, and resigning to go into the United States Senate, left John L. Helm in his stead. He was succeeded by Lazarus W. Powell and John B. Thompson, who largely in his success overran his party strength and was made Lieutenant Governor of Kentucky, from which position he was soon after transferred to the Senate of the United States, his term of office as President of the Senate of Kentucky being completed by Henry G. Bibb.

While the country was enjoying this civil prosperity, it was also making rapid strides in material progress, in which Mercer was having no more than the reflex advantage which one county of the commonwealth derives from other members of the same body. Railroad making was almost a mania then, but we were not included in any of the successful roads made at that time. The Military Asylum was broken up at Harrodsburg early in this period, it having been ascertained that it would be more economical to allow our disabled patriots

"To shoulder the crutch and tell how fields were won,"

on the tapis of the Galt House, Willard's or even the Fifth Avenue in New York, than in the provincial town, Harrodsburg, Ky. We missed the figures of the old soldiers hardly distinguished from the iron sentinels that adorned the roof; we missed the military presence of Major Anderson, of unblotched escutcheon and Sumpter fame; the dash of bluff Buford, and the court circle of the handsome, genial Alexanders, to the society that mingled in the Harrodsburg Springs in its various stages of existence, the sentiment,

"I feel like one who treads alone,' etc.

of that plaintive melody must come with exquisite sadness. To me the green twilights of the forests, the thick matted verdure that overspreads the lawns, are but the adornments of a graveyard in which are buried the ashes of the splendid architecture of that place and around which lingers the memories of the beauty and chivalry of southland in its dashing life of long ago.

During these years, David Dale Owen was appointed to investigate the condition of the banks of mother earth and find what dividends we might, with fair management, get from our stock in her; i. e., was appointed State Geologist in '54, and gave Mercer the credit of having in her most centennial farms—the Chapline hills—the finest cereal producing lands in the state, and some of our farmers—notably Mr. Elliott—have demonstrated that in the culture of the vine they may yet prove the Switzerland of America.

The only military event that marked this period in Mercer was in the raising of a company of volunteers for Utah on a call of the government. The service was rendered by Capt. Benjamin Trapnal; the company was accepted, but never called out. Who were the sub-officers in his company I cannot recall. Capt. Trapnal was one of the younger of the numerous sons of Dr. Phillip Trapnal, of this vicinity, who was a successful physician, and several times represented Mercer county in the legislature. The wife of Dr. Trapnal was of the well known Casey family, a woman of uncommon good sense, business efficiency and unparalleled popularity of manner.

Capt. Trapnal was a lawyer, of fine personal appearance and pleasing address. He represented Mercer in the legislature; and died unmarried and in the prime of life.

But during all these passing years, whatever had appeared on the surface of the stream of time, there had long been an undercurrent of agitation on the subject of slavery, and its political rights and wrong, separated from the abstract question of its neutrality and religion, had come to be widely and warmly discussed. Its political value and expediency to north and south was the question to be settled.

From the time of our nation's first and great debates in forming a constitution for our United States we had forced the recognition of our independence from the reluctant mother country, the abolition of slavery had been a question that like Banquo's ghost, would not be downed; and was forever rising for discussion in some state or church convention.

The election by which Mr. Lincoln came into office, brought these questions upon the country for summary settlement. It could not again be laid on the table. It can not be said truthfully that emancipation was a plank of the platform on which Mr. Lincoln was elected or that when inaugurated, he expected or desired to cut the Gordion knot of slavery. The act was simply the result of public opinion and the pressure of circumstances that surrounded him.

Abolition had been a cloud not larger than a man's hand in its beginning, but ever floating, ever growing and darkening the perspective of the future, and had now by '61, so overspread our horizon, that while all apprehended a storm, none foresaw its nearness or fury, and when on April 17th, '61, the first bolt from it fell, it gave an electric shock to all the nations of the earth; and at home, paralyzed at once the man in the field and mart, the bride at the altar, and pierced even the dulling ear of death. Kentucky was stunned, dazed; for on no one single state were so many counter influences working. Georgraphically her borders were exposed on all sides to the horrors of war; the most convenient great highway over which the belligerent armies must cross, and on which they would naturally camp to watch each others movements. A thorough belief in state sovereignty as set forth in the resolutions of 1798, was the very groundwork of Kentucky's political faith; but in her heart of hearts she was devoted to the Union, and if her journal should have been truthfully written from the beginning to end, "lawful but not expedient" would have been her verdict on slavery. Kentucky was not wedded to the institution as the south was by interest; she had never made it profitable. Her great chief, Mr. Clay, and other eminent men in church and state, had strongly advocated gradual emancipation, and all unconscious to himself, Mr. Clay had sown broadcast in his advocacy of human freedom, as applied to South America and Greece, the seed that in home soil as surely bore the fruit of abolition sentiment. In fact, sympathy was the only strong tie that bound Kentucky to the south; sympathy and that self respect which made her feel that in a war waged to maintain an institution in fact, which was also her own, she ought to stand shoulder to shoulder with its defenders.

Mercer county did not differ from the rest of the state in her sentiments. She had a considerable non-slave holding population; and her largest slave holders were so weary of the moral responsibility of this nearly profitless institution, that they would gladly have accepted legal relief from it with most moderate compensation for loss of property; indeed, would have hardly rebelled at peaceful deliverance without recompense. Mercer's purest loyalists were those who valued as the sum of all political good, the Union above all domestic considerations. Her purest rebels were those who valued the Union, too, far above the domestic and pecuniary value of the peculiar institution, but would brook no interference with the rights of the southern states any more than they would with that right of habeas corpus, or trial by jury. And again, as it had always been whenever a crisis had come in the state, a Mercer man was always at the helm. In 1859, Beriah Magoffin had been elected and duly inaugurated; the condition of the atmosphere not wholly serene, but giving no portent of the violence of the coming storm. But when it broke, in spite of his sympathies and connections, he exhausted every effort to maintain Kentucky's independence, clinging desperately to the right of neutrality, which the north and south alike promised to respect, and which they alike disregarded.

An armed neutrality was for a long time the popular scheme of the state; the Courier-Journal leading in its advocacy. General Simon Buckner, with plenipotentiary powers, conferred with the loyal authorities, and reported to the Governor that the "neutrality of Kentucky would not be violated."

This idea took like wildfire; petitions were circulated and signed almost unanimously by the women, and miles of people went in procession with flying banners and beating drums to where acres of citizens were awaiting them to discuss how to avoid the abominations and desolations of civil war, and the beauty of brotherly love and the duty of neutrality. The people had hobnobbed and feasted together, and the masses were built up with orations and resolutions. The authorship of the petition which I append, for its peace seeking spirit and the period to which it belonged, was as much disputed as that of Junius' letters, though finally Garret Davis was accredited with the popular document:

Memorial

"To the General Assembly of the Commonwealth of Kentucky, to be convened in extra session on May 6th, 1961:

"We, the undersigned mother, wives, sisters and daughters of Kentucky, as those who guard the home altars for the chivalric sons of our native state, beseech you on our bended knees to grant us a boon entirely in your gift, and which to us in the receiving and to you in the granting would be more 'precious than rubies.' Oh, true-hearted, gallant Kentuckians! by the memory of your mothers, guard us from the direful calamity of civil war by allowing Kentucky to maintain inviolate her 'armed neutrality.' Her present position wins for her and you immortal renown.

"How does she stand today? A Peace-maker among Brothers—bound by the closest ties of blood, linked by the same majestic memories of the past! Kentucky stands guarding the dust of our great commoner, Henry Clay! His immortal "never, never, never," when asked if our Union should be broken, trembling on his lips. One hand she stretches to the balmy South, and one to the pine-clad North, and so standing she presents a sublime spectacle of moral power before which every other history of the world grows dim. Your honorable body has power, we are defenceless. Grant our petition for the sake of hearts that are breaking with anxiety; for the sake of happy homes of which civil war would only make desolation."

PART IV.

CHAPTER XX

Biographical Sketches of Prominent Men Who, During This Period, Mingled Largely in the Affairs of the Day—Governor Robert P. Letcher—Thomas P. Moore.

Having brought our readers to the verge of the great war of the Rebellion, appalled by the outlook, I retrace my steps to linger awhile in the sylvan shades of civil life, to give place to those who served their country chiefly in her state and national councils in those times, and were spared participation in the practical strife which so soon afterwards crimsoned with blood our country's soil.

Governor Letcher

Robert P. Letcher was not, as often stated, a native of Virginia, nor yet of Garrard county, but of Mercer, as I think will be shown in the very interesting forthcoming sketch of Burgin, by John H. Grimes, Jr. In this belief I am strengthened by circumstantial evidence. I cannot say that I remember, as the ballad hath it, "the day that I was born," but the very first recollection I have of this good, green earth, was of our moving from the country to town, an epoch of unparalleled importance to me, scarce a weanling. I remember our worldly goods were packed on a wagon very much unlike the Avery's and furniture cars of today, and how the strong, patient oxen stretched forth their necks against the heavy yoke, and that when we, the family, had mounted single and double on a train of horses, that a handsome, cheerful young woman dashed to the door holding a pound of golden butter on a plate, and exclaiming: "Mrs. Thompson, you have left a plate of butter," and that ever careful and managing woman stowed it away somehow, somewhere in her caravansary arrangement; that maiden was Miss Sally Letcher, a belle and beauty, and everybody's favorite of her day, who stepped across the field like a good woman as she was, to help a neighbor in a great emergency and throw her slipper after her for good luck. Of course the young Robert was sheltered under the same roof-tree with his sister.

The next step of Mr. Letcher in history is as a bare footed vagabond sort of boy who has had sudden qualms of conscience over misspent days, and sudden inspirations of ambition for higher things. Somehow and where Mr. Letcher got his modicum of education and intelligence, and I opine, as his father was a substantial farmer and mediocre, that the student, Robert, passed through the Troy Academy on his daddy's dollars.

The men of old times had such a way of talking about their hard times and early struggles; and book makers have such a way of providing self-made men for the emulation of our boys and the glory of our institutions with its free highway from the begger's hovel into the presidential chair.

The next time we came up with Governor Letcher, he has, reckless of consequences, married the beautiful and trusting Charlotte, sister of George Robertson, and occupies that historic lucky cabin in Lancaster. From that point he went back and forth between the bar and legislature and congress. He was a speaker of the house of representatives in 1838, and served eight or ten years in congress. He wound up his state services as Governor from

'40 to '44. Good stories followed Mr. Letcher's canvass course like a trail of light. Electioneering was his element, and he was ever ready with a bon mot, or to turn aside a shaft of malice with a ready rejoinder. When some one called General Harrison "a granny;" "Ah, yes," he said "boys, which of you is not glad when granny comes? Doesn't she always bring goodies in her pocket? Yes, boys, granny's coming and we'll all have goodies."

He and Col. Moore had many a test, and on one occasion, Moore said they found themselves together in a country house; he could not keep up with Letcher in kissing and tucking and riding the little unwashed gang on his foot, so he stole down early in the morning to hunt kindling or go to the well for water, but, behold! The housewife stood a kimbo, dying with laughter, her half filled bucket setting under the cow and Letcher sitting astride the calf and holding it by the ears, while he patted Bettie and praised Billy and that coffee they had had the night before. One morning he paused before our door in Frankfort and pressed my husband to be punctual at his rooms that evening. Mrs. Letcher, he said, was going to make herself very agreeable. The air of mystery in such an invitation struck me as peculiar, but the Governor passed on down the corridor delivering his invitations with a nod and a wink which were responded to rapturously, and my lord enlightened me with the information that Mrs. Letcher was making herself agreeable by going to Lexington. Judging from the time the hotel guests came in, they had wine and wassail to the "we sma' hours" at the Governor's mansion.

The last public service the Governor performed was national. He was sent minister to Mexico in 1849. He died in January, '61, not before the storm cloud of war rose, on the horizon, but ere it swept the country in its fury. His wife survived him many years, and was a beloved and honored citizen of the capital until she took her honored place in death, as she had it in the chances and changes of life, by his side.

Colonel T. P. Moore.

Col. Moore was of Irish extraction, but born in Virginia and brought while very young to this state. He was, with another brother and sister, orphaned while very young. His parents resided in or near Danville.

I do not know under whose guardianship he was reared, but without this guardian's consent or the use of his small hereditary means, he entered, when sixteen years old, in the war of 1812. He saw severe service in the northwest and received complimentary notice of his conduct at Mississenawa, both from his regimental Colonel and General Harrison.

He then returned home and studied law with Judge John Green; but again volunteered before the close of the war, and by the promotion of his captain was left in command of his company and was recommended for a commission in the U. S. Army. He again volunteered in answer to Governor McArthur's appeal for troops, made a good record and was offered a captaincy in the United States Army, but as peace was soon after declared he declined, and returned to the practice of his profession at Harrodsburg, being decided in his location by the residence of his only sister, Mrs. Hanna, here. He entered too soon into politics to have much practice in his profession, being elected to the Legislature so soon as he was eligible, and was afterward sent eight years to Congress. His chief work in the Legislature was the successful advocacy of abolishing imprisonment for debt; and his best work for his congressional district was the procuring of a large grant of valuable land for the Deaf Mute Asylum in Danville.

While an intensely partisan man, Col. Moore was always a vigilant, faithful guardian of the interests of his whole constituency. He was in the beginning an adherent of Mr. Clay, but split off to the democratic wing when

Clay, being out of the question, choice had to be made between Adams and Jackson. He became a bitter opponent of Mr. Clay and a zealous and efficient partisan of General Jackson, and was with him a prime favorite, and was appointed by him minister to the Republic of Colombia, South America.

After his return to the United States he was Commissioner's Agent to some of the northwestern tribes of Indians; but the rumor of the Mexican war having reached him, he resigned and was made a Lieutenant Colonel of Cavalry, and had some hard active service under General Scott in his celebrated brilliant and successful march on to the conquest of the city of Mexico.

Col. Moore had quite his share in the dangers and hardships of that campaign, his command being detailed as escort for a long train of stores and a very large amount of money, which he carried successfully, showing as great a disregard for personal danger and exposure as the youngest of his corps.

After his return to the county he remained in private life until 1849, when he served in the convention that revised and remodeled the second constitution now in force in Kentucky.

Col. Moore was thrice married. The first time to Miss Mary Locke, of South Carolina; the second time to Miss Mary, daughter of pioneer Samuel McAfee, who perpetuated in the name of her first born that of her predecessor, the Carolinian. Of this marriage the children of Dr. C. S. Abel and Samuel D. Johnson, of Frankfort, are descendants. Col. Moore married the last time Miss Lake, of New Orleans, who, I think, has no living children.

Col. Moore was a man of small stature and very noble face which, with his quick step and restless demeanor, betokened his nervous, energetic temperament. He was undoubtedly a man of talent, having a wonderful insight into the character of men, and thorough knowledge, binding them to his iron will. He was accredited to have almost the talent of Tallyrand in combination and contrivance in political scheming; but he was impatient and imperious, and finally did cope successfully with Letcher's good humored raillery, or Thompson's silent, vigilant tactics, which kept him ever ready for attack or defense.

Col. Moore had some hereditary estate, and his second wife, Miss McAfee, a good patrimony of land, and of course the emoluments that came with his political success were large, but he spent lavishly. He made very large investments in Indian lands, which except for the immense territory brought on the market by the conquest of Mexico and California, must have made him immensely wealthy.

He died in '53 of paralysis, and was buried in the New Providence graveyard where so many of the McAfee clan are gathered that supported him in his political career, with such fidelity and unwavering devotion.

CHAPTER XXI

Biographical Sketches Continued—John B. Thompson.

John B. Thompson

I am not the person who should write the memoirs of this man. At once my memory steals back through the corridors of time to the cottage in the wood where we were born, and instead of the lawyer and statesman, of whom my readers would have me talk, I am with the pale, resolute child that hunts hares with Caesar through the tangled thickets, or sits in the stilly midnight munching his cold biscuit as the flickering faggot betrays him to my scared vision, gesticulating with his hands and shaking his head as imperially as in later days, for has not nurse made me feel already that he is a wierd thing, not like the rest of us? But morning reassures me, and I go with him tracking rabbits and hunting berries, or maybe see him a little later bending over his pretty sweetheart at school, or meeting his grave father, suddenly scudding around the corner as he was caught in the very act of carrying her books home gallantly, barefoot and with torn hat, as was likely, for he always carried the marks of the campus on him; was as fond of balls as of books, and took part in the wrestlers' ring heroically. Sometimes we were sent out punished by the mother, and build real rubbish play houses and castles d'Espagne together, concocted rebellions and escapades; and then, scared by the goblins that came round the dark house, crept in, in forced penitence, and played Barnum's money in the happy family. But years lapsed by, and John had his study and play under several teachers in the Academy on the old Fort Hill; and then some rollicking times with the Daviess and Marshal and Trapnel boys, where Dr. Trapnal always kept a first rate teacher, who in John's time, was Mr. Daly, an educated Irishman, whose specialty was mathematics. To that place he always looked back as an oasis, never forgetting the motherly spirit with which that princess of good women bore with the mischief of a score of boys, of which he and his brother, Henry, were two. These brothers took their finishing course with Dr. Polin, a graduate of Dublin University.

John had no college advantages, but studied natural science from taste, and belles lettres at discretion. He was very fond of history and the impassioned poetry of Byron, as it came out in our day, giving sensation after sensation to the literary world. He had finished the reading of law by the time he reached his majority and had commenced practice in his father's office. His father's death, so disastrous to his family, proved a sad but golden opportunity to John. Left so young to the administration of several estates of his kindred, who fell by the fatal plague of '33, and to close up his father's extensive practice, he had ample opportunity to develop and exhibit his ability. He gained professional distinction rapidly, and had he kept in the line of his profession he might have found usefulness, fortune and distinction in it, but he marred this by early embarking in politics, which left him little but barren distinction, the guerdon of his success. His pre-eminence at the bar was as a jury lawyer. He depended not so much on his profound knowledge of law, nor upon the fullness of law in the particular case which he had in hand, as in reading the character of his jury and moving the main spring of their biases and prejudices to his purpose. In fact he often purposely steered wide of the law in his case, and maintaining his jury men each on his hobby, sent them ambling off like Don Quixote in search of discoveries in their own favorite fields of adventure.

He was also a successful electioneerer, without much distinction of taffy in the shape of kisses to the children and flattery to the mothers. His entire freedom from egotism, his earnest convictions of the right of the political policy he advocated, and his inexhaustible fund of good will to men, made them very tolerant of very plain, hard truths which he good humoredly enunciated. I do not remember ever hearing John, until he reached his mid-career as a politician, ever say a hard thing about a human being, though, like Rhoderic Dhue, he would

"Right a wrong where e'er 'twas given,
Had it been in the court of Heaven."

But no threats preceded, no boasting followed the blow. It was said he was a relentless prosecutor as Commonwealth's Attorney, claiming, as history vindicates his opinion, that the surest pity to our race, the only preservative of national purity is in the sure, swift retribution on real crime. In society he was very diffident at first, and from a kind heart always devoted himself to the wall flowers. He had some cases in Cupid's courts and was always sure to appear before a worthy tribunal, but finally gave society a sensation, when considered a hopeless bachelor, by unexpectedly marrying Mrs. Mary H. Bowman, the widow of Dr. Benjamin Bowman, a native of Mercer, but afterward an eminent physician in Mississippi. Strangely enough that only a garden wall had separated these mature parties for years, and why the strong affinity which bound them at last had not earlier drawn them together is inexplicable. Any way they spent several years of golden wedded life, and then the inexorable reaper gatherd in our tall sheaf. His illness was brief, painful and under singularly trying circumstances. But his ears were deafened to earthly sounds and he heard not the storm of the wrathful skies, such as shook Helena the night the great exile went out on the wings of the death angel.

He was a believer in the Christian religion, and during the last years a daily reader of the Scriptures and a constant attendant on the services of the Methodist church, of which his wife had been, from childhood, a member. Mr. Abbott, resident pastor of the church at the time of his death, made as a funeral service a fine argument for the immortality of the soul from that all important text,

"If a man die shall he live again?"

He was buried amid the arctic splendors of such a morning as is rarely seen. The blue dome of Heaven rose up from a field of spotless snow while the multitudes of funeral pines bent down with their weight of flashing gems, as though in their royal state they were bowing in solemn sympathy with the cortege of mourners that gathered around the grave.

I have given briefly a few of the memories that come to me of the early and again the last days of my brother. From the committee delegated by his brothers of the bar I will append their memorial as rendered. It is a better synopsis of his public service than I could make.

In every stage of his life he was honest, in his political sentiments and in the rebellion unfaltering in his loyalty to the federal government. The places he filled were high and responsible. I have never thought the winning of any of them, although Col. Moore was experienced and had been successful, was so much an honor not even his over running his party ticket as Lieutenant Governor, as was his election over Hon. C. Wickliffe, a man who had the prestige of family, experience, and high national reputation.

Of national reputation Mr. Thompson had himself a share that grows surprisingly as the distance grows from home. He was better known as a statesman and orator in the distant states than here. His Cuban speech is often called up to illustrate the force and peculiarities of American eloquence.

In Washington society he mingled little. He was a long time of the coterie of Mrs. Crittenden and Mrs. Webster. Mrs. Crittenden was always his model of excellence, elegance and propriety; Mrs. Webster of taste and fashion. He had a set of jewelry copied from one of Mrs. Webster's for his wife. Below I append the memorial referred to above:

First after the preliminary order of Judge Keller this morning, W. O. Bradley, Esq., rose, and suggesting the death, but two hours before of Hon. John Burton Thompson, of this city, stated that he desired, on the part of the attorneys for the Commonwealth, to make a motion. A man who stood high in the estimation of his countrymen; a personal friend of the speaker; a man whose memory Kentucky would delight to honor, one whose voice was wont to charm the thousands who hung upon his lips, had crossed over the dark river into the silent land. The members of the profession which his genius had so elevated and adorned, desired to pay the last sad rites of honor and affection to the distinguished dead, and hence Mr. Bradley moved to postpone any further proceedings with the case in hand until such day as the proprieties of the mournful occasion might suggest.

Gov. Bramlette joined Mr. Bradley in his chaste and earnest expressions of sorrow for the noble dead. His great heart was pulseless, and his brain no longer troubled with the inspiration which had made his name a household word throughout Kentucky; and it was eminently proper to give as many of the members of the bar as could do so an opportunity to pay tribute at the bier of the great lawyer, John Burton Thompson. He therefore suggested that the court adjourn until tomorrow morning at 10 o'clock, when resolutions of respect will be passed, and, if by that hour the funeral services were not concluded, the bar would take such necessary steps as the occasion might demand. Judge Kellar, at the instance of C. A. Hardin, Esq., therefore named Judge O. S. Poston, Judge Robert M. Bradley and Gov. Thomas E. Bramlette a committee to prepare the necessary resolutions, and instructed W. F. Robards to drape the inner pillars of the court room with the customary emblems of mourning.

Biographical Sketch

John B. Thompson was born December 14, 1810, near Harrodsburg, as was his father, for whom he was named, and his mother, formerly Miss Nancy Robards. He was the second of ten children, among whom are his brother Henry, Capt. Phil B., John and Charles. He was educated here, read law with his father, admitted to the Harrodsburg bar in 1831, and has never resided elsewhere than in this county. When twenty-five years of age, in 1835, he was first elected to the Kentucky Legislature, and a second time the following year. In 1840 he made a brilliant canvass as candidate for Congress, beating Hon. Simeon Anderson, his competitor. His constituents insisted upon a second term, and in August, 1841, he was elected over Hons. T. P. Moore and J. Kinkead; in which position he served until 1843. When he was appointed Commonwealth's Attorney for the district; and the Mexican war breaking out, he organized a company of colunteer cavalry in 1846, which was not accepted; his brother, Capt. Phil B. Thompson, having raised a company of infantry which was accepted. In 1847 he was again elected to Congress over Hon. C. A. Wickliffe, and in 1849, without opposition. He was a prominent candidate for Governor before the Whig convention of 1851, and though failing to secure the nomination for the higher place, was put on the ticket for Lieutenant Governor with Hon. A. Dixon, made a brilliant canvass, and while Mr. Dixon was distanced, Mr. Thompson ran in by a handsome majority over his democratic competitor, Hon. R. Wickliffe. This was a triumph which at once lifted Governor Thompson into distinction throughout the country, following, as it did, a campaign which had already attracted attention by its brilliancy and enthusiasm. The elation of the Whigs over their success in this quarter was dashed by the reflection that had he held the first place on the ticket their triumph would have been more conspicuous, even if he had not dragged the entire ticket through with him. The election of Gov. Hendricks, of Indiana, in 1872, while the remainder of the nominees (with the single exception of Superintendent of Public Instruction), furnishes the second instance of a double-headed state executive, or "split magistracy."

His Election as Senator

Finally, in 1851, he was honored with a seat in the Senate of the United States, which he held for six years, his last and highest official position. During this term he delivered his celebrated speech on the Cuban question, which for wit sparkles till it dazzles has never been excelled, if equalled. It can be found in the Congressional Globe of that term, and those who delight in this character of oration will begin, now that its distinguished author is dead, to re-peruse and re-enjoy this remarkable production. What other state than our own can boast with us the glory of having produced even a single orator approximating that peculiar genius which electrified the country and set its sides to shaking, first over "Cuba" and lastly over "Duluth?" What geographical antipodes! And yet the kindred genius of Kentucky's gifted son has linked them together in glorious fame-weaving from the bluebells and water-cresses of the sunny isle, and from the vine and myrtle of the land of Knott, a wreath of Immortelles! The gem of the gulf; the "con centric-circled" city, near the palace of the ice king—are silent no more. Another voice mingles with the carol of star-winged birds of musical throat that join in nature's merry-making among the orange-groves of Cuba; set now to mirthful music are the brooks.

"That chatter over stony ways,
In little sharps and trebles,"

down the sun crowned hills of Duluth!
At the time of the delivery of "Cuba" (rare also, as an argument), Senator Thompson was in such feeble health that he was compelled to sit through a portion of it. When it became known that he would speak, the Senate chamber was crowded with citizens and various members of the Foreign Legations, who joined in the hearty zest with which the speech was received by his colleagues.

His Personal Characteristics

I find that here at home, where Governor Thompson was best known for his personal worth, he was most highly esteemed. His social and domestic virtues endeared him to his family, and to a host of friends. He married, five years ago, one of the most accomplished and gifted ladies of the state—Mrs. Mary Hardin Bowman, daughter of Judge Chinn. Had he joined his fate in early life to such a woman Governor Thompson might have had a prominent career second to but few men in the country, and attained to a ripe old age. His splendid constitution was impaired, and no doubt his intellect to a small extent, also, by what seems to be the bane, almost inseparably, of the most gifted of our race. I do not mean that Governor Thompson ever so dissipated his talent as to excite serious apprehension, or to interfere with professional or other duties. His convjviality never passed into what we called habit; but being of an eminently social nature like every other political campaigner of rare genius in this country, he indulged an occasional "good time" with his companions. Indeed, if indulgence had become fixed he could not have exercised the control over himself which he did; for I am told that since the hour of marriage to his death he was temperate almost to abstemiousness.

Members of the bar of this place never tire of recounting Governor Thompson's

Achievements of Stump and Rostrum.

They describe him as pre-eminently sui generis; he was his own pattern and no one could imitate him; consequently the bare outline of the prominent epochs and public events of his life serve but tamely to illustrate the man. The world, those who knew him, say they know all that was said, and done by him during his life, but the world can never know John B. Thompson. The same original individuality which characterized him was alike prominent in the most commonplace social gathering, the contests of the court room and in the halls of Congress, where he often held his audience entranced by his eloquence, or convulsed by his wit. In his mental organization well defined opposites blended harmoniously, and his physiognomy clearly indicated. I never met him but once, and then only for a few minutes. The square face and heavy jaws, indicative of the combative, if not the aggressive were pleasingly modified and toned by the upturned corners of his expressive mouth, the very picture and exemplification of mirthfulness and good humor. He was emphatically a genius, but not of the erratic or sky-rocket type. His whole mental superstructure, splendid and dazzling as it was, was based upon an extensive substratum of common sense; hence, as a lawyer, he was noted for his sound practical judgment.

As a wit and humorist he has rarely if ever been equalled; and his wit was part of himself and partook of his own individuality. One can describe neither without the other. To relate his anecdotes, sayings or witticisms, would be unjust to his memory, for no man could say them but himself, and the very recital by another would knock the pith, soul and brains out of them.

For instance, a case was once being argued in which he was counsel, and the question was as to the value of certain services rendered by a corps of engineers in building a bridge.

Divers witnesses from a certain county in his old district were examined who proved that the work on the bridge was worth only so much. The weight of testimony was against him, such testimony as it was. But when he made his arguments, he said: "Well, let us come up to the point; here they are—clever men—who vote for me in the elections. But how do they know anything of engineering? They live in log cabins; they are honest and clever; but even in their fishing they are not apostolic; for the fishers of men set their nets, and these men use a spiked iron barb, with which surreptitiously they approach the finny tribe in summer when water is low, and, feeling feloniously under the shelving rocks, they, with murder in their hearts and malice in their copperas cotton breeches, assassinate catfish. Now, gentlemen of the jury, how can you take the testimony of such men against my clients—experienced, educated engineers—when they don't know a perch of rock from a concealed catfish?"

His style was simple, inimitable. By a look, nod or gesture he could convulse his audience with laughter; yet he never indulged in the common mimicry of the clown. He imitated no one. It was simply the magnetic inspiration of his own original genius speaking in the twinkle of his eye of the magic movement of his finger. He was a profound lawyer, and always fond of his profession; yet in his practice, and in his logic, he knew no given form or rule, except as he often said himself, "To come up to the common sense of it;" and woe to the antagonist who shielded an unjust cause behind a legal technicality when "Old Jack," as he was often called, turned his batteries of hot shot and shell upon it.

Who that heard that memorable defense of the boy charged with stealing ten chickens, and hunted down by police officials, will forget the picture of country-town police courts, when he said that "God Almighty in ancient days had permitted Shadrack, Meshack and Abednego to be tried in the fiery furnace as the severest substitute in the absence of that modern invention called police courts, of which history gives no account of any one who has passed through unscathed;" or who that heard the case of the Commonwealth vs. the Shakers can forget that eulogy on morals and religion which fell from the lips of the old man with an impassioned eloquence akin to the voice of inspiration.

All minds have their own peculiar, fixed channels, grooves and methods of thought. He was specially peculiar in his, that it had no fixed channel or method.

His sequences and description were neither attained nor presented in any known or anticipated line of logic; to him in their conception they seemed as by intuition, they appeared axiomatic. His most intimate and well known friends could never anticipate him beyond the sentence he was uttering, for he thought like no one else.

In his social life he was ever agreeable and pleasant, having a kindly greeting for all, and, unlike most men who possess to a great degree the faculty of wit and power of sarcasm, he died without an enemy, for he provoked an honest smile even from his victim writhing under his excoriation. I have heard lawyers of the Harrodsburg bar say that Governor Thompson often made an excellent speech after he got through. That is, by the manner he would back himself to his seat, indulging, meantime, a series of original pantomimic delineations, bowing first to the right, then to the left, and all the while gesticulating with his hands in a manner that could be read by all. And yet, strange to say, in all this there was not the least lowering of his dignity nor discoverable the least approach to the vulgarity of the clown. It is doubted whether the best living actors could imitate him, even by hard study, since he never delivered the same pantomime more than once, his gestures, like his speeches, being suited to the special case and character in hand.

For the anecdotes and characteristics of Governor Thompson, collated since his death this morning, I am indebted to members of the bar here, and more especially to P. W. Hardin, T. C. Bell and Col. Nat Gaither.

During His Last Illness

he was happily surrounded by all those sweet charities which a wife, sisters and brother know so well how to administer. Dr. Davis M. Thompson, his nephew, and Dr. Thomas Kyle, attended him professionally throughout his sickness. Henry Thompson, Esq., of Hillsboro, Ohio, a brother of the deceased, and of Capt. Phil B. Thompson, Sr.; his sister, Mrs. Kate Dunn, also of Ohio (a lady, by the way, who is said to bear a most remarkable likeness to Mrs. Martha Washington); Mrs. William Daviess, another sister, of this city, besides Captain Phil Thompson, Phil B. Thompson, Jr., John B. Thompson, Jr., with other relatives and friends, were with him in his last moments.

C. E. M

CHAPTER XXII

Loyal Mercer—Camp Nelson First Recruiting Station in Kentucky—Organization of Several Regiments in Mercer and Boyle—Names of Officers From Those Counties in These Regiments—Remarks of Adjutant General Lindsay on the Conduct of These Troops—Sketches of Officers of These Regiments.

The many measures resorted to toward Kentucky's complications in the Civil war have been detailed in Governor Magoffin's' life. The legislature which had temporized and delayed so as to render the arming of Kentucky almost a farce, suddenly toned up to the highest key and quickly and rudely dispelled the illusion and voted men and money to the government and passed stringent resolutions disfranchising adherents of the South, making active sympathy treason, and recruiting in the state for the south a penal offense. In August, 1861, the United States Government took military possession of the state; establishing by General Nelson, at Camp Dick Robinson, Garrard county, a post which served first for a recruiting station for white volunteers, and afterwards for the same purpose for blacks and making for that race a place of refuge throughout the war.

I quote from memory, but I think Kentucky furnished a fraction less than 70,000 men to the Union army of white soldiers, and of colored, 15,000; no account being taken of the large numbers that straggled off and enlisted from other places; but deaths and removals have so scattered the remnants of the companies that composed the Union forces that were furnished by Mercer and Boyle, that I could not from authentic sources, official or private, derive matter belonging purely to Mercer and Boyle as counties. I was therefore forced on to public records of the state and have found from them who constituted the rank and file of such regiments as were organized in our bounds, or that were officered by our men, and shall enlist in proper place the names of any of our citizens who signalized themselves on any field, on either side, by their valor or humanity. I have gathered and somewhat condensed the accounts I found in General Lindsay's very complete official reports to the state of the different regiments in which I recognize the names of officers as Mercer or Boyle men.

The private, the bone and sinew of all armies whose achievements are the ground work of all the glory of historic pages, must, as in all other annals, be left out as too numerous to cumber the record.

The rolls of the army are starred with Kentuckians who were in command in both armies. Of course, I only mention those in our county enlistments. For the use of Lindsay's reports I am indebted to the courtesy of Dr. J. R. Cowan, of Danville. I also acknowledge the kind services of Mr. Samuel D. Johnson, of Frankfort, and valuable aid of our townsman, Mr. George Passmore.

The 4th Regiment of Kentucky Volunteer Infantry was organized at Camp Dick Robinson, under Colonel Speed S. Fry. Company A, of this regiment, was commanded by Captain Wellington Harlan, of Boyle county. Company C, of this regiment, was commanded by Captain Lewis C. Lancaster, of Mercer county. Company F, of this regiment, was raised and commanded by Josephus H. Tompkins, of Mercer. This regiment saw exceedingly active service. It was organized at Camp Dick Robinson and mustered into service, October 9, '61. Before the close of that year it

Hemp Standing, Spread and Shocked

A Field of Burley Tobacco

fought and defeated the rebels under Crittenden and Zollicofer, remained in that section for a while, and afterward continued in very active service, chiefly in Kentucky and Tennessee, until '64, it returned, and after a short furlough, re-organized as a cavalry regiment and fought to the close of the war, its base of operations being chiefly in southeast Kentucky. This regiment from the first to last saw hard service and bore it with persistent bravery. The 4th was in Mill Spring, Rolling Fork, Corinth, Miss.; Tullahooma, Chickamauga, Chattanooga, Missionary Ridge, La Fayette, Mason's Creek and New Mont, Ga.; Pulaski, Lewisburg, Pike, Franklin and Lynchville, Tenn., and Shoal Creek, Alabama.

Brigadier General Speed S. Fry having served in various civil and military capacities from Boyle county, might as properly belong to a future chapter of Boyle biographies, but it seems to come more naturally in the records of this regiment. He is directly descended from Joshua Fry, the head of the extensive and respectable family of that name that pervades Kentucky under various names engrafted on it. General Fry was educated in Centre College, and saw military service first in the war of Mexico. Again, at the breaking out of the rebellion, he raised a company and was in command of a regiment at Mill Spring, and had much to do with the discomfiture of the rebels there, by depriving them of their commander, General Zollicoffer, who fell by his hand. He continued in service to the close of the war, and came out with the rank of Brigadier General. General Fry has always ranked high in the benevolent orders, and has been a member of the Presbyterian church. He is still in the prime of life, and I leave him with the rest of his contemporaries, the chances of going up many rounds yet on the ladder of promotion to the highest honors of his country.

Ninth regiment of Kentucky Volunteer Cavalry, was organized at Eminence, Ky., by Col. Richard T. Jacobs. In it Company J was commanded by Harvey J. Burns, of Mercer county, who raised this company in Mercer. Company K was commanded by Capt. William Edwards, of Mercer. Company M was commanded by Capt. William G. Connor, of Mercer. This whole regiment numbering 1,250 men, was enlisted at different points in the state and concentrated at Eminence in three weeks. The officers were reported as very efficient and fine disciplinarians and the soldiers gallant. This regiment fought successfully at Geiger's Lake, also at Camp Colman, Todd county, Ky., and upon Bragg's invasion, were ordered into Buell's command and performed the arduous duty of guarding the supply trains in that critical period; they afterwards served in southwestern Kentucky and Tennessee. This regiment and a battalion of 3rd Kentucky Cavalry, under command of Colonel Bristow were sent in pursuit and gained the laurels of capturing the celebrated chief, Morgan, in his raid on Indiana and Ohio.

Tenth regiment of Volunteer Infantry, was organized by John M. Harlan, in Lebanon, Ky., and was assigned to the second division of the army of the Ohio, and had active service in Tennessee and Mississippi, in the seige of Corinth and in pursuit of Bragg. Col. Harlan was certainly a native of Mercer, and I think, Harrodsburg. He resigned his command in consequence of the death of his father, Hon. James Harlan, the business interests of his family imperative requiring his attention. In his resignation he expressed strongly his regret and undying devotion to the Union. Col. Harlan rose steadily to the highest position attainable in the legal profession. He is in the prime of life and has time to accumulate the well deserved honors he wears so well. He left in his native county the impression of decided talent, high integrity and I think of religious proclivities. His wife and daughter, Miss Edith, were considered women of unusual solidity and excellence of character. Soon after her marriage, when the Master was gathering lillies, he took the daughter to his own fadeless garden.

Justice Harlan was the son of Hon. James Harlan, a native of Mercer county, who for a number of years resided in Harrodsburg. He was a prominent lawyer, and for a number of years was Attorney General of the state. He also represented the district in which he resided for a number of years in congress. James Harlan, of Louisville, was also a son of Hon James Harlan.

The 11th Regiment of Kentucky Volunteer Cavalry was recruited in the fall of '62, at Harrodsburg, under Col. Alexander W. Holman, and Company C was raised by Captain Jacob Cozatt, of Mercer, and Company F was raised by Captain Robert S. Curd, of Mercer. This regiment was recruited in the fall of '62. Capt. Milton Graham opened a camp at Harrodsburg, and the companies A, C, D and F were recruited from the counties of Mercer, Washington and Madison, and reported at rendezvous about the 11th of July. In the 27th of July this camp was removed to Frankfort in consequence of the invasion of the state and the difficulties attending the equipping and mustering recruits at the former place. On arriving at Frankfort they were ordered to report to Major A. W. Holman, and during their stay Company B was recruited, and from Frankfort they were ordered to Louisville Fair Grounds for recruiting, drilling and picket duty, and were there mustered into the United States service and remained in Louisville during Bragg's invasion. This regiment was on duty in Tennessee and southern Kentucky, garrisoning towns to July '63, when it went in pursuit of Morgan and was present at his capture at Buffington, Ohio. General Riley having resigned, Major Graham took command and went in pursuit of Scott's rebel cavalry to Somerset, and from there joined General Burnsides in his East Tennessee operations; was in all the engagements of that campaign, and in '64 sustained severe losses in killed and wounded. Col. Graham was severely wounded at Seviersville, Tenn. At Mt. Sterling, Ky., this regiment was joined by Col. W. C. Boyle, and being filled and fully equipped, was engaged in skirmishing and scouting at Lexington. From this point they went to Stonemen's brigade in East Tennessee, and there and in West Virginia suffered greatly, many officers and privates being disqualified for service by severe frost bites. December 18th, Lieutenant Boyle was killed leading a charge at Marions, Alabama. At the close of the war this regiment was with the army operating in Tennessee, Georgia and Alabama. It was mustered out of service at Louisville, Ky., July 4th, '65, the recruits and veterans being transferred to 12th Kentucky cavalry.

The 19th Regiment of Kentucky Volunteer Infantry was recruited and organized at Harrodsburg in the fall of '62, by Col. William J. Landram, of Garrard county, and Lieut. Col. John Cowan, of Boyle. Captain Aaron Blakeman raised and commanded Company B of this regiment. Said Captain and company were from Boyle. Hannibal Downey, of Mercer, was Captain of Company E. Captain Josiah J. Mann, of Mercer, commanded Company F. Captain Henry Hicks, of Mercer, commanded Company I.

Officer of the 19th Cavalry, Col. William J. Landram, has not a place on these columns by birth or residence; but in looking over the records I noticed that he was promoted and complimented.

Lieut. Col. John Cowan was a lineal descendant of the Cowans of the pioneer period; and I have heard through a private source that Col. Cowan was as tender as brave, and that where he was posted in the south the people were not made conscious of the presence of an enemy.

Captain Josiah J. Mann was of a family better known by its undivided devotion to the Presbyterian church than to the Union. Some fought on each side and bravely . Capt. Mann reached the rank of Major before the close of the war.

But in the main our loyal provost marshals prevented and mended all possible trouble; especially to the late Capt. Wesley Cardwell do southern sympathizers owe lasting obligation, for he threw the broad shield of his kind heart over every possible offender.

Dr. De Camp, I believe, distributed the wounded Confederates from Perryville, whether in malice or humanity it mattered not, it was received by them as a gracious privilege. He doubtless acted under orders, and in their intercourse was unexceptionable. Of Capt. Black, in that office, we are bound to record soldierly conduct and forbearance. On one occasion it was said Capt. Black met at a social dance several of the Confederate boys who were always making stolen visits to sweethearts and home. "Did you have those rebels arrested you met at the party last night?" enquired one of those many, always more vigilant than valiant, stay-at-home patriots. "As provost marshal I did not attend the party last night," replied Capt. Black, "and I saw no one there but the invited guests of my hospitable host. This morning you can have any rebel soldier found in Mercer county arrested." The two grand excitements of Mercer county during the war, were the Morgan raid and the presence of Bragg's army in our midst before the battle of Perryville.

John Morgan was of our state, and many of our Mercer boys were with him; so when the repeated rumor of his coming raid took wind amongst us, it was hard to say whether joy or dread predominated. To one side he was coming an angel of deliverance; to the other as an avenger; both sides recognizing in him the dominant leader that the London Times had said, "Was the star that was steadily rising to the zenith obscuring all others." During one of these invasions, Will Messic, who carried within him as wild a spirit and brave a heart as ever animated a soldier, wishing to take a glimpse of his home folks, elected himself courier and announced to the startled citizens of Danville, the speedy approach of Morgan and advised the surrender of the town at discretion. What the city fathers did belongs to the future history of the county, but down our way, the roads were soon strung with foot and horseback refugees, who had not remained to wait the current of events, and every unusual and nondescript vehicle was met, filled with people, valuables and trumpery that the fleeing gathered up as people do things wildly in a fire . A hearse came by one person clinging to the steps and one inside almost smothered with valuables and invaluables, amongst them millinery goods, the feathers within nodding to the plumes without this strangely desecrated equipage. One darkey was halted with a coffee sack full of photographs, gallery fixings and dentist wares, while a wagon came careening down the road with no standing room left in it, the men singing at the tops o ftheir voices:

"We will rally 'round the flag,"
We will rally once again."

A humorous man by the wayside threw up his hands to stop them and the horses fell fairly back on their haunches with the sudden check.

"Boys," the interrupter said, "I judge from your song, you are going the wrong way, hadn't you better rally before running?" "Whoop! whoopee!! Morgan's taken Danville, and is shelling the road, ge-et up!!" and with cracking whip and swelling chorus they dashed on. The Danville rumor had been contradicted and Harrodsburg had succeeded to the sensation and that had also subsided, and Sunday morning between the ringing of the first and second bells, the people had peacefully sought their various temples of worship. Before the invocations were made there came some whisper in the air that Morgan was entering the town and suddenly the churches were filled with mingled lamentations and cheers.

The congregations of the churches retired and there was seen entering the village streets a wierd, wild cavalcade, such as no war ever saw before; horses of all kinds and colors; boys of all ages and sizes, and no uniform, save the general grimy gray, that dust and wear had given. There were shaking of hands and tears and kisses, and such unsoldierly demonstrations, as never were shown. The horses were soon disposed of, and under the magnificent elms of the old Graham Springs grounds (now known as the Military Asylum) there was improvised a picnic that was indulged in with the wildest abandon. The fat of the land was furnished in rich abundance, milk and honey literally flowed and the larders of the loyal yielded up their stores as freely as the most rabid "secesh." In fact they only saw the return of prodigals in their neighbor's sons and ate, drank and were merry with them. Meanwhile some of the provident rebel soldiers were recruiting and exchanging horses in places conspicuous enough to have them seized by these free traders, and the loyal could find no screen close enough to hide theirs from the levy. I do not remember ever to have had so romantic a scene pass before me as on that evening's close.

We had all come out to the roadside to have a farewell glimpse of the passing band. A mile distant in the town, they were singing "The Bonny Blue Flag," etc., which floated clearly out on the night air, the several parts well sustained by male voices of all ages from deep bass to shrill tenor, some fine baritones carrying the chief burden. There were wild cheers again and again repeated, then we heard the tramp, tramp of many horses' feet and soon the band began passing by steadily, silently as a phantom host. A few of the boys who knew us swerved aside in the dark for a brief word and a farewell, and one little maiden wringing her hands, declared she would never, never wash them again until the boys should come back to imprint them with fresh kisses.

The next day my liege lord followed this band to bring back a fugitive contraband negro that had mounted a cannon and gone, little recking whether he followed the grey or the blue. He found little trouble in reclaiming this chattle, but lingered along watching the novel scene. The boys were lounging and sleeping in every possible position on the ledges of the cliffs, while those detailed were swimming the horses across Shryock's Ford. He said that George Arnold, that we all soon after nursed with such interest down to his grave, was the finest specimen of humanity he had ever seen, and that he crossed and recrossed the river scores of times, the wonder growing each time that he should come out alive from amongst those rearing, plunging, kicking horses. The next day after the bivouac on the Spring's grounds, the town was reeking with that previous day's adventures; how that the daughter of the most loyal citizen was wearing on her watch chain a button from John Morgan's coat; how Greenfell Ledger had given a gage d' amour to a certain beauty; how unshorn, unwashed Texans had graced the daintiest village boards; and Morgan's name proved an open sesame to the closest closed parlors. This next day I chanced upon a household of the worthy dames of the village; in answer to the question of news from the village, I said: "All the town is crying shame on the way the women kissed Morgan's boys." "Who kissed the soldiers?" they answered in chorus with uplifted hands and scornful lips. "Every one of you, I suspect," I said. "Come, make clean breasts. Mrs. T——, did you?" "Of course, just Mary's sons." "And you, Mrs. B——?" "Why, law! yes; there was a lot of college boys there I used to take care of like my own children." So every woman in the room confessed to a score of such transgressions, and thus was explained the story of the indecorous kissing of the Morgan boys by the Harrodsburg women.

CHAPTER XXIV

More Adventures of the Boys—Incoming of Ledbetter's Command—Bragg's Invasion and Brief Occupation.

There were Mercer boys in Morgan's band that now and then, for love of home or adventure, or of a bonnie bright eye, would slip into the county, often giving trouble, and sometimes making narrow escapes from serious danger. I have heard some who were reckless enough even to come out gallanting their sweethearts to dances, or to church in broad Sabbath noon. One of the most amusing adventures that I remember in this line was of the young man who helped hunt himself through the hills and hollows of Kentucky river cliffs. He had been hid in these cliffs for some time, fed chiefly by the rebellious daughter of a deep dyed Unionist, who had at that time at home a soldier son on sick furlough. The home guards at length got information of this Confederate and came to this loyal house for clews to his whereabouts. Our heroine hastily equipped her hidden Confederate in her sick soldier brother's uniform of blue, mounted him on his horse, and he boldly joined the home guard pursuit. He amused himself for a while in exploring the crags and bushes until presently, suddenly crossing the river and reaching a bridle path he well knew on the other side, he turned, waved his adieu with three cheers for Jeff Davis and dashed off and was lost before the bewildered hunters understood the situation . But many of the escapades were not so successfully managed, and the captured adventurers repented their temerity at their leisure in prison.

It was curious to see with what ardor searches for these adventurers would be made; then the repentant, frightened efforts these same captors would make to have the ensnared boys released. One Sunday morning just before dawn we were aroused with a thunderous knocking upon the front door. My husband went forward, I hastily dressed and followed. A Federal officer sat upon the steps; the tale he was telling was half stifled with sobs. "He had taken a Morgan boy that he would not have arrested for the world! Would we not hasten in and see the loyal powers and try to avert the captive's incarceration, for Danville prison, his destination, was not accounted a pleasant abiding place in those days, not exactly a place for the indulgence of pleasant anticipation of the future in this world." It was thought, perhaps, a woman might make a better intercessor in this case, and I went to the home powers for words of aid and comfort. I went to Major James Taylor first. "Yes, he would exert himself, certainly. Where was the boy? Whose boy? Where were pen, ink and paper; no where was his horse; he would go anywhere, everywhere." Next, to Dr. Smedley. First, a lecture on the sin of rebellion, and thanks to God none of his blood had been carried off in the delusions, but "certainly he was not the man to refuse a neighbor a helping hand." Then I was charged especially to see James D. Hardin. I stated my errand. He exploded like a bomb shell and excoriated rebels and rebellions. The storm was soon spent, and I arose, saying, "But you will go with me to the soldier's home and see the boy's mother?" He would not refuse me everything; he would go, and he reluctantly entered the carriage. We found the mother lying on her couch, exhausted with grief. In a half hour he was so excited, so sympathetic, that I could not induce him to leave with me; he gave me his instructions and stayed until the setting sun. But a wiser friend took the cause in hand and went to Jerry Boyle, and our captive was at once paroled.

The first body of southern troops that came amongst us of any number were those of General Ledbetter, who had probably participated in the battle of Richmond, and though the engagement had proved a Confederate victory, these men were foot-sore and weary. They were clothed and fed and feted, and many a merry story was again told of the ever gushing southern women; of how they came out with fruits and flowers, and basins and towels for the travel-stained pilgrims of war, and how patiently the poor fellows bore the often repeated infliction, one of them saying drearily, "O, certainly, Madam, certainly, wash my face if it will do you any good, it has only been washed fourteen times this morning." And O, tell it not in northern lands, it has been said that the beautiful banner given and received with so much prestige in our burg, was quietly sunk in the flowing river by the boys in grey as they passed over the Kentucky, their patriotism being too little, or their speed too rapid, to induce them to undertake the conveyance of such a cumbrous souvenir, however handsome.

But the time approached rapidly when Mercer was to look "grim visaged war" face to face. In 1862, General Beauregard, having taken a rest of a few weeks, General Bragg, of Mexican experience, was left in command, which arrangement President Davis made permanent by displacing Beauregard.

Bragg, to relieve West Tennessee and Alabama, concluded to move on Kentucky for supplies and to protect the people and a confidently expected uprising for the Confederacy. He was expected to take Louisville and hold Eastern Kentucky. This invasion was preceeded by raids of Morgan and Forest. The first with less than two regiments passed through seventeen towns, destroying millions of United States stores, and returned to Tennessee without the loss of a hundred men and these fully replaced with new recruits.

In early August, General Bragg rendezvoused at Chattanooga. Kirby Smith was detailed in co-operation with Humphrey, then in southwestern Virginia, to to hold the Cumberland Gap region. This division tougnt the battle of Richmond, August 29th, entered Lexington September 2nd and Frankfort the 17th. But to return to the chief command. Bragg himself meanwhile had moved to intercept Buel, then massing his forces in Tennessee. Polk and Hardee took Mumfordsville and gained control of the Louisville & Nashville Railroad.

A general view of the situation of Kentucky in '62 would have shown General Bragg, commander-in-chief in Kentucky, in position to press on and capture Louisville, or else to force Buel back into Tennessee. In fact, to a mind unbiased by military knowledge, the wonder is why either of these leaders did not exterminate the other's command, Bragg, having such decisive advantage in the position of his forces and backed by a country of abundant supplies and hearts largely in sympathy with him; while on the other side it seemed that Buel, had he understood, might have crushed by masses the lines of Bragg, weakened by extension in so many directions. But Buel wended on his uninterrupted way to Louisville, and General Morgan made good his march from Cumberland Gap to Cincinnati, and then it was but a question of time how soon the Confederates, with all their aid and comfort must retreat from Kentucky, leaving all military advantages and thus forever extinguish the political prospects of the Confederacy in this state. But the end was not yet; there was yet a foolish farce and bloody tragedy to be enacted. Bragg went on the old plan of selling the lion's hide while hunting him, and so proceeded to take the Provisional Governor to Frankfort, that military Vanity Fair, to install him; but before the Governor bent the supple knee to take his seat, "wars and rumors of wars" recalled Bragg in inglorious haste to order in his command to where General Buel threatened several points on a line of sixty miles. Distracted by these feints, there was variances in counsel and uncertain movements; but learning that General Hardee was sorely threatened at Perryville, General Polk was ordered to move on with Cheatham's division to his support; and now Mercer and Boyle stood face to face with war. For some days there could be no thicket treaded, or by-path ventured into that some grey spectre was not met straggling from the main body, but with full intent of rendezvous at the battle; and the highways presented the spectacle, at a distance, of a murky grey river flowing, flowing on over to the rumble of wheels and the occasional wild bugle blast and roll of drum. For sometime the environs of the town were the camping grounds of men whom hearts and ardent imaginations had, before their coming, invested with forms and souls of heroes, now manifested to our eyes in all the grime and rags with which time and hard service had covered them and which the sympathizers were powerless to clothe with their well earned—a treasonable uniform.

I shall never forget one calm, delicious October morning while we sat enjoying our farm breakfast with a rollicking set—for such were always happening in, whether the blue or grey camped near, our house was always full of guests for it lay between the camp and a distillery which both sets were prone to haunt—the door bell rang. My liege lord went forward and I heard a warm welcome given, closing with "I'll not call your name, let's see if my wife will know you." In a moment the folding doors were withdrawn and my parlor was the gay background to the sorriest specimen of gentlemanly humanity I have ever seen. A chivalrous young Mississippian, who had passed his college life with us, and became as one of our children, stood before me, hatless, almost shoeless, his knees protruding from lindsey pants a world too short, and his fluttering shirt held on by a coat of perfect freshness and fineness. After a cordial recognition and hearty breakfast, he said: "I must go into town and finish my outfit. You see, I met my coat you sent me." He had left it, his Sunday best, when he stepped out from college life into camp, and I had sent it to him. "Come into my room," I said, "and see whether you can not be equipped out of my box." Sympathizers those days always kept a box for wayfarers. "No," he said, "keep those for the strangers and friendless; auntie will be sure to provide for me when I get to town." It was Singleton Garritt. He left me his knap sack to fill with provisions, and came by in the evening finely mounted and well dressed, the work, doubtless of his aunt, Mrs. Dr. J. A. Thompson. He was accompanied by a young kinsman, John Singleton, who had been expelled from West Point for refusing to take oath of allegiance. A marble bears his name in our cemetery in Harrodsburg. He was desperately wounded in one of Morgan's bloody raids on Lebanon, Ky., and died in our town. Singleton Garritt survived the war and lived to show that southern men could work as well as fight, shielding his family as far as laborious and successful devotion to journalism could from the disastrous effects of the war on their large estates.

CHAPTER XXV.

Battle of Perryville—Hospitals—Incidentals of Hospital Life—Guerillas and Regulators—Mention of the Boys—J. Q. Chenoweth.

The next morning we heard of the premonitory guns of the bloody 8th of October at Perryville. It was General Sill as he skirmished down to the west of us to the support of the Federal troops already formed in line at Perryville. About noon the battle work began in earnest, and as volunteer scouts flew back and forth between the town and scene of action, the wildest and most variable rumors prevailed. Meanwhile the extensive buildings of the old "Harrodsburg Springs," property of the old soldiers of the United States, were reclaimed from the owls and bats and hastily prepared for hospitals; and from Perryville to Anderson county beds were turned down ready for disabled occupants; and carriages stood on the outskirts of the battlefield ready for the wounded, while deft fingered women were making lint and bandages at home. The churches were also converted into hospitals, and by sunset the ghastly victims were coming too fast for the surgeons. By ten o'clock that night the legs and arms, that had been amputated, rose like a pyramid to the floor of the second story gallery of the Spring's ball room which was one of the chief hospitals. We have a heroine amongst us yet, who assisted the surgeons from early dawn to the evening hours in tieing veins, dressing wounds, etc., etc.

We cannot diverge from our own proper county lines to follow the evolutions of battle of that day. History records that, that night the Confederates held the battlefield, and it is equally truthfully recorded that in twenty-four hours afterwards Bragg found himself confronting Buel's three divisions, outnumbering him two to one. At midnight he fell back on his first line, and the next morning concentrating at Harrodsburg where he met Kirby Smith hastening on to re-enforce him, and commenced from here his retreat via Bryantsville to Cumberland Gap, south. It is said he carried a train of supplies from Kentucky forty miles long. His horses drank our town branch adsolutely dry, and few sympathizers had more clothes when they left than they stood in. The commissary department was certainly the most efficient wing of Bragg's army, but n'importe, had the fighting wing been better manipulated it would not have changed the issue. God rules, and not a sparrow falls without his His knowledge; ergo, the fall of the Confederacy and maintenance of the Union, however distasteful to us, were unquestionably His will.

Mainly the hospitals were comfortable, for the daintiest quilts and spreads were doing service as bed ticks, and the sufferers were generally cheerful, though daily the dead were carried out to fill unmarked graves. Now and then a humorous thing would lend a momentary light to the sombre place. One day there was a general distribution going on of clean clothes, mostly of the second hand sort, however. A merry, boisterous Irishman was literally crawling around like a serpent; a pair of good pants were offered him; he took the bundle, contrived to tuck it under his arm and made off to his couch saying, "Well, on my soi'l, this is five pairs today; I think I shall have enough to last through the war and give moi ragged Captain a pair." Another poor fellow amused himself by giving a new cognomen and state to every enquirer for his local habitation and name. But there were very sad happenings. Some days after the battle, a poor fellow was found off in a solitary room who had been brought in amongst the first wounded from the battlefield, and by a sad mischance was never visited again. He was too exhausted from wounds and hunger to live, and we were all horrified to find he was the young brother of an excellent clergyman, Mr. Sherrill, of Mississippi, who had served in the Presbyterian pulpit in our town for some years, and whose brother should have been as our own had we known him.

One evening there were said to be five men in the ball room hospital who must soon die. When asked what could be done for them, one replied, "Send me a hot breakfast so long as I live," two turned their faces to the wall silently; and one asked eagerly to be taught to die willingly. The lady talked to him earnestly, and to his question, "Is there no test by which I know I'm ready?" She thought a while and said, "Forgiveness is the threshold over which we must all pass into Heaven." He shook his head sadly. After a day or two she was there again, and he beckoned her to him; "I could now," he said, "put my arms around the man who shot me and go into Heaven with him into the presence of the Saviour and ask forgiveness for us both." He folded his arms as if clasping someone within them and they never opened from the imaginary embrace.

Presently many of these men were distributed around to the homes of the disloyal. Hearing a lonely and delicate woman had had twenty-three sent to her, I called on Dr. DeCamp, the Provost Marshal, to ask a division in our favor. The Doctor laughed, and handing me a list of ten, said, "Perhaps this consignment will be as many as you can care for." I did not reply like the brave lady hostess, that I wished to relieve, "As long as there is an unoccupied plank in my floor they can send on the wounded to me." They really never sent us but five, and part of these were from the overtaxed house. Two fine young Tennesseeans came among them who were exchanged a few weeks later and fell at Chickamauga. It was a curious coincidence that these two young men were the nephew and grandson of a man who had had his law training in the office of Capt. Daviess in early times. Of the others that came, one was a young Mississippian who laid down after his bath in his fresh bed in supreme content and never waked again. There was one of them, a soldier of the line, brave, as he was true to his cause, that afterwards died in the old Gratiot prison in St. Louis. A Frenchman was sent, because it was supposed he could make his wants known to me, which he could do by slate, but we proved in viva voce communications to be utter barbarians to each other. Poor fellow, when they came for him at last, as the officer said "Arms or no arms, legs or no legs, with or without heads;" I spoke to him of the home beyond the river to which I knew he was rapidly tending. He took a French testament I had given him from his bosom and said in his broken way, "I believe this and God will show me the way."

CHAPTER XXVI

"Our Brother in Black"—His Early Days and Advance in Living, Etc.—How Some Grew Taller in the Field of Life Than Others—How Some Bought Their Freedom and Some Had It Given Them—Anecdotes of Them—Effect of the War—The Enrollment—The Enlistment—The Emancipation—Its Effects—Prospects of the Race.

All through this long web I have woven of the History of the fourth period of Mercer and Boyle, the Blue and Gray have glinted profusely on the surface, while the Black warp on which it has been woven has continued almost invisible. But it was there, strong and indestructible. And since the colored race which formed it has been lifted by the action of our government to a place of perfect political equality with us, I can no more ignore their existence as one of the factors of history, than I could paint the portrait of man and leave out some prominent feature of the face.
From all the different slave holding states from which our pioneer population came originally, slaves were brought in varying numbers, and remained chiefly in unaltered status until the rebellion. Their comfort as to lodging, clothing and provision advanced pari passee with that of their owners. Their hovels were abandoned for the hewed log houses of their masters, these again for the frames and plasters, and finally when the baronical bricks were built, kitchens and servants' rooms always had a place on the ground floor. So with clothing; tow linen was shed for domestic linsey and cottons, these for prints, as they became cheap, for working wear; and the fine dress the mistress dropped to her favorite, or its imitations, have kept men and maid servants only at respectful distance behind my lord and lady in apparel. The food for all was usually wholesome and abundant; the house servants faring, as now, with trifling difference much as the family did and does; the quarters having abundance of meat, milk and vegetables, and before the war, coffee, sugar and molasses became the regular rations for all. As to their personal treatment, it depended much on the temper of their owners and a good deal on the conduct of the servant. I think the type of slavery in Kentucky was as mild as ever existed in the world. Women rarely worked in the fields; mothers had care of their own children, and married relations were little interfered with, and social intercourse ran into dissipation in the dance, and they had the unlimited privilege of religious meetings.
Slavery was capable of terrible abuse, but these outrages were the exception and not the rule. We have all heard sensational horrors answering to those in Uncle Tom's Cabin with which Mrs. Stowe helped to almost split wide the Union, but we all as well know that such tragic occurrences were not near so frequent or dreadful as the daily press show as occurring in domestic life all over the land now. As in a field of grain there will always be some heads that rise above the rest, so it was even on the natural dead level of slavery. Every owner who had many around, found himself surrounded by persons of very different capacities, efficiency and trustworthiness, and these qualities, as in the white race, seemed to inhere a good deal in the blood. Every here and there a slave would buy himself by exercise of persistent industry, self-denial and management. Our well-known citizen, Mat Harris, paid $1,000 for himself, as did his father before him, and an uncle, for themselves. Mat, too, by marriage, was once a slave holder (He

bought his wife from her master.—Editor's Note) and has owned lands and houses about town, some of the best and finest in it. He has always shown public spirit enough to bear his part in the expenses of improvements, giving $500 to Bacon College, although he had to send his own children out of the state to be educated. The Dorams, of Danville, were also of this family, successful and large property holders. Conspicuous among them I must mention one woman who has done more for the education of her race than all the school agencies yet organized—Sallie Ann Taylor. A faithful slave to the sunset hour and the careful tender of her master, and then of her aging old mother, she gave all the evening hours of her servitude and the days of her freedom to the teaching of her race, with hardly nominal compensation, to the present time. In testimony of the appreciation of her faithful services to him and the cause of her people, her master, the late Major James Taylor, left her a school house; she has beside a comfortable home, and surely by her many pupils uplifted by her from the depths of ignorance, she will have a memorial stone and on it written,

"She hath done what she could."

Every plantation had its Uncle Remus to beguile the boys from their evening's lessons, and every household its black mammie on whose bosom the household pet, when snubbed, could cry itself to sleep, and some of the nicest children I have ever seen in the past or present have had their sole mother-care from these sable aunties. The counties, too, were spotted with cabins embosomed in clumps of fruit trees and truck patches, where masters had left their old servants to die free from the yoke. Old Mr. Morgan left several such devices. Peter Dunn, too, I think. My paternal grandfather freed all his, but the pitiless pestilence came and in a few days laid him under the sod and gathered his retainers all around him on the dead level of the graveyard. I think I have elsewhere told of Major Handy's freeing Logan Dupeye and buying his daughter for him, and of Dr. Graham's famous brass band and their fate, but I am sure not of "Old Mose," who lay around a limp mass of rags and humanity, a very caricature of all African ugliness, the unfolding of whose face into a rose of wrinkles was the untiring monkey show around which the village children gathered every day, and all the time with inexhaustible pleasure. Mose was of high descent, his "Missus" being the niece on one side of Patrick Henry and granddaughter of Judge Spencer Roan, whose office Mose kept and swept until he " 'lowed no sputifying, argifying er law pints with him by no po' white trash."

Sam Blackburn also claimed to be a f. f. s., (First Family of Slaves) but I cannot show his geneological tree. He was a dapper little old darkey, at first indispensible around all "quality" tables on company occasions, but with age fell into disuetude. He always wore somebody's cast off regimentals and a cocked hat and stately plume, and carried his blacking brushes and violin about with him. I do not remember precisely when Sam flitted out, but I do remember seeing the town wild over his supposed death. One bitter cold morning he was seen astride the comb of the tallest house of the store row, with drawn bow, but no sound of music was heard. It was a clear case: he had been drinking, as all gentlemen of his school are apt to do, had ... out of his loft window and taken that perch and frozen to death. Th... ...e not changed entirely; ladders were no more apt to be in place th... than now, and some time elapsed before the adventurer on the roof reached the old fellow who meanwhile remained deaf to all the shouts of the excited, pitiful crowd. The rescuer, when he reached the victim, turned with infinite disgust and pitched the straw figure down amongst the expectants, where by this time Old Sam had come to claim his violin and military toggery that some practical joker had stolen while he slept.

There were also freed amongst us both in Mercer and Boyle, some quite large bodies of negroes that gave rise to important law suits and much dissatisfaction in the neighborhoods where the manumission took place. Major John C. Meaux, of the staff of General Jackson at New Orleans, lived on a fine plantation somewhere in the vicinity of Danville. He had lost the wife of his youth, was childless, and from conscience or sentiment, freed all his negroes when he died, all but one who at the battle of New Orleans he had armed with the promise of immediate freedom and whom he had found, when the smoke was lifted from the battle field, hid away in a cask. He always had some factotum, who followed him on horseback with holsters and pistols. On one occasion, returning from one of his sporting tours with General Adair, he dropped in the tavern where they were dining, a very plethoric pocketbook, which the valet picked up and put into his own pocket, but handed over intact at the end of the journey. Sometime afterward General Adair meeting him again, said: "Meaux, what did you give that boy for saving your pocketbook?" "Nothing, I declare; here, Watt," and taking from his pocket a splendid gold watch, he handed it to the elated negro. This watch is said now to be in possession of Abram Meaux, a son of Watt, a colored barber of Lebanon, Ky. It has another history back of this. General Jackson was also a boon companion of Major Meaux, and it was said that one morning at breakfast at the Hermitage, General Jackson said: "Major Meaux, I dreamed last night you gave me that splendid black horse you are riding," "It is yours, General," he replied, "and I, too, was dreaming last night; I thought you gave me that fine repeater in your pocket." The General laughed and handed over the timepiece; and that is said to be the watch now in possession of Abram Meaux that was given his father, Watt. Whether from natural or undue influence, Major Meaux had his father, the finest possible specimen of Old Virginia grandeeism, free his negroes, bequeathing them a large body of land on which to live, and I think some of those freedmen are living on that bequest yet. They made mainly quiet, orderly citizens, and gained comfortable supports by small farming and trucking. One of them was ordained an elder and had the oversight of his brethren in Dr. Cleland's Providence church. They were always respectful in their intercourse with the whites and effusively polite, so much so in their everlasting response of "Ya's ma'am," that a merry colored girl of ours called them "ya's ma'ams," which sobriquet attaches to them to the present day. My father had been the attorney for their freedom, which always kept a link of friendship bright between them and us. Always having a tincture of emancipation in my composition, the scheme of colonization addresseed itself strongly to my judgment. It seemed the only way to free, and better the condition of the freed, without demoralization to the country. But this was not a generally accepted theory in the country. I addressed myself zealously to the Meaux settlement, trying to get them to send an envoy to Liberia to inspect the country and arrange for their colonization. Johnnie Black, the chief of the settlement, came to see me about it repeatedly. On one occasion Capt. Daviess was present, and Johnnie ask him: "Maas Sam, what do you think about this Liberia?" Capt. Daviess was a good friend to negroes, had no faith in Liberia, but hated to oppose me, so he said: "Johnnie, my Gilbert's a sensible nigger, ask him." Johnnie went down and planted himself before Gilbert as he sat wiping the sweat from his brow at his noon rest. He was a princely looking specimen of his race, carrying in his veins and brains some of the best blood in old Old Virginia: "Johnny Black," he said, after Johnny had summed up my arguments to him, "do you reckon there's a place on the face of the yearth where they make two craps in one year and the white folks hain't took it?" Johnny turned slowly away and stopping before Colonel Moore, asked his opinion.

HISTORY OF MERCER AND BOYLE COUNTIES

The Colonel said, "Liberia was a fine country and colonization a splendid scheme, if the pirates were not sure to get the emigrants as they crossed the sea." A prospector from the Meaux settlement did go, however, to Liberia and died after two years residence there, and his wife, coming back for recruits, died here.

Rev. William Jones, of Greenville Academy, and Dr. Stephen E. Jones, his brother, and William Thompson, then of Cane Hurst, now of Florida, sent perhaps in all a hundred emigrants, and so ended Mercer's connection with colonization so far as I know, but Boyle, I think, furnished many emigrants.

But to return from our digression to our Brothers in Black as a race. I do not think any general discontent prevailed previous to the war. Occasionally there was an escape to Canada and I remember one or two persons who expressed a passionate longing for liberty. One, a young wife and mother, who said she would die willingly if she could be free one-half hour before she died. Generally they seemed contented and cheerful and when they began to apprehend the change, a mixture of hope and dread took possession of their minds and for a while they stood still, dazed in their places; then the men, learning their backing, went to the war and the women, freed by this enlistment, began to straggle to and from the camps and rapidly the whole system was so demoralized that it became intolerable and the Emancipation act, however great an outrage on property rights, was hailed as a rift in the cloud of relief. This generation has surely seen two spectacles as marvelous as any in the history of miracles. First was seen two great armies fighting for the liberty of a third party that continued quietly working for the maintenance of the families and soldiers who were boldly battling to rivet upon them the chains of slavery, and then their going off and leaving their own wives and children to the care and mercy of their deserted masters. Surely none can have been so blind to the dealings of an over-ruling Providence as not to have noticed while this deadly fray progressed how God held the passions of both races in check, even as He held the lions harmless while Daniel shared their den. Outrage and insurrections were never beard of—only collision and blood on the battlefield.

In October, '63, Mr. Lincoln called for 300,000 troops but exempted the negroes from enlistment.

For February, '64, James B. Fry, United States Provost Marshal, ordered the enlistment of colored soldiers. General Woolford denounced this action and the Governor demurred, but finally recommended the people to submit and trust to future legislation for just compensation. The work went on then, but the compensation is still in the future. By the death and division of the estates of Col. George C. Thompson and Peter Dean and the removal of W. M. Thompson, my husband had been left the largest slaveholder in Mercer county, therefore I select our place to illustrate how things went on in those days. Every male past twelve years of age left us one by one. The first and most prompt were two men, my father-in-law, a very tender heart, had bought at their earnest entreaty to prevent their being sold south, the negroes' horror or horrors. Both returned and served us as freed men, and one has passed on to my pension list, the government having failed to place him on its roll, although four fine young men, his sons, who donned the blue and answered not to the call of the discharge roll. The women, of course, who were wives or children of these soldiers, were freed by this enlistment and took their chances in the country and camps or stayed at home as they chose.

September 22nd, '62, Mr. Lincoln had issued his warning emancipation proclamation and in January, '63, he issued the final dicta of freedom.

Kentucky had not seded, but the edict was practically as effective as in the seceded states and again the world saw a stupendous passage of history having no counterpart since Moses led Israel out of Egypt with a high hand. Four millions of people, with only the Heavens above them and not even a claim to the earth on which they stood, nor the promise of any Canaan beyond the wilderness, were disrupted from their homes. This act of emancipation might have been done justly without the expense the war entailed and if wisely done would have been a mighty beneficence to all concerned. Had the old been left for the masters to maintain, who had had the labor of their days it would have been but just. Had the young men and women gone out with their little children it would have been humane and fair, had the great band of children, especially those who had no legal fathers, been put into coercive schools of apprenticeship, we should have amongst us today a class in sufficiency of such laborers in physique and intelligence as no land on earth could show. As it is the picture is reversed. The old and trained are dying out and they have not had the will or means to give to their children industrial education, and a Christian's world has not put out a very friendly hand to help, and the shrewdest politicians in the land do not see a hand's before them into the future of "our Brethren in Black." They have now the right of suffrage, of bearing witness in court, in fact equal protection in acquiring and holding property and equal political privilege with the white race without knowledge to use it. They have also the favor above the old masters in having all their taxes devoted to a fund for schools for themselves, and their need is a coercive and industrial feature to these schools. Many of them are property holders, some have farms, a number of them have not only a home but own tenant houses and the town has a large number of snug cozy little homes in which these new citizens live.

Old Centre College, Danville.

Kentucky School for the Deaf, Main Building

CHAPTER XXVII

Towns of Mercer County—Harrodsburg—Its Location—Its Extension—First Buildings and Successive Styles of Private Buildings—Public Buildings—Old and New Court Houses—Jail, Etc.

Having followed the history of her people from pioneer to present time, I turn back upon physical Mercer and give in this chapter her towns, giving Harrodsburg the just precedence of antiquity, and present it very much in the same guise of locals as two years since furnished to the Mercer Enterprise, as advance columns of this serial history.

It has been decided by impartial investigation that while Boonesboro was first laid out, the overt act of building a house was first committed in Harrodsburg. In 1774 Capt. Harrod, Abram Hite, the two Sandusky's and some two score other men floated down the Ohio, penetrated into now Central Kentucky, and on June 16 laid off Harrodsburg and built several cabins. The nucleus of our city was first called Old Town, then Harrodstown, and finally by its present time honored cognomen. The lots within and without the town were distributed by lottery, but for a long while these lot owners continued to live in the fort, for the settlement was continually subject to the attacks of Indians, who very slowly and eventually withdrew from their great hunting parks known as "The Dark and Bloody Ground," from the ever recurring desperate conflicts of the tribes from outside its bounds that contended for its exclusive possession.

The Old Fort Hill on which the pioneers clustered their huts, was originally a noble elevation, from the north side of which twin brooklets leaped merrily down the shelving rocks into the town branch that meanders on to its confluence with Salt river, receiving by the wayside at the foot of the Old Fort Hill, the unfailing and abundant waters of Gore's Spring, which still in seasons of drouth, slakes the thirst of the land for miles around.

When and how the stockades, the cabins, and even the Old Fort, disappeared, the writer of this sketch cannot recall. The hill was as described when it was for years the play ground of the mixed school held in the old Academy on its summit. A few straggling large apple trees lingered on the hill side, and originally a nice well built hewed log house in dilapidation, stood between the school house and the spring, and to the south lay God's acre. The twin streams are lost; the hill has been blasted into hideous quarries. The first school house was smitten to the earth by the tempest; its successor has been razed by man; and the graveyard where some out of the fort and many of our rude forefathers sleep, is only redeemed from utter desolation by being private property; it is kept covered with thickly matted grass, in which the gentle cows graze, little recking on what sacred or heroic dust they tread. During the Fort life of Harrodsburg and while cautiously extending its agricultural ventures outside of the stockades, it was subject to continued harrassment from Indian attacks, but yet had a steady access of population.

During the year of 1777, the census of Harrodsburg was taken and showed a population of 200 and the Fort dwellers began gradually to spread out diagonally from northwest to southeast, said diagonal, however, being laid out in regular squares.

As we have said, in pioneer times, the first houses were of log, next plastered, and then began the building of frame houses with weather boards without and plaster within, all classes being direfully guiltless of paper and paint.

The first brick house in Harrodsburg, certainly over eighty years ago, was on the corner now occupied by one of the handsome store houses built by Dr. W. P. Harvey, which the fire fiend has spared, now used commercially by Marschall & Geffinger. I cannot give the succession of brick houses built in Harrodsburg either for business or residence. Of the old business houses on Main street only the remnant is left on the square of which the First National Bank is the conspicuous corner and ornament. These buildings are easily classified by their styles and so the succession without the exact date preserved.

First were built square, double two-story houses, with ample cellar and attic; such as the beginning of the Morgan row, Capt. Daviess and Joel P. Williams' homes on Main street, the interval between being filled with a long, white plaster building, which was replaced by a substantial row of brick ones, burned and again replaced by the present National Hotel and the fine row of brick stores facing the Court House yard. These are still the property of Dr. Augustus Jones.

The next style which captivated the home makers of Harrodsburg, was a kind of composite, Italian villa order; long, low winged with portico in front and extensive gallery communication in the rear; such as the houses of Dan Curry, built by James Haggan; John Lafon's by Madison Worthington; the Chinn place, by Dr. Robertson; Ben An (present Spilman farm house) by Judge Bridges; the Payne place, by John B. Thompson, Sr., and Litsey home, by Col. R. M. Sutfield—the last two, however, somewhat varied in their architecture. These houses were built between 1820 and 1830. The next style that came in may be classed the Bank or Church order, the large columns giving them the appearance of such buildings. Of these are the houses of Judge J. M. Tebbetts, Mr. W. H. Riker and Dr. A. T. Stephenson. This class of building was quite popular in the county and fine specimens were built by Robert Davis, David Thompsosn (Mr. Neal's), Abram Bowman (Dr. William RoBards). Abram Bonta has made a departure and advance on this style in his palatial home on the Danville turnpike.

Since then the builders have been divided in their following between the handsome brick houses of the Isaac Pearson and Thomas Marimon kind, and the frames cottage ones that so brighten and beautify Lexington and Danville end of Main street. The first of this style was that of Judge Hardin, and now these pretty and convenient houses you have glimpses of in the country, too, from every turn of the road. None of these buildings wear a Mansard roof, except Governor Magoffin's and D. J. Curry's, which doubtless were adopted by them rather as crowns to their buildings than from its French origin of economy of space, both places having such ample and beautiful lawns around them .

In running one's memory back over this list of properties, and thinking of who built and who owns them, it is impossible not to be struck with the certain uncertainty of American life. Only one or two of these valuable homesteads remain in the founders' families to the second generation. But there is also reason for self-congratulation in this, that we live in a land of such possibilities that a man can, by his own work, ere meridian life, possess himself of such homes as these; for with one remembered exception, these places are all owned by men who have been the artificers of their own fortunes; and we must record it to the honor of our people, these changes have not come from spendthrifty, but from natural business causes. Further, we state to the praise of these home-makers, that they showed sound sense and foresight in building. Handsome as some of these houses are and as comfortable as they all are, the designers of them were not seized with such passion for "gorgeous palaces and cloud capped towers," as to invest as the manner of some is, the whole of their capital in a mass of architecture that they cannot justly devise to any one heir, and that could not probably be sold for cost of material when death should make a sale necessary for the distribution of the estate.

Public Buildings of Harrodsburg

The Court House has always stood on a square reserved in laying out the town for that purpose. It is naturally a fine site, though unfortunately having been denuded of the magnificent forest trees that sheltered the pioneers in their conflict with the Indians on that spot. The forest kings have been replaced with the locust which seems to have had universal favor notwithstanding it is the last to assume and the first to drop its at best inferior foliage. The first Court House was rather a rude structure of stone; a jail of the same material, having its location a little southwest. While we hold that as correct sentiments of justice and humanity ruled them as now, still we think there were more fear and shame mixed with the apprehension of being condemned to that ancient penal abode, than was felt concerning the prospect of a sojourn in the now airy, comfortable, inviting looking refuge from the toils and privations of life of honest industry outside their walls.

The Stone Clerk's Office

was situated on Main street southeast of the Court House and the loft of this important building was kept filled with earth as a precaution against fire, slate, tin nor iron having put in their claims to usefulness as a roofing material. There had, however, been a Clerk's office two or three miles east of Harrodsburg on the place of Elias Tompkins, near which the writer of this went to school, and whether this office had been the adjunct of some early station (Froman's was nearby) or the Clerk felt bound to keep his papers in bodily possession, is not remembered, neither when they were brought into the town office on deposit.

A Market House

was on this public square, bordering Main street, nearly opposite the business house of Matheny & Poteet, where Wednesday and Saturday mornings was dispensed from rude shambles, beef, and beef only. Other days this house was the boys' gymnasium, in which ball, marbles, etc., were indulged by all the unkempt, unwashed, uncombed rabbles of white and darkey children whose absence was more enjoyed than their presence at their homes. The first humble Court House served, as its more imposing successor has until recently, all theordinary uses of a town hall, being used especially for preaching, before "meeting houses," as all church exercises in those days were called, were erected. The strolling player, and the enlivening church festival never lighted its auditorium as they have the more spacious halls of the present building.

The present Court House was built by contract with Joel P. Williams, an enterprising citizen, who was wont to keep many irons in the fire, usually running simultaneously a store, a farm, a mill, a building contract, a turnpike, and would not have hesitated, at three score and ten, to have undertaken to build the Cincinnati Southern. I have heard him say that by the contract he was to forfeit $10 every day he failed to work on the building. He lost the first day; but brought a wagon, horses and teamster before breakfast the next morning, and never allowed another day, rain or shine, to pass without doing full work on some department of the building. The house has been remodeled and renovated in the last few years. The exterior is respectable, of red brick, covered with slate and surmountd by that incalculable convenience, a town clock, that gives notes for miles around how time is ever flitting, flitting. The house itself has every convenience for the furtherance of business, including the County Judge's office, and still lends itself literally to be used for social and benevolent purposes, and also gives friendly shelter to an excellent, but not fully appreciated Town Library. Perhaps in no similar edifice in the west has been unfolded more interesting cases. Suits continually trying in which men's lives, character and fortunes were all at stake. In this house gladitorial contests of devouring tongues have stirred the depths of men's souls. A central position in the state; the habit the members of the bar had of itinerating in early days, brought the best talents of Kentucky, to Harrodsburg. Besides our own far above mediocral bar, Clay, Crittenden, the Breckinridges, Hardin, Pope and McKee have all spoken here. Perhaps there never has been a more interesting trial in the state than Wilkinson's, not because of its own interesting details, but from the talent employed in it, in which trial this Court House was the forum in which for once was heard the splendid forensic display of the immortal and matchless S. S. Prentiss.

The Clerk's Office

just south of the Court House, is a low, substantial iron roofed brick building, which will, with the vaults constructed for safe keeping of valuable papers, and if not so comely a structure, answers the ends of a Clerk's office as fully as any similar building in the country. There is no remarkable record to be made of this office. Its honors and emoluments have been held in one family. Major Thomas Allin was the first Clerk in Kentucky, and the office has remained in the family with one single interregnum during "the late unpleasantness" for nearly a century. The continuance of this office in this family by election speaks strongly for the patriotism of our people, who have not allowed party spirit to rule competent and trained men out of a place where so much depends upon the accuracy and fidelity of the officer.

Major Thomas Allin, the first appointee to this office, had served on the staff of General Green during his southern campaign. He was a man of fine sense and good address and served in several civil capacities notably, being a member of the convention that framed the constitution of Kentucky.

Harrodsburg Jails

The first jail of our county was built in Danville in 1783, but when the seat of justice was removed to Harrodsburg, a jail of stone was constructed near the old Court House. The second jail was built of brick and the third, of the same material, stands in the rear of the second on Chiles street, and is more pretentious in its architecture and apparently more commodious and secure, but answers the purposes no better than the first one of stone. Perhaps by superior comforts it tempts the indolent to break in, and keeps the county wondering why so much tramping and vagabondism is allowed to burden the town while an ex-jail stands empty with fitness for a work house written all over it. The engine house is small and inconviently situated, but serves to shelter our bright little engine and as a rendezvous for our brave boys that answer to the fire bell. It serves as a police court room.

The Market House

The market is on Water street; and would be sufficient for town market purposes, were not the community's wants forestalled by numerous provision stores, which are abundantly supplied at all seasons of the year from all sections of the country with everything that can cater to the most capricious appetite. Flesh. fish and fowl; precocious vegetables from the sunny south and island fruits are so abundant that it would be easy to imagine yourself in the corner of the New Orleans market, if only the old negro's cry of "feele, feele" were heard and some pretty creole would flash a basket of violets under your nose. Sea shells are all round with their hearts of rare murmuring about the merits of the luscious oyster that hide themselves in more modest mansions. A striking contrast all this to the beef only, which was displayed on our first shambles. The rent of the house is a part of our city revenue, and it sometimes hoists the sign of a provision store, sometimes a fuel and ice store.

CHAPTER XXVIII

Harrodsburg Continued—Public Private Buildings—Morgan Row—Greenville Springs—Chenoweth Hall—Opera House.

Public Private Buildings

This heading seems paradoxical, but there are a class of houses which come strictly under this head, such as have been built by private enterprise for public purposes. Thus

The Morgan House,

a long, substantial row of brick buildings, was built and used for a hotel by Squire Joseph Morgan, a merchant of the early days, also a landed proprietor of the vicinity, whose lands have descended even to the third generation, and who, but for the statute of limitation interfering, would have been a millionaire, he having had valid claims to thousands of acres of land in a few miles of Cincinnati. The Morgan row was purchased and extended by John G. Chiles, who had stage contracts extending largely over Kentucky, that kept our town wide awake with the rattle of wheels and echoes of the merry stage horn. This staging was so profitable a business, it was said, that Mr. Chiles found it too tedious to count its profits of nights, but swept out the money drawer by hats full into his strong box. A part of this row is still the property of Squire Morgan's descendants.

There was the

Old Stone Tavern,

that long held fashionable stand, on the corner now occupied by the Commercial Hotel. Again, the old

Greenville Springs,

the nucleus of which was in the close of the last century, a group of log cabins in which invalids who desired the benefit of the water, lived, bringing their own furniture and supplies of food. To these were added quite commodious frame buildings and numerous cottages. This establishment was jostled out of place by its gay successor, the

Harrodsburg Springs

It was then converted into the Greenville Female Academy, as property of Rev. William Jones, and by him, I think, sold to Samuel Mullins, under whose care it was burned; rebuilt partly by subscription, and then passed by sale into the hands of Dr. C. E. and John Aug. Williams, of Columbia, Missouri.

The Frame Hotel

situated on the eastern side of north Chiles street, was one of the earliest hostelries in Harrodsburg. It was known as Stone's Inn in its last years as a tavern, from Nathan Stone, the proprietor, whose inventive genius and hobby was a flying machine. He spent much time trying to evolve a lighter-than-air contraption, a strange eccentricity for a man so slow and deliberate of action as he was. The story is told of him that one day he was on top of the house preparing to test his work by jumping off and an excited man ran to his wife to tell her to prevent it as he would kill himself. She said, "Let him alone. He will fall so slowly that he will hit the ground easy enough not to hurt himself." The two-story frame building was used as a sort of family apartment house for years, and was finally left to the residence of negroes.

The Wingfield House

was built as an investment by the Roger Thompson family, and was kept by a succession of bonifaces, chiefly broken down gentry; hotel keeping and school teaching being the unfailing resort of that unhappy class for which, by want of economy, executive ability and a surplus of pride they were peculiarly unfitted. This was a popular and fashionable house in its day. It was the place where Burr concocted his conspiracy, and headquarters during the war of 1812 for General Scott and his staff ,who for some reason was a while stationed at Harrodsburg.

Jemmie Noble's then was where the

Poteet House

afterward stood, and "mine host" always kept a bear and had for the delectation of the crowd and such a spectacle as would attract, annually a bear fight and afterwards a Christmas dinner of slaughtered bruins. Of this the elite of the village men were always fain to partake; a sort of memorial feast to pioneer times. These have been burned as also the substantial and handsome store rooms which replaced them.

The present home of Mr. Robert Coleman, for a number of years wearing the name of its transient proprietors, opened its doors hospitably to the wayfaring public.

But these have all passed away, and only the quiet, substantial

Mercer House,

reposing in the shade of its maples and in sound of the gurgling waters of the stream near which it is built, and the handsome and commodious

Commercial House

with all its comfortable appointments, are the sole havens of rest open to the pilgrim world. They are supplemented by numerous boarding houses proper, and private houses that take boarders, that large class in all American communities, who weary of home cares and restless for ease and change, give up that most blessed gift of Heaven—a happy earthly home. Neither need the day's man perish; our restaurants are numerous, reasonable and satisfactory. Under this classification, we cannot omit the

Harrodsburg Springs,

although a solitary little white cottage, a few scattered stones and the groves are the only vestiges left to tell that this once fashionable place ever existed. Dr. C. C. Graham, since dead, who has eaten his centennial dinner, acquired the site of these celebrated springs by marriage with the only daughter and only child of Capt. David Sutton, a woman of fine personnel, unusual excellency of character, and fully her husband's equal in executive ability. The grounds themselves were the creation of marvelous and tireless industry. They came into his possession rugged, broken, full of pits, barren of grass and treeless. He first made the ground ,then planted the forest, which even in its uncared for state of today, is the admiration of every artistic eye. He first covered the premises with extensive frame buildings and long rows of cottages; these, after a time, he supplemented with a costly and handsome brick hotel and a ball room of corresponding dimensions; and in that day no watering place in the Union was so complete in its appointments for comfort, or had half the attractions for the pleasure seekers that then filled the south and west. The driving on our splendid roads whiled away the morning; sumptuous dinner gratified the most pampered appetites at noon; and music, moonlight, mirth and flowers lent their fascination to every evening. Dr. Graham had trained in music, for his own establishment, a band of colored men of whom he required nothing but to report well equipped and render service in music during the gay season. After years of this hardly nominal service, they were lured by mistaken friends into Canada, impressed into the British army, and fell victims, one by one, to the deadly climate of the West Indies. This Springs was open from May to November. The first and last few weeks brought refugees from a warm climate and real health seekers in large numbers. It would be hard for the present generation to realize the rush and glitter of midsummer in Harrodsburg; the road alive with dashing equipages; the streets with gay pedestrians, and ever and anon a strain of music floating by like a waft from Fairy Land. Much demoralization of our village has been charged to the influence of the springs. Doubtless it had its power. There was much pleasure and culture at this Springs, and the steady streams of people that ebbed and flowed through these halls were not merely the dissipated and frivolous pleasure seekers; the excellent, the great and good were there also, and left a residium of refinement and intelligence. This place was finally sold to the Government for an Old Soldiers' Home. For awhile a few officers' families kept up a faint echo of the gaiety of olden times. Amongst these were Major Alexander and Captain Wood, of genial memory, and bluff General Buford, of the turf and church. But first in command was Major Anderson, whose name will ever stand on the commerative marbles of the rebellion, being commandant at Fort Sumpter, where the opening gun of the war was fired. A few old soldiers basked in the sun and lounged in the shades of these beautiful grounds,

"Shouldered the crutch and showed how fields were won."

But it was found more expensive to maintain them here than in Washington City hotels. The Military Asylum, for which, as in all cases of purchase, an enormous price was paid, was discontinued, and from then 'til now the grounds have been rented as pastures. The buildings were left to silence and the ravages of time until the battle of Perryville filled the halls and cottages with the ghostly wounded, and for months it sheltered the miserable wreck of that senseless system of righting wrongs called war. These poor victims were there many months prisoners to the victors and objects of tender compassion to our Christian people, but

"When wild war's deadly blast was blown,
And gentle peace returning,"

these poor men, like Arabs, folded their tents and moved silently away. Finally, the devouring fire, which has so often swept our village with its destruction, again singled out the handsome vestiges left of this doomed place, and some scattered heaps of stone remain to mark this a monument of folly of the Government that holds so large an investment of the soldiers' money in almost total unproductiveness. There has been several sales of this property advertised, but it has always been withdrawn on account of inadequate offers. It was an evil day for Harrodsburg when an irresponsible company overbid fabulously the genuine offer of Kentucky University. Had the property been acquired by that institution we should probably have had a flourishing college for the education of our sons; and the complications which this University drifted into in Lexington might never have been.

Chenoweth's Hall.

This hall was built, as its name suggests, by the Chenoweth family and some kindred capitalists. It is roomy, well finished and well furnished, but its success even before completion was marred, by its incapable position, lying as it does above business buildings and reached by a rather intricate way.

The Opera House

of L. D. Cardwell, has a frontage of stores somewhat in the arcade style. The conversion of a church into an opera house rather offended the critical sense of or community. It is a transformation of frequent occurence in the cities and vice versa, and the proprietor very courteously allows the use of his house to the church to which it once belonged and to other churches in emergencies.

CHAPTER XXIX

Harrodsburg Continued—Post Office—Its Local Habitations—Succession of Postmasters — Names and Notices of Some of Them — Statistics of Harrodsburg Post Office. Names of Other Offices in the County—Cemetery.

The Post Office

Has always had a name, but not always the same local habitation, but is movable at the pleasure of the postmaster, and has dispensed its eagerly sought favors from various points. For a while the post office and the first Harrodsburg Library kept house together in the old plaster row that was described as filling the space between Capt. Daviess' dwelling (present drug store and opera house of L. D. Cardwell), and Williams' corner, now Jones' block. Mr .Sargeant kept the Library; I am not sure he was postmaster. It was for a long time, until lately, nearly opposite the Mercer National Bank, and previous to that location had place in the Wingfield building. Once it took lodging by the town pump near Lexington street, and for a while in the building lately torn down that was occupied by Ranz Craig, barber and raconteur to the young men of society of the legends of old times. During its first sojourn in this house the mail was distributed by Andy Kyle, bachelor, a man of very marked character. He was honest as steel-yards, crabbed as a cross-cut saw, but like a walnut, the rough and bitter was in the outside rind, while the rich kernel of sound sense and humor were inwrapped within this blustering covering. I might paraphrase a line from that fine old ballad and say,

"Auld Andy Kyle was very gude to me."

I did not wait under dripping eaves for letters, nor did "first come, first served," prove the ruling motto when I laid my burden of books down on his counter at delivery hours. In defiance of his inexorable rules, one summer afternoon some of the Southern chivalry attempted some freedom in his office. The sudden snap of a flint and outthrust of an opened muzzled shot gun from the window produced a stampede that kept the county's sides shaking with laughter for a fortnight. He died very suddenly.

His successor was Mr. John Donehy, who kept the post office for a number of years.

Then Mr. Whitney was his successor, who was a New Englander by birth and of one branch of the President Cleveland family, of which Mr. H. Cleveland Wood, our fellow townsman and poet, is the representative.

Our post office next took its stand on the Wingfield corner under the charge of him who gave his name to the building; a dapper little man and as obliging a person as ever answered the post office catechism questions.

Then the Wheatleys succeeded and from it the family have scattered to various places and destinies. Walter, chief clerk, was, I think, a consul at some port in South France.

Next in order of succession came Mrs. Carter, who though very competent, took into partnership to aid and comfort her, E. B. Head, Jr., a staunch Republican, a staunch Methodist, and a staunch friend also

The mantle of descent has fallen upon the shoulders of Thomas Cardwell by appointment. Our postoffice is now on Poplar street, two doors west of Assembly Presbyterian church, and we have never had a room of such perfect convenience before, with all of its arrangements so complete, nor have the office duties been more regularly and politely performed.

Thomas Cardwell, postmaster; Mrs. Nannie Cardwell, assistant postmaster; W. Thompson Grimes, general clerk. Five daily mails; one tri-weekly and one semi-weekly. There is an average of 8,500 pounds of mail matter handed per month. About 147 money orders sold per month, amounting to $866 per month; 99 postal notes, amounting to $605 per month; 60 money orders paid per month, $606; 94 notes paid per month, $206; post master's salary, $1,500; clerk's, $300; money order and note fees. $100.

Other offices in the county (thirteen in number), all fourth class except Harrodsburg: Bac, named for E. B. Head; Tom, named for Thomas Cardwell; Rose Hill, from wild roses abounding; Cornishville, for a prominent citizen of the vicinity; Dugansville, for a prominent citizen; Bohon, for an extensive respectable family; McAfee, for the pioneer family; Salvisa, blended Indian names of Salt and Kentucky rivers; Stewart, Pleasant Hill and Burgin take their town terms, the origin of which has been given elsewhere.

The improvement in no department of civilization has been more marked than in the mail facilities of our county. When the writer of these reminiscences first remembers, mails were not daily, but were brought periodically on horseback, on the same horse with the carrier, as is now done by some of our little post offices; sometimes on a separate horse that would presently become so trained that he would come in in advance of the carrier, greatly to the delight of the children who had not yet been initiated into the capabilities of the equine race by a single attendance on the circus—not yet!

The great thundering mail stage, with its rumble and clatter and merry train came next, and our ears are still tingling with the first shrieking whistle of the first railroad that brings its tiding and express packages and friends and drummers and duns every hour of the night and day.

But there has been no greater advance in the facilities of the post office than in the material transported. The blueish tinted paper, not even smooth edged, compared in quality to that now used about as delf to pure French china, no water or other lines, but the pen wandered over the blank page at the will, or rather the skill, of the penman. The quill, fresh dropped from the goose wing, having gone through the process of oiling and boiling, was the implement that preceded Gild's invention, and woe to the man who owned a good penknife, and was accounted a good pen-maker, for the calls on him were by legions. There were no nice, secure envelopes, and folding a letter neatly was an art, and to many remained a mystery all through life. Wafers, a dry composition of paste, colored and cut out like bullet patches, served to seal these missives; sealing wax, of various colors, after a while, came into use, and stamps, with various devices and mottoes. Post stamps had not been adopted until near, or more than, a third of this century had passed . Postage was high and not prepaid, and so your letter lay at the post office of its destination at the mercy of "whom it might concern."

The Cemeteries

After burials in general ceased at the pioneer cemetery on Old Fort Hill, a plat was set apart for the dead known as the Magoffin cemetery, as it occupied part of the property owned by Gov. Magoffin in the southeastern part of town. This was used from about 1840 to the neighborhood of 1860. It was on a steep hillside situated in such a way that in order to bury the dead facing the east, as is the custom, the body had to be placed in the grave with the head down hill in most instances.

A good deal of dissatisfaction was occasioned by this, and Meaureau

Pulliam (father of the late Mayor J. G. Pulliam—Ed. Note), then a member of the city council, tried to get a measure through to purchase a more fitting place of burial. Failing to gain the attention of his colleagues in office, he made a deal with his friend, Squire Burford, for a tract of land to be cut from his property in the northeastern section of town. Later several influential citizens joined him in the purchase and the new cemetery was privately owned for some weeks before the town decided to take over the property as a municipal burying ground and called it Spring Hill Cemetery. The deal broke up the lifelong friendship of Mr. Pulliam and Squire Burford, who did not know for what purpose the ground he was selling would be used.

There remains but one more public place to which, alas! alas! all our ways inevitably tend, the

The Spring Hill Cemetery

To this, through an orchard gateway, we often pass in sad procession, bearing our kindred and friends, one by one, and soon they shall bear us to that same bourne from which none ever return. On either side of the main way lie two squares of well kept garden and shrubs; then, by winding ways, we pass the homes of the silent dead. Costly monuments or plainer tablets mark their resting places. The grass grows green upon them, and countless evergreens, emblems of immortality, point upward to remind us that they, over whom we sorrow, are not here, but in the many mansions He went to prepare. All burials are sad, and amongst the saddest in this garden of the dead, have been the keepers of the ground, poor Michael McCabe, of skillful hands and warm Irish heart, surrounded by his young wife and innocent bairns too young to be conscious of the loss; and Glakken, poor Glakken, save on the morning when a ravening bear rent from its bed one of his children, I have seldom heard such wails as he made, beating his breast and tossing his great arms in the air as he followed his fair wife and a grown young lad out in the grey of that winter morning.

This cemetery is now in charge of and in keeping by James H. Stagg Unfortunately for those who keep the homes of their dead sweet with fresh flowers, the conservatory has fallen into dilapidation, and no available supply of water can be had for those who with hands of love, would themselves keep these graves covered with verdure and bloom.

It was very much the custom of our country in its first days, to bury the dead on their own homesteads, a sure deed to neglect and oblivion; for homes in this country rarely descend to the third generations, and no sight is more common or desolate looking than the old family grave yards, glimpsed from the roads, which have fallen into decay, these graves of strangers having no sacredness to the new land owners.

But the association of the ideas of graves and church yards lingered in the memories of emigrants to these wilds, and there was a yearning desire in the hour of bereavement to lay the remains in sacred ground; hence there are few churches in our county, however small or obscure, around which are not gathered the precious dead of the vicinity. These places tend, too, to almost certain neglect and oblivion; hence the growing custom of citizens from all parts of the county having a lot in the chartered grounds of the towns, of which our own and the extensive one of Danville are beautiful samples.

Around old Shawnee Run meeting house there lay a dead host. The rank, green grass assuming the office of England's famous "ivy green," has gradually stolen over palings, the humble tombstone and every mark with which affection strives to perpetuate the memory of the beloved.

New Providence has yet a larger concourse sleeping in the forest that shadowed the first historic church. This primitive building and its successor have succumbed to time, and the new and handsome inheritor of the name and fame of this pioneer church occupies an eligible and accessable site on Frankfort turnpike. This burial ground has, I think, been chartered and a new "McAdamized" way is being made leading to it. Doubtless there will be a revival of the old memorial stones, and whatever taste and liberality can devise will be done to perpetuate the memory of the many honored dead who rest in these grounds. A sure mark of advancing civilization is the provision of and care of these silent cities, where the heart may build its shrine and memory forever lay on it the votive flowers to those who are
"Not lost, but gone before."

CHAPTER XXX

Danville

Kentucky, it will be remembered, was formed into a district, and afterwards this was redistricted into three counties, and in one of them, Lincoln, the future Mercer was inwrapped. In these courts of justice were organized, and the first court met in Harrodsburg. But centrality of location being desirable, Danville, that lay midway between Harrodsburg and the forts in Lincoln, was selected, and a log Court House was erected, and there crime, for the first time, was made responsible to law, and from thenceforth there was a visible improvement in "honesty, probity and good demeanor." These courts did not hold jurisdiction over life.

The original plat of Danville is said to have belonged to Walker Daniel, who laid the foundation of a splendid fortune in this investment, but did not live to realize the value of his forethought. He was cut off in his youth by the Indians. He was a young man of talent and fine education, and the field for his professional success as a lawyer before him was even fairer than that of a land speculator, Christopher Greenup being then his only competitor. Captain Harrod is said to have built the first cabin in Danville. There may be some lingering who remember that over sixty years ago there stood an old Presbyterian church, of stone, surrounded by graves, and afterwards used as an African church. This stood on the very site of the fort, and afterwards a county seminary was built on the same spot, and strangely enough, like the first building of the same class in Harrodsburg, was blown down by a storm. Storms, like dances, came square in those days, not taking on the waltzlike gyrations of the modern cyclone, but just as irresistible in power.

When the actual survey of Danville was made for the purpose of platting a town, very sensibly the Jacob's staff was stuck into the town spring as a center, and for many years the spread of the town was eastward, until the passing by of the railroad seems to have suggested a reconsideration, and now the fever for business buildings seems, like empire, westward to take its way. However, the colored element seemed disposed to colonize southeasterly, and Duncan's hill is the site of quite a flourishing suburb.

But to return to our legitimate bounds. Old Danville: it was laid out by Major Thomas Allin, an aide of General Green in the Revolutionary war, a member of the convention that framed the first constitution of Kentucky, and was clerk for life of the Mercer Circuit Court. Danville had little of the dangerous and growth-depressing experience of Harrodsburg in Indian warfare, but had her full share, however, in the dread; and her men were in the danger of that period, for danger was a tie that linked all the first settlers in one band of brotherhood of arms. On one occasion John Cochrane, returning from Bullitt's Lick with a sack of salt, was about where Prof. Failles now lives, set upon by an Indian. His horse was shot from under him, and he fled on to Crow's station. Scouts were sent out from there and found the dead horse, but the salt was gone and never a trace of the Indian was seen. Captain Pogue, too, it will be remembered, was shot in the vicinity of Danville. The contrality of Danville and the existence of a suitable building there decided it as the eligible point for the meeting of the conventions which continued to debate and petition for the separation of Kentucky from Virginia and for her admission into the Union. Over all these conventions Judge Samuel McDowell, of Mercer, presided and never, since our Commonwealth had being, have debates been held of greater interest or importance. The simple points of separation and admission were not only ones discussed, but Kentucky's rights in this western world and her future relation to the Federal States. There never has been in our state a body of men assembled of finer talent or more political experince, many of them having heard and participated in the debates through which the Federal constitution passed to adoption. In fact, when our last state convention met to form the constitution, it had but to digest the previous debates, sum up and select from them our political creed, and in these conventions, first or last, every man of eminence in Kentucky of that day served.

But to come back to physical Danville, it had no growth different from Harrodsburg at the same stage. It was laid out in blocks as now, with wider streets, and gradually faced with the same class of buildings, wooden, stone and after a while with some brick interspersed; and it is with rueful steps that we turn back from this erection of Boyle county as our limits, from this period of extension over beautiful grounds on which stand so many handsome cottages ornee and fine brick residences.

Now, my first impression of Danville is very distinct. Under the wing of one of the saintliest of the Presbyterian sisterhood of our village, I came up to one of the Synods that were wont to gather almost yearly in the Mecca of our church. The famously hospitable house of Mr. Yarce received us under its roof, teeming like a bee hive with the faithful, chiefly of the order clerical. From thence I was appropriatetd by the clannish Rochesters, who lived in a brick mansion which has been superceded long ago by a more spacious and imposing building, in which the Talbots, Grahams and Jones have successively lived. I remember there was a glitter of cut glass and silver on the Rochester board, and that their's was one of the few carriages that went to and fro from the church, and what with Synodical debates and teas and dinners and college boy gallants, Danville took on a glamour its society has never lost to my eyes to the present day.

For many years the career, if a progress so quiet and slow as the advance of Harrodsburg and Danville can be called a career, was about equal, without any natural commercial facilities, they seemed doomed to the slow developments into respectable inland towns only useful for living in. But the location of first, the Deaf and Dumb Asylum, then of Centre College, and its adjunct the Theological Seminary, decided Danville as a literary center, and the growth of these institutions and the number of learned men that have come with them, has made it one of the most desirable places of residence in our state. It has become a favorite point for persons wishing to educate their children, or wishing desirable social and religious privileges for home surroundings.

Long before the erection of Boyle into a county, the most of the denominations having a foothold in Kentucky, had their places of worship in one town. The sites of some of them have been changed, and all nearly have undergone modern renaissance of Gothic windows, fine painting, fresco and all the luxurious furnishing that modern self-indulgence and aesthetic taste demands. The second church was not in most places the result of schism, but a natural and necessary division from increase desiring extension. These churches though do rank under different banners and pronounce Sibboleth differently when they come to the book.

It would be impossible for me, "not to the manor born,'" with so few less lingering around to point out old places and tell me old histories, to trace out the growth of streets, the changes of the architecture and occupation of homesteads, the extension of the town and trade, the organization of the churches, etc., previous to the creation of Boyle county. The present ville I could more easily and accurately describe were it in the scope of my history. But I shall not essay into these bounds in this serial and will, as heretofore, confine myself to a notice of the institutions which were founded in Danville while belonging to Mercer, and to brief sketches of the dramatis personae who were connected therewith.

The Deaf and Dumb Asylum

Was amongst the first of this class organized in the United States. It was created and went into operation in 1823, in a frame building on Main street, with a very limited number of pupils. Col. T. P. Moore, the representative of our congressional district, then procured for it a grant of public land in Florida, which with the state's appropriations and some legacies and gifts from individuals, have enabled it to develop into one of the best institutions, in every respect, of its kind in the states.

It is located on Second street, and presents a very imposing array of substantial and handsome brick buildings, completely convenient, and comfortably furnished. It has extensive grounds of quite farmlike proportions, where the unfortunate tenants of these elegant homes find recreation and usefulness in cultivating. By the purchase lately of a fine and ample property, just across the street, the colored unfortunates of this class have equal opportunities with the whites for learning. So, now every deaf mute in Kentucky is provided with educational privileges, and it should be the voluntary mission of every Christian to carry this gospel of redemption from utter uselessness and inanity to these unfortunates—that is to inform the ignorant that there are these places for them to be sent to.

The Rev. John Kerr,

was the first superintendent of this establishment. Circumstances brought me into close association with this family. Of course Mr. Kerr was, as all Presbyterian clergymen, well educated, and he left·on my childish judgment the impression of one whose motive power was love for his kind. I think his second wife was a Miss Jacobs, and that his successors of that name were trained under him or imbibed from him their devotion to this noble vocation in which they were so eminent and successful.

Mr. Kerr furnished several sons anad at least one grandson to the ranks of the ministry. John A. Jacobs went through the training hardships that seem necessary to success. He taught school in youth, graduated at Centre College, and devoted the whole of his life to the closest following of his divine Master, literally spending his life and largely his means in doing good. The silent objects of his life-care gave him the gratitude of hearts redeemed by his teachings from the helpless hopelessness of ignorance. Beyond this, his particular field of work, he wrought just as diligently for the feeble-minded who could never know or appreciate his labor of love for them. The establishment of the Institution for "feeble-minded" was very much through his influence, and for these and all kindred charities he prayed and worked and gave of his substance until the Master called up higher his faithful servant. He was succeeded by a kinsman.

John A. Jacob, Jr.,

A man of ability and marked financial integrity. His administration during an interregnum, of Mr. Dudley, of Carolina, and of Mr. Argo, belongs to the history of Doyle since its independence of Mercer; but I cannot forbear the pleasure of mentioning that from recent observations its outward and inward management seem all that the most exacting philanthropist could desire and I think much of its internal beauty of life is due to the executive ability and conscientious care of Mrs. Dudley, who sharing collaterally the

McDowell Residence and Monument

Covered Bridge Over Dix River, Boyle County.

talent of her distinguished kinsman, Benjamin West, and in addition to her duties adorns her room with such work as would do credit to a professional artist.

The Theological Seminary

of Danville, belongs wholly to modern Danville. It had great possibilities of usefulness and brought some eminent divines to Danville, with whose names I would fain adorn my columns. Now it is a silent witness to the Master's wisdom who said: "And if a house be divided against itself that house cannot stand." This property has been in ecclesiastical litigation long enough for its patronage to drift away, and I think it has performed only duty vital to its existence for some years.

CHAPTER XXXI

Centre College—Its Origin and Presidents—Chamberlin, Blackburn, John C. Young, Lewis Green, William Breckinridge, Dr. Beatty—Boyle Biography The McDowells, the Greens, Joshua Frey, Judge Bridges, Judge Fox, Joshua F. Bell—The Boyles—General Jerry T. Boyle—Colonel John Boyle, William C. Boyle, Etc., Etc.

Centre College

This first literary institution of Mercer, to which Joshua Frey's Academy had been a successful and valuable unchartered and unconnected preparatory, was founded in 1823. In 1824, the board of trustees agreed with the Synod of Kentucky that upon the payment of $20,000 on the part of the Presbyterian Church with funds of the institution, that the church should forever have the right of appointing the board of trustees. This virtually made it a Presbyterian College. and it remains that to the present time, belonging to the Old School in the schism of which the New School was but temporary, and now belonging to the church adhering to the General Assembly. A valuable result of this division has been the founding of the prosperous and growing Central University, of Richmond, Kentucky, belonging to the Southern Presbyterian Church, and competition between these two institutions reduces a first class collegiate education in either college almost to free school terms. (Centre College and Central University are now merged into one institution at Danville.—Ed. Note). The first buildings of Centre College were very plain, but fronted with an ample campus. These are now used as a college home for students, and new, spacious and convenient college buildings have been erected by Danville and the church.

The College Library

is a building provided by the late David Sayre, a devoted Presbyterian of Lexington, Kentucky. This library contains several thousand volumes. The college has two flourishing Literary Societies and an Alumni Association, swelling and spreading every year over the land. I have met every successive President of the institution, but was too young to receive impressions of the intellectual calibre of several of the first, except through others. I remember Mr. Chamberlin's fine personal appearance and pleasant manners in the home circle, and that some circumstances proved him a Christian of the highest type.

Dr. Blackburn

rises to my mind as a very, very able man and powerful orator. I remember seeing him in an impassioned description of the Savior's resurrection, raise a snowy handkerchief slowly, representative of the clouds that embosomed the Blessed One, so effective that there was a visible motion to uprising in the magnetized congregation.

Dr. John C. Young

succeeded him in A. D. 1820, and here my pen always needs a check. I have never met a man who so indelibly impressed me. Of intellect equal to any; of deep erudition, profound conviction, and of unequalled power of language, which was driven to the heart by his irrestible earnestness. It requires an effort of memory usually to remember what most men say; what Dr. Young said you could not forget.

Dr. Lewis Green

succeeded Dr. Young, and though upon his accession Centre College no longer belonged to Mercer, I write him as a Mercer man by both birth and education that naturally group with the Danville men of Old Mercer. He was one of Willis Green's numerous family and educated in Mr. Frey's famous pioneer Academy, graduating afterward and then going through the Presbyterian stereotype process of a course of Theology in Princeton. He spent some years also in Europe, and was probably the man of the most varied attainments and complete education of any of Danville's literary celebrities.

Rev. William D. Breckinridge

succeeded Dr. Green and shared in full the talent of that noted family. He was very handsome, and said himself that he was a representative Kentuckian "who had the best wife, finest children, fastest horse and best dog in the wide world." His election to this presidency vouched for his education and intelligence, and I thought him of the sweetest spirit I have ever known. He had quite a long and mixed career of pastoral and literary presidencies, I think, in Missouri to which he went.

David C. Proctor

presided during some interregnum as also did

Mr. Beatty

until his formal installation after his appointment to succeed Mr. Breckinridge. Mr. Beatty has discharged the duties of tutor, professor and president of this college, come next commencement day, fifty-five years, having been previously educated in the college. It is not my want to expiate on unfinished lives, but I must be allowed to say Mr. Beatty has filled his place fully, his thorough training, experience and faultless morality making a fit setting for his intellect and ripe scholarship.

To preserve the harmony of our narrative, we have come adown the stream of time to the present hour, and now must retrace our way and would I could, with the truthful photograph, portray pictures of the great departed, instead of sketching with the dim ink of tradition, characters fast fading from the memories of the oldest living citizen. Some of these figures seem to gather naturally in family groups. Thus the McDowells, of whom

Judge Samuel McDowell

is the central and head figure. He was of Scotch descent and of Virginia nativity, and seems to have been called naturally and continually to the front. I do not find where he was educated, but presume he was bred to the law, as he was a member of every grade of first courts in Kentucky, presided over every convention and helped make the first constitution of the state. Judge McDowell, like the good man of Uz, had not only a princely estate, but had sons and many fair daughters, the fairest in all the land, who transmitted his blood, without his name to many well marked races in Kentucky, and who carry their dower of beauty to the galleries of the present day. His son,

Dr. Ephraim McDowell

came here with his people in his childhood. He had every advantage of education this country afforded, and afterwards took a term in Edinburg and one in Halle, Germany. Dr. McDowell had the courage and skill to achieve that in surgery which had never before been attempted, and ranks in the old and new world in the front ranks of surgeons and the benefactors of mankind. He, as well as also a brother, married a daughter of Governor Isaac Shelby. His remains rest in the grave yard of Traveller's Rest, the old Governor's home, and a handsome monument has been erected to his memory by the medical fraternity of the state, in Danville.

Dr. Charles McDowell

was of the same family but not a brother of Dr. Ephraim McDowell. He was a co-adjutor of the distinguished Dr. Drake, of Cincinnati, and married his sister. He afterwards removed to St. Louis and founded the college called by his name, in which is preserved an excellent portrait of him, and there lingers around in his fraternity and the society of St. Louis many an anecdote illustrative of his marked peculiarities—especially his sayings and doings during the late unpleasantness in which he signalized himself as a rebel.

Mr. James G. Birney

was an affinity of this family, a lawyer, a professor of Centre College and an unsuccessful politician, but was the entering wedge of abolition into American politics, and had strength enough to cause the defeat of Mr. Clay by withdrawing from him the abolition votes. His sons' names will be found on the list of "Distinguished non-residents of Mercer and Boyle counties."

The Greens were another family of mark in Mercer, now Boyle.

Willis Green

was from Virginia, and for a long while a clerk of the court in Danville. His marriage to Miss Reed is mentioned as the first occurring in Kentucky. I think it was later than Capt. Lynn's in Harrodsburg. They had a numerous family, and their home was what is known as Wavelend, property now of Mr. John Craig, a descendant in the female line.

Judge John Green,

his son, was a man of fine mind, strong prejudices and sterling character.

Lewis Green

was also his son, whose life has been sketched as President of Centre College. By maternal ascent this line goes up to

Joshua Frey.

This gentleman belonged by some official connection to General Washington's military family. Determined, in his search for wealth in the wilderness, that his children should not lose their chance for education, he took upon himself the arduous duty of instructing them himself, and from pure good will to his kind, gradually extended the opportunity to his neighbors, and gave vent to nearly all the forest of great men of this section while in the "tiny state." The Bells, Bullitts, Speeds, Greens, Barbours are all descendants from this literary Samaritan as well as several men of his patronymic already mentioned in other parts of this work, and few men of note of this section but had their training in his school.

The Harlans,

who have been mentioned in these columns, as also the Cowans and Caldwells, who gave name to the Female Institute of Danville, were of that part of Mercer now known as Boyle.

Judges Bridges and Fox

have both been honored residents of Danville, as also

Judge Payne Mitchell,

who began his usefulness in Mercer, and continued it in various offices when Boyle became separate.

Judge Durham,

his son-in-law, but a generation younger, had the same local record, but has been a lawyer and politician in Boyle of many years standing and is making most satisfactory record as Comptroller of the Treasury in Mr. Cleveland's administration of national affairs.

Joshua F. Bell

was born in Mercer county in 1811. His father, David Bell, long time merchant in Danville, was of Irish birth, and married one of the daughters of Joshua Frey, who himself had married the daughter of Dr. Walker, one of the first explorers of Kentucky, who surveyed the line that gave his mark to the geographical division mark between this state and Tennessee. He was educated in Centre College, took his law course in Transylvania, and enlarged his knowledge by a leisurely travel in Europe. He was strongly marked with the characteristics of his father's race. Sensitive and poetic; full of both humor and pathos. He mingled largely in the complex and civil affairs of his day. He served a term in Congress; was Gov. Crittenden's Secretary of State; was chosen almost unanimously for the peace conference held at the National Capital, and labored earnestly to avert the horrors of civil war. Mr. Bell died in the zenith of his usefulness and fame in 1870.

The Boyles,

of three generations, were of Mercer birth, the dividing line between the counties by a purpose divergence, throwing the home and grave of Judge Boyle, now the home of Alex McKee, into the county named for him. His life constituted an important and interesting part of the struggle between the constitutional and usurping Court of Appeals, styled the New and Old Courts—relief and anti-relief.

Jeremiah T. Boyle

was born in Mercer in 1818. He had his literary training in Princeton and his law course in Transylvania, Lexington. He commenced the practice of law in Harrodsburg, but afterward came to Danville, but had his most conspicuous career in Louisville, Kentucky. He was an emancipationist in principle, hence fell naturally to the Federal ranks in the war of the rebellion. He raised a regiment for the service and was afterward made Brigadier General for merit. He was appointed Military Governor of Kentucky, and in his zeal issued some of the most stringent orders of the period, from the consequences of which his own nature so revolted that he resigned. He went enthusiastically into the internal improvement so needed in the city of his adoption, Louisville, and the state. He was talented, genial, and left recollections of him as a true friend and charming society man. He married the daughter of Simeon H. Anderson, once a representative from this district in Congress. She is now the dispenser of the generous and graceful hospitalities of the home of Mr. Beatty, the President of Centre College, having married him several years ago.

Col. John Boyle

was also in the late war of the rebellion as we have seen.

Col. William Boyle

fell on the field of Marion, Alabama.

Alas, for the wreck of life war makes, and yet, after all, peace must be the fruit of concession and treaty.

In closing this biography of men whose lives were native of Mercer but spent in Boyle, I feel like a prisoner who comes to the inexorable bars and looks out on the sunshine and verdure in which he would fain revel—so much would I like to still make sketches of the fine men and fair women of present Boyle.

CHAPTER XXXII

Towns of Mercer County Continued—Pleasant Hill—Perryville—Lucto—Chaplin—Nevada—Bohontown and Cornishville—McAfee—Duncansville Dugansville—Rose Hill, Etc.

Pleasant Hill

This is a small, but neat and pretty village, situated on the highlands which head the cliffs of Kentucky and Dix rivers. The Lexington turnpike bisects it and wends its way on to the handsome and substantial bridge which overspans the Kentucky river, near which the busy amphibious little hamlet, Brooklyn, with its post office, planing mills and warehouse stands. A branch of this same turnpike diverges from the east side of the village and leads down to Shaker landing, across the river and up to High Bridge, the station from which the various products of Pleasant Hill find outlet on the Cincinnati Southern to the country's markets. The Lexington turnpike and a smooth broad flagged pavement on either side for foot travel, constitutes the broadway and only street of the village.

The dwellings, all of choice materials and good construction, stand on either side of this street, fronted with matchless blue grass lawns and backed with well cultivated kitchen gardens and flourishing orchards, and have that air of abundance, neatness and thrift that ought to belong to rural life everywhere. Their house of worship is a simple, large, pure white frame building, without steeple or ornamentation, in which the Shakers meet to practice their unique rites. The post office, a quiet colored little frame, stands pretty central in the village, and near it the free flowing town pump for the hospitable refreshment of the weary wayfarer, and the same benevolent provision of water is made by their road sides for the toiling mule and dashing span that fly or drag their weary ways over this once thronged, but now comparatively deserted highway; deserted by reason of that railroad magnetism that draws all commerce to itself. This modest post office is overshadowed by a large, handsome brick house that has lately taken the character of a hotel in self defense, so numerous have become the guests that the facilities of the railroad brought—pleasure seekers in avalances upon these quiet people. And now refugees from city dust and heat, and their children, flittering about like butterflies, afford vivid contrast to the quakerly figures that glide about in the cool twilight in their long corridors.

The costume of these people is quaint and peculiar, as is everything else in the place, exquisitely neat, and very noticeable is the transparency of their caps and kerchiefs. Once the whole village wore materials as distinctive as the cut of their clothes. Now they use fabrics found in the manufactures of the world, but confine themselves chiefly to neutral tints.

This community is rich in land, having a large body around their village, and owning fine farms at intervals all along the road to Harrodsburg. They confine themselves chiefly to grazing, as farmers, keeping the best of stock and having comfortable quarters for all they keep.

They still pursue several industries, but to a more limited extent than formerly. They were pioneers in silk culture in Kentucky, having engaged in this fascinating industry in 1822. They carried it out so far as to manufacture the product into silk handkerchiefs of beautiful texture and lustre. They give it some attention still, only, however, making their own sewing silk, and send their surplus cocoons to market. Garden seed and preserves are their chief exports; though they still manufacture brooms for the trade, and the sisters make a few ornamental articles by way of recreation, which are carried off by visitors as souvenirs of the place, as bead and bark work are by the pilgrims to Niagara.

This society is a branch of religionists that originated in England, and a society was formed in this county very early in this century. It first owned and occupied the fine farm, now the property residence of Mr. John L. Cassell. I do not know in what year they changed to their present base. One of the leading men in the movement was Mr. Dunlavy, a prominent Presbyterian minister, who went out in that extraordinary religious disturbance in that ordinarially staid church in the beginning of this century. Barton W. Stone also diverged about this time into Unitarianism, and was long the leader in this state of that denomination. This society is, we believe, governed by elders, of both sexes, of whom venerable Benjamin Dunlavy, a descendant of the founder of that name, and Paulina Bryant, a woman of striking physical and mental proportions, have been representatives since the writer's earliest recollection. The titles of property and conduct of business is in the hands of a committee elective or appointive. Of managers they have had a safe and respectable succession—some of exceptional ability. Francis Voris having shown, after leaving them, wonderful financial ability, having first its need of success, then its common feature of failure, and finally the more extraordinary one of full retrieval.

Rufus Bryant had less scope, or, perhaps, was less speculative, but he was safe and successful and had the full confidence of his own community and the respect of the gentile world around him. By his death the business of the society has passed chiefly to the hands of younger men, on whom the future center must set the seal of value. The Brothers Pennebaker are men of good capacity and culture, not inferior in intelligence or enterprise to their predecessors or the world around them, and it is hard to foreshadow, with the many forces of this age acting upon them, their destiny. The habits of these people are simple and their ways are kindly. Their hospitality has been extensive in time past, and expensively imposed on, and one can never leave them without a sentiment of regret that a life of comfort and thrift is based upon principles subversive of the Heaven ordained family institution, and that we must diverge from them in the paths we take to the better land.

Salvisa

The name of this village is a combination of the names of the two rivers that flow not far from it. Sal for salt, and Visa, the terminus of Levisa, the original name of Kentucky river; and I think, Dr. Cleland was said to have suggested the combination. It is the second size secular town of Mercer county. Shakertown being larger and classing as religious. Salvisa is bisected by the Frankfort turnpike with several streets crossing it that divides it into squares. It has four churches—a Baptist, Presbyterian, Methodist and Reform—and a full complement of stores, a mill, distillery, and postoffice. It has about 300 population; fine roads and thickly settled neighborhood give it a large and most excellent society.

McAfee or El Dorado

is another point of the Frankfort road, where the neighbors have carried New England fashions and have a pretty village, affording all the conveniences of life and trade. It was named in memory of the pioneer McAfees.

Burgin

is the next largest town, and I regret that each of the places I name, bore not as loyal a citizen as Mr. John H. Grimes, who, in response to my request for items, has hunted enough tradition and history to make an entire and interesting chapter about his town.

Oregon,

on the Kentucky river, Cornishville, on Chaplin river, Lucto, Bohontown, Duncan, Dugansville, and Rose Hill, are all centers of trade, precincts and have postoffices.

Perryville

in age, ranks after Danville and Pleasant Hill. It had its beginning in 1815 on the lands of W. Hall, east, and Edmond Bullock, west of Chaplin river. It took its name, it is presumable, from the hero of Lake Erie, Commodore Perry, who was at the zenith of his fame about the time of its beginning.

One incident of interest has come down to us when that dread was realized in blood. The fort that stood where Perryville now stands, was called Harbison's. The man whose name it took was lame. One day he and a fellow fortman named Ewing, were in the field together when a party of Indians attacked them. Ewing would not outstrip his unfortunate companion, and while delaying to shield and help him was killed by one of the savages. While the Indian who had killed Ewing was scalping him, a man in the fort named Potts, shot the Indian who fell dead across the body of his victim. The rest of the band took Harbison off as a captive. He was never heard of again, and it is probable that as his lameness would retard their movements, he was sacrificed to their haste and malignity.

Perryville has now about 500 inhabitants, two Presbyterian, a Baptist, Methodist and Reform churches; Ewing Institute for male and female pupils is very flourishing. The common school holds a limited term and the colored people have full advantage of educational privilege the law gives them. Perryville has its full complement of stores, groceries, mills and shops, and of course its post office. The Masons have a regular organization there, and temperance flourishes there, as in all own towns, fitfully. The troubles of Mercer and Boyle during the rebellion, headed at Perryville, October 8th, 1862. That conflict and its consequences have elsewhere been glanced at in these columns. The battle belongs to the nation, state and future historians of Boyle. Perryville wears many scars from that deadly collision yet. She had her part in the civil affairs of the country, as will be found by the names of her citizens on the legislative rolls that will be hereafter furnished.

Roads of Mercer County

Mercer county was amongst the first of the counties in the state that secured the benefit of the "McAdamized" turnpikes that were first made between 1825 and '30. Our well known Lexington pike is an extension of the celebrated Mays road, which was the representative road that made claims for national aid, and which occasioned General Jackson's celebrated veto. Beside this road there are a number of others leading into Harrodsburg. The Frankfort and Crab Orchard passes through and constitutes our Main street. Connecting Harrodsburg with the named points are turnpikes called Cane Run, Cornishville, Mackville and Bloomfield. The county is in fact almost a net work of fine turnpikes, yearly extending and of which in most cases the county owns one-half the stock. The comfort and commercial value of these roads cannot be appreciated. These roads are in all nine, leading out to the heart of fine districts of the county and which, of course, have tributary veins of commerce emptying into them from many sections and having in fact but two roads coming into town without grade or metal.

For many years these numerous turnpikes were subservient chiefly to the domestic trade of the county, the capricious rises of the Kentucky river, and wagons connecting with not very near railroad stations, affording the only outlet for commerce outside of the county. But the South Western Railroad has given a new and wonderful impulse to trade. The once almost deserted streets are constantly traversed with teams which bring products of a large back country to the little road which works like a giant, night and day, to transfer the accumulating freight to the great commercial artery to which it is a feeder. Our South Western is a peerless thing of its kind, admirable in construction, with fine rolling stock, needing only turning table at the Junction to make its completeness in convenience and safety. It has spacious depot room, large elevators, all conveniences for receiving and keeping stock, and well paved courts around it, making it easy of access for freight or passengers.

This road is said to furnish more freight than any station in Kentucky except Lexington. The road has been peculiarly fortunate in having always been in the management of men of rare energy and executive ability. The road was built partly by a self-imposed tax of the town and by joint stock subscription. It now belongs to a company, the stock being chiefly managed by the president, Dr. M. Tabler, a man of large experience, executive talent and financial ability.

CHAPTER XXXIII

Burgin—History of the Ground on Which It Stands—Distinguished Men of the Vicinity — Its Name — Number of Inhabitants — Manufactures, Schools, Etc.

Burgin

The historic spot upon which Burgin is situated deserves a passing notice. In the year 1778, a stockade was built around the big double spring enclosing a cabin or two. This spring which now supplies a large scope of country with water, was then called Harlan's Spring as it and all the land surrounding it, including about one thousand acres, had been entered and claimed by James Harlan—one of the very first settlers in Kentucky, who was the grandfather of John M. Harlan, now a Justice of the Supreme Court of the United States. This land was purchased by Alexander Robertson, a Virginian, of Harlan, and the original patent was issued to Robertson.

A cabin within this stockade was for a long time the home of Alexander Robertson, and in it some distinguished persons were born, among them the children of the founder of the Fort, viz.:—Elizabeth, Margaret, Jane, James, Alexander, Martha, George and Charlotte Robertson. Alexander Robertson, the father of these children of the wilderness, was a delegate to the convention which adopted the constitution of the United States. He served also as delegate from the county of Mercer—then one of the five counties which afterwards comprised the State of Kentucky—to the House of Burgesses, which separated Kentucky from Virginia. He was also the first sheriff of Mercer county. It is not generally known that the late learned lawyer and judge—Chief Justice George Robertson—was born within a stone's throw of this big spring. It was here, also that the first frame house ever erected in the state was built. It burned about twenty-five years ago upon the spot where William Gregory's house now stands. In this old frame house, Governor Robert P. Letcher was married to Charlotte Robertson. He was born in the house where Mr. John A. Huguely now resides; was member of Congress three times, and once minister to Mexico. In the old frame house mentioned, in 1807, another sister of Chief Justice Robertson—Martha—was married to Samuel McKee, a member of Congress from Kentucky from 1806 to 1819. He was succeeded by his brother-in-law, George Robertson, who in turn served three terms—a singular coincidence—three brothers-in-law, each serving so long and succeeding each other in rotation.

But from this digression, let us return to the village which must now occupy our attention for a while. The neat and quiet village of Burgin is situated on the Cane Run and Dix River turnpike at the point where the Cincinnati, New Orleans & Texas Pacific R. R. intersects said road, and near where the Shakertown and Danville pike crosses at right angles the Cane Run pike. Its birth dates with the completion of the Southern Road to Danville in 1877, when only one log cabin marked the spot where now about fifty houses loom up in the distance, giving evidence of thrift and enterprise. In return for his liberal donation of "the right of way" to the Cincinnati Southern Railway Co., through his splendid blue grass farm (which was about the only recognition for his munificent gift that Mr. Temple Burgin ever received), the station was named for him.

Mr. Burgin—peace to his ashes—only lived to see his namesake pass through its infancy and emerge into childhood when he received his final summons.

When the town was laid off into lots and streets, the territory on the north side of Main street was owned by Messrs. D. L. Moore and John A. Huguely; and that on the south side by Mr. Temple Burgin. It now has a population of nearly two hundred, and while its inhabitants and business men are of rather contracted means, yet Burgin is a thrifty village. It has four stores all in prosperous condition, and two cooper factories in active operation, which employ from ten to twenty-five mechanics daily during the busy season in the manufacture of whisky barrels, kegs and tobacco ho sheads. One is the property of Hon. D. L. Moore, the other of Mr. John A. Huguely. A high grain elevator of 40,000 bushels capacity towers above all other buildings, and is a monument to the enterprise and capital of the Burg. n Association, a corporation composed of John L. Cassell, John Nichols and D N. Rue, who also own the largest store house in the town, and command a fine trade.

The absence of any church within the corporate limits of Burgin is not to be attributed to any indifference on the part of its Christian people, but rather to their membership in the various denominations in Harrodsburg and Danv. le, and to the Cane Run (Christian) church just beyond the limits, and to the Shawnee Run (Baptist) church only a short distance from town. It is more in accord with the inclinations of the good people to continue to wo hin where they were wont to serve their Master before the existence of ~ the places are so accessible, rather than sever the affec....... heir first church loves. The town was surveyed off into squares u. _ eets, and the plat shows more streets and squares than have yet been ut.. The business houses are constructed more on the idea of cheapness than . ' grandeur or display, and scarcely come up to the standard of ordinary ap earances. Over two of the principal stores are halls, designed for lodge r ns, public lectures, or entertainments.

The incessant ring of anvils continually remind one that in this pleasant village "Two Village Smithies Stand."

The health of the community bids defiance to the struggles for livelihood and eminence in their professions of two prominent physicians, Drs. J. M. Dalton and John L. Price, who are ever ready to tender their aid and skill to the afflicted in this and the surrounding neighborhood, and the absence of any cemetery in or near the town may be taken as a criterion of the merits of the M. D.'s.

Burgin is a shipping point of no insignificant proportions—hemp, gram and stock—from portions of Garrard and Boyle counties are sold here, or loaded on cars for a better market.

Over one hundred and twenty-five thousand gallons of "Old Bourbon" are shipped from this point annually, the product of the distilleries of Messrs. D. L. Moore and J. A. and Cabbell Huguely. Some idea of the magnitude of these industries may be gained by stating that these two manufacturing houses of whisky together consume annually about forty-five thousand bushels of grain, employ each about fifteen laborers at wages ranging from $20 to $100 per month. While upon the product of these distilleries, based upon an average of fifteen hundred barrels per annum, or 135,000 gallons, the U. S. Government receives as tax one hundred and twenty-one thousand, five hundred dollars—or ninety cents per gallon—equal to three times the cost of production.

These are simple incidental facts en passant and not intended to indicate the drift of the prohibition or anti-prohibition sentiment that prevails, in the neighborhood.

A new school building is now almost completed in which Mrs. Rosa M. Payne, a lady of rare education and accomplishments, and of enviable reputation as an instructress, teaches the "young ideas." The house has been christened "Payne's Institute," in honor of Mrs. Payne, a just compliment to a most worthy woman.

The dwelling houses are all of modest pretensions, and their external appearances do not indicate wealth and aristocracy, but it does say for cheerful and happy homes they are as well suited as are mansions more conspicuous for wealth and elegance.

When Burgin was scarcely two years old, seeking to imitate her rivals along the great artery of commerce, the C. S. R. R., and to carry her head as high as the highest, she became an incorporated town, and holds an annual election for city officers—judge, trustees and marshal. Whether any special advantage has been derived from this other than to increase taxes, I am afraid the records would be loth to tell.

There is one thing to the credit of the citizens of Burgin that should not be unwritten, for while the fair fame of Kentucky has been blotted by deeds of violence and murder, but one stain of blood has ever yet disgraced her history, and the courts decided that the slayer of Jerome Gay was justified in the deed.

Situated in the very center of a magnificent scope of country where blue grass, hemp, grain and tobacco—emblems of the most fertile soil and of industrious muscle attain their most luxurious growth and reach the highest perfection, and upon one of the greatest thoroughfares on the American continent, where the tropical fruits of the south and the choicest products of the north are laid down at her door, is it a wonder, then, that the people of Burgin are contented? The landscape as far as the eye can reach in any direction, can be seen dotted with hospitable residences, homes of people noted for their social, moral, religious and literary proclivities. Indeed, the neighborhood immediately surrounding Burgin is worthy of some boasting. The culture, refinement and intellectual graces distinguish the residents, and mark them as f. f. k.'s.

It is hardly reasonable to suppose that Burgin has attained its growth, when situated in the midst of such a country and such a people; and if the increase in size and population shall continue in the same ratio, by the time it has reached the present age of the county seat, this page would scarcely contain space to chronicle its dimensions, population and wealth.

Her merchants are prospering; her work shops give evidence of industry; a thousand brooms, and twenty-five barrels are the products of her several factories; the town is as well lighted by night as many others of much greater pretensions and recently the enterprise of Mr. John Nichols, assisted by public help, has given every family a copious supply of fresh, cool water at their doors—thus guaranteeing the permanent success of her water works. Having attained this much at such an early age, and with future prospects growing brighter daily, that Burgin, now but a small meteor on the face growing brighter daily, who doubts that Burgin, now but a small meteor on the face of the earth, will in time expand into a star of great magnitude and brilliancy.

CHAPTER XXXIV

Schools and Colleges of Mercer County—Mrs. Coomes' School in the Fort—Schools of Early Times—Classical Academies for Boys—Bacon College—Kentucky University—Mr. Prather's Classical School—Mr. Hogsett's Common School and Academy.

Nowadays a colony may be organized so completely with its mechanics, professional and merchantile men, all included, a through ticket obtained, and in a few days a town or neighborhood may be set up like a lot of portable furniture, or a yankee clock, wound up and set running, the sleeping passengers hardly aware of the transplantation. It was not so in pioneer days. Emigrants came out in detached parties; were crowded in together like a lot of trees from a nursery and took root slowly. Nevertheless, they seem to have been ambitious to give right things precedence, and first amongst useful things initiated, we find a school in the Fort. This was the enterprise of Mrs. Coomes, wife, we presume, of the man who figures several times in skirmishes with the Indians, and fortunate in always eluding his subtle foes. Her school was, likely, for both boys and girls, probably met in her own rooms, and the books used very primitive and far from allowing classification. Probably the infant class (of pretty large physical development), used, instead of crimson and gilt illustrated card boards as now, real clapboards with letters marked thereon with fire coal. We heard the mother of one of our most prosperous and successful families say she taught her boys on that sort of lesson board, and I know a large family in which all the children down to number six, used the same copy of "Webster's Spelling Book," and the little Jeshurans "waxed fat and kicked," and the children of today could not, I am sure, count on their fingers the primers and readers they have used up without ever getting "head" of their careful predecessors.

My first experience was in a low, dingy room where long rows of girls and boys, on backless benches, sat kicking their feet on dusty floors and murmuring every one of them more than audibly their elementary lessons. From almost "early dawn to dewey eve," the good man held session, and beginning at his desk, went round and round, hearing the sing song recitations of his unclassed scholars. We little ones would give him our hand with perfect freedom, place our foot on his, and with a little deft toss he would seat us on his knees as a preux chevalier assists a young lady to her saddle, and we would spell on in our primer until our time was out. A good lesson was often rewarded by a bit of candy or gingerbread, and when we wanted a holiday we had it. We barred the doors and windows, the master capitulated, and we sought minnows in the creeks and wild flowers or nuts in the woods, a set of as wild, barefoot, sun-burned gypsies as ever were seen outside of Bohemia. Ah, those old days! Praise to the memory, and peace to the ashes of good Nathan Harris, who taught that school.

The next teacher we had shall be nameless; he clearly taught for his meagre living, and so humbly asked pardon for the wrong in his very demeanor, that I can not hold him up to ridicule; he was so poor, so ignorant, so craven spirited.

The successor to this poor man added a good many studies to our list, without much regarding the fitness of things. He employed himself chiefly in talking to a big boy he called Socrates. Under this administration I committed a hard grammer to memory, and by guessing, and keys, and other extraneous aids, parsed even in Milton's Paradise Lost, and never had a dawning idea that my grammar was expected to exercise the remotest influence upon my tongue or pen. In old times there was a general practice of utilizing all professional failures by making teachers of them. In consequence of this policy, I had a term of tuition under an abortive lawyer. I lived in such mortal dread of this knight of the birch lest he should cut off my ink stained fingers, across which he was wont to draw his jackknife threateningly, that I have no recollection of his educational processes, save that evenings the whole school stood up in a semi-circle and spelled—and that a handsome, gallant young fellow, Overton Thomas, one of the sons of historic Mrs. Thomas, nee Poage, ended head nearly every evening, and by virtue of a usage of the times, gave me his place, which I took as triumphantly as if won by my own merits. That school master allowed the doctrine of substitution fully and practically. There was in this school a nearly simple child, the daughter of a harsh mother, who herself kept an A B C school near by.

One day that pedagogue stood the child up before him for the third time for chastisement, and throwing up his hand impatiently, exclaimed: "I'm tired of whipping this girl, will any one take this whipping?" Up rose a sturdy boy of some fourteen summers, red haired and freckled, but with undaunted eyes; stepping before the girl he drew off his coat and received the thrashing. Oh, great hearted Vance Noel, where are you now? I know if you had been a little older you would have felled that brute and trampled the life out of him. If you live, wherever you are, I know the world is better for your helpful presence, and

"If that brave heart has gone down,
It carried sunlight into the tomb."

The girl, with a scream, bounded out of the window, and I, with a heroism unaccountable to myself to the present day, to aid and abet her, threw her bonnet after her.

The town schools were usually presided over by the teacher who sat in the door that was the passway between two large rooms. These two rooms were filled respectively with the girls and boys of all ages from the village. They recited together, and at play times, having no bar upon their intercourse to stimulate to disobedience, instinctively separated from difference of taste; the boys to play bandy and ball, the girls to play dolls, munch green apples and read some threadbare novel clandestinely, because ashamed of the tears they were sure to shed over the sorrows of the "Children of the Abbey," and unfortunate "Thaddeus of Warsaw." They had, however, their loves and hates, and it amuses me now to remember seeing one of the great big boys dart around the corner as in the act of gallanting his pretty sweetheart from school, he suddenly encountered his very dignified father who it was not supposed would tolerate this precocious gallantry in his wool-hatted and bare-footed heir of promise. The wheel of time turns; the girl passed on to a brilliant career in city society; the boy to have his wool hat displaced for the highest civic honors his state could give.

I have now a little dirk some four inches long, that was made with deadly intent in a school feud between two stripplings scarcely in their teens. I sought the peace-maker's blessing, and the dirk was given me in token that the hatchet was buried.

These schools were held in the old Academy on Fort Hill. Some of the teachers whom I remember were Rev. George Moore, of Arkansas, now; Mr. Bohon, of our own county, and Mr. Tyler, a New Englander, who never could catch step with the Kentuckians, as the term goes now, but who worked up a very large and successful boarding school in Pittsfield, Mass. One of the pupils in one of these schools, I do not remember which, was Monroe Edwards, a very celebrated forger that figures in western detective stories; and years after in the preparatory, I believe, of Bacon College, we had of the same ilk, Sam Berry, the one armed guerilla that kept fearful people awake during the days that tried men's souls as also women's, during the late active misunderstanding between north and south.

After these, I can not trace a clear succession of schools, especially for boys. But I know the first generation of Kentucky men, at least professional men, had as good classical educations as their college bred sons, i. e. had Mathematics, Greek and Latin for their courses. Natural science was ignored, and the general intelligence of each individual depended a good deal on observation and contact with other men and precarious access to books. Newspapers, magazine, etc, did not lend as now their very superficial ready plating to all kinds and often very cheap metal.

There was Fry's Academy in Mercer, and a classical academy in Jessamine, and another in Nelson, in whose halls the prominent lawyers of Kentucky took their finishing course, of which tradition names the Alma Maters of the Breckinridges, Crittendens, Thompsons, Daviesses, Hardins, Rowans, though probably some of the wealthier students went back to the old states for a diploma. The first schools of this classical grade in Mercer county were taught by foreigners. Notably among these was M. Gurin, a Frenchman, by whom the men of the second generation were taught; James Taylor, and his contemporaries, etc. Mr. Gurin taught French as well as the dead languages, and probably went out somewhat into the field of natural sciences, as I remember that a pair of globes which used always to adorn the desk of the best school in the village, had been a part of the apparatus bought by the city fathers for his school.

After Gurin, Dr. Trapnal imported an educator named Daley, under whom his numerous sons, several of the Marshalls, including the celebrated Tom, and his scarcely less known brother, Ed Marshall, as well as some of the boys of the village were educated.

Next in prominence as a male school was that of Dr. Polin, an Irish graduate of Dublin University, a very competent and successful teacher. At intervals, all along the line of descent from Gurin to the building of Bacon College, there were schools at which by resolute selfhelp the lords of creation might equip themselves for their sovereignty if they would, for good as schools may be, one fact is patent to all generations ,that men and women can only educate themselves. A sketch of

Centre College,

the first chartered literary institution of Mercer, has been given; and material for a fuller sketch had been furnished me of Bacon College and Kentucky University by President Williams, but somehow in the confusion of the late destructive fire which swept our village, it was misplaced. Before this serial takes book shape I hope to recover it and make the amende honorable to the Alma Mater for many prominent and useful men of the current day.

Bacon College.

Bacon College was organized at Georgetown, Ky., in 1836, under the presidency of D. S. Burnet and the patronage of members of the Christian Church. It was without endowment or property of any kind. The board of trustees soon offered to locate it permanently in that city or county which should pledge the highest or best foundation in the way of endowment and buildings. Through the exertions of Major James Taylor and other enterprising citizens of Mercer county, the college was finally removed to Harrodsburg in 1839, and placed under the presidency of James Shannon, aided by Prof. S. Hatch, M. D.; Prof. S. G. Mullins; Prof. H. H. White and Prof. G. W. Matthews, as faculty.

The institution was conducted for a few years in the building on College street at present owned and occupied as a residence by John Lafon. In the summer of 1843 the new edifice was ready, and commencement exercises were held in it for the first time. The buildings, planned and constructed by Maj. John G. Handy, stood in the center of the beautiful grounds now owned by Mr. George Alsop; they were destroyed by an accidental fire in February, 1864.

The endowment which had been secured for the institution was found to be wholly inadequate, encumbered as it was with scholarships made transferable; so that after several fruitless attempts to endow it properly by appeals to the members of the Christian Church in Kentucky, it was virtually suspended in 1850. During the twenty years of its career, it had accomplished much for the higher education of young men in Kentucky, and throughout the South—and many of our most useful men claim with reasonable pride, Bacon College as their Alma Mater. But of its earliest class of alumni but few are living; of the first class that graduated—1842—only John B. Bowman survives, and of the second class—1843—only John Aug. Williams; while of the noble old faculty, all are gone save Prof. H. H. White, now of Lexington, Ky.

In 1855-56, John B. Bowman, then living on his beautiful farm of "Old Forest" in Mercer, began the work of resurrecting the College, making use of its endowment, amounting to only $9,500, as the nucleus of a University fund that should be adequate to the educational demands of the brotherhood and the State. Unwilling to make his appeal to the brethren of Kentucky until the citizens of Mercer, who were most interested, should show a proper zeal in the matter, he called on Maj. James Taylor to begin the work in that county. In a short time $30,000 was subscribed in cash notes, to which amount Mr. Bowman added $8,000 more by subscriptions obtained. With this amount pledged by Mercer, he went abroad, and in one hundred and fifty days he swelled the cash endowment of the new University to one hundred and fifty thousand dollars. After its resumption the College, under the title, changed to Kentucky University, had quite a prosperous career. Even during the war the bell rung in its fair attendance of students with unfailing punctuality. After the resignation of Mr. Shannon, the Rev. Mr. Milligan, a native of the Emerald isle and a graduate of Dublin University, filled the presidential chair with great acceptance, so long as it continued in Harrodsburg. In broad noon in January, 1867, the University was reduced to ashes.

Mr. Bowman, with his characteristic energy, commenced a fresh canvas for funds to rebuild the college, and succeeded so far as to feel authorized to bid for the old grounds of the Harrodsburg Springs that had been bought by the United States. Unfortunately he was over-bid by an irresponsible party, and thus passed from Harrodsburg this institution of untold value to the youth of our county. The contention and funds that sprang from the removal of this institution to Lexington, Kentucky, belong to the history of the Reformed church of Kentucky. The State has drawn out its stock and established the Agricultural College of Kentucky, and law has decreed the ownership of the Literary College to the Reformers. But one can hardly refrain from regretting that Regent Bowman was not allowed to carry out his magnificent conception of a University that had already drawn to its support several hundred students. After the destruction by fire of the buildings of Bacon College, by unfortunate management it was lost to our county, and for a long interval the opportunity for the education of our boys and girls was inadequate and unsatisfactory.

The Lincoln Cabin

J. Newton Prather, a native of our county and a graduate of Centre College and Transylvania Law School, kept steadily a classical school for boys, which has always and continues to sustain excellent reputation.

Lately the Presbyterian College, nearby the First Presbyterian church, which fell by division of property to the Second church, has been purchased by Mr. J. J. Hogsett, a gentleman of Centre College education and training in his profession. The common school is under Mr. Hogsett's care, and thus far his management of this institution has been eminently satisfactory and prosperous, and the town certainly owes thanks and patronage to the Professor for redeeming the handsome property from decay and unsightliness.

CHAPTER XXXV

Female Schools in Mercer County—Dr. and Mrs. Essex's School—Mrs. Holcomb and Miss Ben Ali—Spurill's and Peebles' Methodist Academies—Greenville — Presbyterian Academy — Daughters College — Common Schools—Female Schools.

To run a parallel page of the girls' schools is hardly possible except in a very desultory way. The elementary schools of early days and those immediately succeeding were generally mixed and of a very poor character, as I have said in the previous chapter; the mixed feature, however, not being objectionable to my mind, on the contrary the sexes exercise, I think, a reciprocally good influence, the girls refining the boys' rude natures, and the boys infusing by example a courage and endurance needed to strengthen female character. Yet there were favored eras in the line of female education. So far back as the beginning of this century, Dr. Essex, an Englishman, assisted by his wife, kept a boarding school in house now occupied by Nimrod Harris. (Now Ingram Garage corner.—Ed. Note). In this school the substantial base of an English education was given; "the three R's, Reading, Riting and Rithmetic," were three corner stones and English grammar the fourth, and as our modern advertisements set forth, "upon this foundation would be raised a splendid superstructure of accomplishments." I have a specimen of the fancy work of this school. It is fairly well done embroidery, of which cloth and floss were home made. It is a counterpane, snow white, and the work of a variety of beautiful tatting and lace or open stitches.

Next in line of prominent principals of female schools, came Mrs. Halcomb, from the east, accompanied by Miss Ben Ali, a lady of Turkish extraction, as her name indicates. She brought with her a piano and on county court days the street before the late residence of Dr. A. D. Price, when the school was located, was crowded as at a popular auction; the natives trying to catch a ravishing strain from the piano within. Miss Ben Ali remained with us a highly esteemed member of our society, as wife of Terrah Haggin, a member of our county bar, and mother of the young millionaire of California. This must have been a good school from the intelligence and social standing of the young ladies who had their training in it. The writer of this went through it as the clown said he did through college, "in at the front door and out at the back." Having leave from the ever indulgent Pater Familias of our household to enter this school, I reported one Monday morning; the roll had been called (prayers were not in the program) and a large class circled before the presiding vixen. About midway of the class stood the well grown son of fourteen of the principal; he stammered, floundered, failed. The teacher, his mother, rose, and planting a well aimed doubled fist blow that would have staggered Sullivan, felled him like an ox. With a yell that would have done no discredit to a warwhoop, I bounded over the bench, out of the door and, after a rapid run, fell panting on the home threshold. Whether this blow was given, with malice pretense, or in the heat of passion, or by the way of intimidation to the class, or as a part of the regular exercise of the school, I never had the nerve to inquire; but the school prospered and was solicited from one town to another, retaining its popularity until the principal (her courage rising with experience and success), undertook the sole management of one of creation's lords, and I have heard, made a success.

HISTORY OF MERCER AND BOYLE COUNTIES

After this, Mr. Eastman, a New Englander, went up as a teacher like a rocket in a blaze of glory and fell as suddenly and in as utter darkness.

Next, Mrs. Polen, wife of Dr. Polen, for awhile kept a school with occasional help from Mr. Smith, afterwards president of some Louisiana college.

Then Mr. Peebles, a minister of the Methodist church, had a full and and flourishing school, the chief impression of which left on my mind is, that it was a fair field of flirtation for the then college boys, one of whom now is a grave and reverend professor who does not much encourage similar divertisements in his well ordered classes.

Again, Mr. Spurill, of the same church, was in full tide of success when the memorable cholera of '33 swept over our village with the bosom of destruction; the days and nights of darkness and desolation, when from every house went up a cry as from Egypt when the Angel of Death touched with deadly wing the first born of every home from the lowly hovel to kingly palace. When the tolling bell brought the fasting and praying people to the sanctuary, Mr. Spurill's noble form bent lowly to lead in confession of sin and plea for mercy. A few days more the bolt had fallen on our doomed village; his flock was scattered, himself in the silent grave, and his accomplished and devoted wife so dazed with the suddenness and entireness of her bereavement, that I know not whether she ever had courage to gather up the broken threads of life and ply the shuttle more, in the darkened web.

Miss Dupey, only, of the corps of teachers was left, whose after successes entitle her to a place on the roll of notable women that we must hereafter give as a partial set off to the great overbalance of distinguished men we have found on our citizen registry.

The next female school in succession was headed by an accomplished member of the distinguished Tappans of New York, assisted by Miss Pomeroy, who was merged into Centre College by marriage with one of its professors, Mr. Nichols. Miss Tappan married Mr. Alfred Robertson, a young man of far more than ordinary intellect and attainments, who did not live to attain his goal, the pulpit.

This brings our best class of male and female schools abreast of the period when Bacon College was founded. Simultaneously Greenville Female College came into existence under the presidency of Samuel Mullins, an ex-Professor of Bacon College while it was located in Georgetown. This institution had quite a successful run. Many ladies of now middle age, and filling well their places in their homes, society and the churches, are living memorials of the efficiency of this school.

About this period the Presbyterian church, then an undivided body, built the Academy, now the property of J. J. Hogsett. This school was a decided success under Rev. John Montgomery, pastor of the church here, and now of the Synod of Missouri.

After he left it was spasmodically successful, and had some chiefs of more than mediocral ability.

Rev. Mr. Beck, afterwards Chancellor of the University of Richmond, Ky.; Dr. Reser, ex-professor of Centre College; Rev. Mr. Cook, now of Louisville, from time to time lifted this institution to the sunny heights of success. There were also several ladies of more than ordinary acquirements and executive ability, occupied its chairs. Miss Raymond, Miss Browning and Mrs. Jane T. Cross, of the number. This school finally went down as all deficiently endowed public institution are bound to do. Greenville was burned down, as has been the fate of almost every edifice of importance in Harrodsburg, and was rebuilt partially by the late Dr. C. E. Williams and John Augustus Williams, his son, then having ownership and charge of Columbia College, Missouri. It is mere justice to say there is not in the wide west, nor in the east, a better school than Daughters College; and I but underwrite the testimony of the most fastidious seekers after good schools I have ever met. The grounds are extensive and beautiful, so retired that the utmost freedom in exercise can be enjoyed in the green twilight of the shade in perfect privacy. The buildings are handsome, commodious and convenient, and kept in exquisite order. In fact, in all its appointments it is more like a well ordered home than any institution I have ever known, and this is saying much after a quarter of a century's intimacy in the establishment by one whose convictions are so strong against all but home schools. President Williams is ever ably seconded by a corps of competent teachers, chiefly of his own training, including teachers in modern language, art, music, and all accomplishments, and is himself without a rival as a teacher of Rhetoric and Belle Lettres. This school never missed a day during the war, and save two years of that time never had a vacant room. It is overflowing. It has graduated about 400 young ladies; about 100 of these are now teaching, and numbers have taught for years as assistants or presidents of their own schools.

The crowning merit of this college is that it yearly sends out free from its halls so many who have desired the benefits of education without the means to attain it.

Mr. Williams has likewise established a Mary Whittington scholarship in memoriam of a gifted lady who assisted in his school for years, on which a pupil is now and some one will ever be in training for teaching; board and tuition being at the expense of this institution.

Common Schools in Mercer County

Mercer enjoys the benefits of the common school system the state provides for all her children. But the provision is entirely inadequate to her needs. The terms are too short, the teachers overtaxed with numbers and underpaid for the amount of work required.

We have now in Judge Hughes a faithful and efficient Commissioner, and the rigid enforced selection of teachers by competent examination, is every year bringing up the teachers' qualification to a higher standard. Mercer county has fifty-one school districts; a school house in each district, of which a certain number each year are being enlarged and improved. We have fifty-three teachers; twelve of them are colored. There are 3,600 children of school age; of these 1,000 are colored; and this last class have every advantage the law provides for them. The average salary of the teachers is $25 per month.

The influence of the pulpit, press, and parental authority should be steadily exerted in behalf of popular education, the main hope for the perpetuity of republican institutions.

Art and Literature in Mercer.

Our notes under these heads must be meagre for these are the outgrowth of leisure and wealth. They do not spring spontaneously from a rich earth or even rich mental endowment. When they come at all in the rude stages of society, they are like the efflatus of prophesy or inspiration of poetry, a something that circumstances and surroundings cannot repress wholly. It was thus with Matthew H. Jouett, who was born in early days in Mercer and bred to the law. But opposition, discouragement and seemingly impending poverty could not wrench the pencil from his grasp. His genius was for portrait painting and the merit of his pieces were their naturalness, and he who owns a Jouett now ranges it on the wall with his copies of the gems from the old masters. He died in the prime of life. He was the son of John Jouett, put on record in these pages as a central figure in the Colonial Assembly of Virginia, delegate to the Constitutional Convention and other posts of honor in early times.

One of the artist's brothers, Capt. Jouett, fell on the battlefield of Perryville; one is a Commodore in the U. S. Navy, and his only living sister is the widow of the distinguished and lamented young statesman, Richard H. Menifee.

Joseph Bush

We claim, too, the successor to Jouett in fame. I know that his mother, Elizabeth Palmer, the sister of Mrs. Gen. Adair, lived with this sister and was married under the Governor's "auld roof-tree." I think they remained some years in Mercer, and afterward lived in Frankfort. Mr. Bush painted with Sully or West, and reflected credit on his master. The coloring of the few portraits of his I have seen is exquisite, and the likeness perfect as the reflection of a mirror. His style is of that smoothness that lately grades work very high, albeit to my uncultured taste it destroys largely the illusions of high relief.

Mr. William Clark,

of our city, has evinced a genius for scenic painting that needs but practice to place him in the front ranks of that branch of art. It is to be deplored that diffidence or want of ambition should withhold his hand from gathering the laurels that would be alike his own and our county's.

Paul Jones.

Although this young man has so lately overstepped the threshold of manhood and a master's studio, his progress in both painting and sculpture has been so rapid and successful that I cannot forbear placing his name on the scroll of fame now, that hereafter when his works hang high in our galleries, I may remind my readers of this and say, "I told you so."

The passion for these fascinating studies is growing to an excess that threatens to exclude solid and domestic branches from the curriculum of our girls' educations. Mrs. Zoe Norris, of the faculty of Daughters' College, and Miss Ovie Smedley, in her private studio, afford every desirable facility for the acquirement of these aesthetic branches, and there are few houses in which beautiful plaques, panels and banners do not brighten the walls, the work of daughter's deft hands. For music we have our own young professors, Aug. E. Williams and Lee Walters, not only ready to teach the facile fingers how to play, but who in leisure hours can give themselves to the mysteries of musical composition.

Literature.

The names of such of us as have been writers for newspaper and magazine articles, handbills, etc., are legion, but few have arisen to the standard of a book. Of these I note as near in succession and time as I can, Col. James H. Daviess: "Reflections on the State of the Country;" a political work of decidedly strong federal doctrines.

"History of the War of 1812," by Gen. Robert B. McAfee, valuable, but unfortunately now out of print.

Dr. J. J. Polk, of Perryville, published an autobiography of himself full of the reminiscenses of the quaint customs of old times.

Dr. C. C. Graham issued a volume of very peculiar views on religious subjects, which I think he mainly retracted in far abler papers in later days.

Dr. Landis, of Danville, has issued, it is said, some sterling theological works connected with the seminary.

Dr. Thomas Cleland also published several works of polemics, much valued and timely.

Nathan Rice was also one of our citizens at the time he did some of his most ponderous work.

Dr. Nelson, too, belonged to Danville in his palmy days of preaching and writing. "Cause and Cure of Infidelity," was his best known book, and

President John Aug. Williams gave a valuable contribution to his church's literature in "The Life of John Smith," one of the noted religionists of his day.

"The History of Highland County, Ohio," by Judge James H. Thompson, of Hillsboro, formerly of Mercer, is a very full and complete local history.

Women of Mercer

Having all my life looked upon women as merely a kind of moon that shown by the reflected light from their husbands, I feel that I have erred in not giving the name of the wife of every man who has been mentioned in this history, giving her thus her just participation in his honors, if a place in this memorial may be called that. This unluckily being an afterthought I must look around for the few who have by their own strength lifted their names to the sunny heights, and of these the most have been strangers and sojournrs.

Miss Dupey came here in the corps of teachers brought by Rev. Mr. Spurill, whose life and school perished in the plague of '33. She was a native of Norfolk, Virginia, of fine personnel, of very considerable talent, brave and persistent as a man, yet lacking none of the distinguishing gentleness and fidelity of a woman. Imagination was her most brilliant gift. She published at fourteen a very readable novel, and to old age always commanded a place in the best magazines of the land, and the New York Ledger is, I understand, reproducing many of her stories. She wrote "The Conspirator," the best of all her works, while living in Harrodsburg. She had been intimate with a novelist of national celebrity, and had shown him the "argument," as the play-wrights call it, of her fourthcoming novel. To her dismay she very soon saw announced from his literature a romance covering this very same ground, Burr's conspiracy, whereupon she wrote immediately to her freebooting friend that if he did appropriate her plot, she would denounce him to the whole literary world. He apologized and withdrew.

Mrs. Florence Anderson Clark

was also a native of Virginia, and resided and wrote here, as the wife of our accomplished and gentlemanly journalist, the editor of our local paper, The Kentucky People. Mrs. Clark's contributions, both prose and poetry, were a marked feature of the paper and she published a quite interesting novel. She has been a continuous writer, I understand, since her change of home, but I am not posted in the names or kind of literature in which she has been engaged. Her answer to "The Moneyless Man" and "Simm's Sword," just now rise most vividly to my memory. Years ago Capt. Clark cast his lot with Texas, where he shines in the legal profession and she gathers the laurels of literature.

Mrs. Jane T. H. Cross

was the oldest daughter of Judge Christopher Chinn, of this place. She had every educational advantage the state afforded and availed herself of them fully, continuing through her life the culture of her mind, and to practice the accomplishments she acquired at school. She married early her very talented and accomplishtd kinsman, James Hardin, the most thoroughly educated man of his age in Kentucky, and rising steadily through politics to a plane where few could have stood beside him, he died ere mid-age. She subsequently married Dr. Cross, then a prominent Methodist, now an Episcopalian minister.

It is probable Mrs. Cross wrote for newspapers and magazines from her girlhood, but her writings never took shape as I am aware until her return from Europe, when her letters from abroad were collected and published, and she also published "Azile" and some other stories; but sweet as any the "Buds and Blossoms," contributed to juvenile literature. Mrs. Cross

was early a Christian, but in her mature years grew more devout and was
a most self-denying and fervent follower of our Blessed One.

Mrs. Nellie Marshall McAfee

was a daughter of Humphrey Marshall of that historic family that stars
the records of Virginia and Kentucky. I am not aware how early Mrs. McAfee became a devotee to the pen. She married under romantic circumstances, and came to Harrodsburg the bride of our handsome and talented
young representative in the Legislature, John McAfee. She published while
among us, "Dan Bixler's Mill," and "As by Fire," and the last named ranks
among the best productions of her facile and fertile pen.

We lost Mr. and Mrs. McAfee in the bar and journalistic field of Louisville; there I believe she finds abundant and remunerative literary work.

Mrs. H. D. Pittman, of St. Louis, Mo., in the past year or two has
issued some dramas and been fairly successful. She has certainly been the
first lady venturer into that field, in the United States. "Manette," "Ravencliff," "The Little Princess" and some spectacular plays have been her most
successful works.

Of beauties we have had several who have taken places in the newspaper
galleries of art and we had some celebrities who have shown in our state
and national capitals and several who had currency even in the courts of
Europe. But by adhering rigidly to our intention of only giving the names
of those connected with the facts and dates of history, I find a host of
our fairest women and best men of our county left outside of this official
circle, and feel to deal full justice to Mercer there will have to be yet written the annals of our folk and their families.

The Press of Mercer County

There is no branch of Mercer literature about which so much curiosity
and interest has been manifested, and on no subject have I so vainly sought
precise information. I give the list of papers and the names of editors
that I can recall, assisted by Mr. Head, of the Harrodsburg Democrat office
now, and who has been always connected with journalism here or elsewhere.

The first paper of which I learn was The Rising Sun, edited by Anthony Hunn, a German physician. He had a good knowledge of natural
science and I think advocated in the press and pulpit some religious eccentricities.

The Eclectic Magazine

A chiefly literary venture by Uriah P. Randal, Its existence was brief,
the conception being in advance of the time. A family paper with a poet's
and story teller's corner would have filled the widest wishes of the community better.

Since then we have had a succession of locals varying with the ability
of the editor. We have had occasionally an independent paper, but generally
partisan and we have had sometimes a representative journal of both parties at the same time. I do not pretend to give a regular succession of papers or editors.

Watch Tower, by Tanner; Americans, by Jesse Head; Union, By Dr. C.
L. Jones; Plow Boy, by Gibbons; Kentucky Press, by Van B. Carter; Kentucky People, by Capt. James B. Clark; Signal, by John Woods; Observer,
by John C. Thompson; Observer-Reporter, by Nield & Grimes; Observer and
Reporter, by E. H. Gaither and C. Hardin, Jr.; Enterprise, by L. D. Cardwell; The Citizen, by W. K. Cardwell; Harrodsburg Democrat, by F. D.
Spotswood. The Pierian was a bright little fountain the college boys kept
up for a while, but as each little rill wandered off on its own way so soon as
the honors of graduations were won, it naturally ceased playing.

CHAPTER XXXVI

Churches of Mercer County—First Sermon in the Fort—First Organization of a Church at Cane Run by the Presbyterians—Its History to the Centennial Celebration '83—The Baptist Churches—Shawnee Run, Etc.—Names of Some of the Ministers—Roman Catholic Church—Father Baden—Location of the Chapel.

Before whatever there was of religious sentiment amongst the pioneers, organized into separate churches, there was an occasional wayfaring messenger of the Gospel passed through and preached in whatever there was opened to him, and to whomsoever it concerned to listen to him.

The very first sermon ever preached in Mercer county was by the Rev. John Lythe, of the Church of England; and doubtless the faithful held in each other's rooms prayer and song service during Fort life, but "The groves were God's first Temples," as the poet has beautifully worded it for the express fitness of such chapter heads as these, and in the grand primeval forests of Kentucky all sects first held their services. Later log houses similar to the pioneer homes were used, serving for meeting and school house and sometimes for magistrate's courts.

Camp meetings were an institution indulged in by all the churches after the Indian dread was lifted from the people's minds. In the course of years these were chrystalized into woods meetings, so services were held for successive days in the woods, but tents and night accommodations were dispensed with private hospitality superceding the necessity for these. The Methodists have never given up camp meetings, and of late years all denominations seem disposed to revert to them and nothing is more common than to see camp meeting bills posted with attractive colors, and excursion rates advertised, as for political mass meetings.

The purpose for which those masses professedly came together was the same that gathers them now; viz: to worship God, but the outward surroundings, and the inner conduct of these assemblies strike one, in whose memory they can be compared, as appreciably different, and if I may be allowed to give the verdict, it is decisively in favor of modern improvements. Horseback being the only mode of travel there would be around a popular meeting place acres of these artless, stamping, neighing creatures, keeping up a general noise and unquietness. Thirst too, seemed to be an epidemic trouble in those days, and between the house and the spring out of doors; and the seats and the bucket of water that sat on the pulpit stairs, there was an incessant passing to and fro to satisfy that seemingly unquenchable want. Then, too, every nurse in the settlement came on in her gay towering turban with her little nursling to claim its mother's kind offices during sermon. The average sermons, too were longer and the music, well—I do not wish to touch a subject so generally productive of discord as church music, but I must say that I have rarely heard a choir, especially if somewhat overtoned by an organ, that I have not thought an improvement on the lining out by a clerk and a simultaneous struggle of all the parts for the leadership in the tune.

There used to be more apparent fervor of spirit and more vigorous practical testimony against worldliness in the churches than now. But the growth of the crowning grace of Christianity, charity, as testified by a more generous support of the gospel at home; more zeal and liberality in spreading it abroad; and the rise of numberless institutions of charity all over the

HISTORY OF MERCER AND BOYLE COUNTIES

land, speaks loudly of the increased power of Christianity over the lives of its professors. After all pocket measure is the severest test of sincerity of faith.

About the beginning of this century there prevailed widely in the southwest of this state a very remarkable phase of religious experience, or involuntary manifestations of feeling. These exercises consisted of violent contortions of the body, dancing, jerking and shooting sometimes terminating in a kind of cataleptical condition that lasted for hours. That much of it was an infectious sympathy and some affectation, was certain, but the subjects of it belonged to all churches and that with many these manifestations were involuntary is equally sure. It was a curious study that no psychologist of that day mastered satisfactorily.

The organization of the very first Presbyterian church in Kentucky was undoubtedly in Mercer county. Dr. Cleland, for many years the pastor of these churches, claimed that Cane Run, now Harrodsburg, was the first. Dr. Davidson, the historian of Presbyterianism, says that in 1785, by advice of Hanover Presbytery of Virginia, Cane Run, now Harrodsburg, was built.

Danville (Concord) and Salt River New Providence, were simultaneously put into being.

Dr. David Rice, of Virginia, a Presbyterian clergyman, came here, lured like other emigrants for rich, low priced lands for his numerous family, but did not invest. He preached while here as opportunity offered. Three years later a call with three hundred signatures, was sent him; his Presbytery advised his acceptance of it as a promising missionary field. The father of Col. Joseph H. Daviess led a horse into Virginia and brought him out. He held for a long time the three first organized churches in charge and has been usually called Father Rice, holding that honored relation to the Presbyterian Church in Kentucky. He resigned from failing health in 1798. He was succeeded after an interval of three years by Rev. Samuel Robinson, who was pastor during the great revival season of the first of this century. He was succeeded by Rev. Thomas Cleland, who was pastor of Harrodsburg and New Providence from 1813 for 26 years, then relinquishing Harrodsburg, resided on his homestead near Providence, and going in and out before his people to the close of his honored, useful and laborious life. The labors of his tongue and pen would fill many volumes. His house was the school of the prophets from which, beside two sons, he sent out a number of useful and some distinguished ministers.

Dr. John Montgomery, of Irish descent and Princeton training, succeeded Dr. Cleland. He was wise, faithful and beloved. The building now occupied by Mr. J. J. Hogsett, is a memorial of the people's vain effort to retain him.

Mr. Sherrill, of Mississippi, succeeded him as a supply, and was followed by James V. Logan in 1860, who was the exemplary minister of the then united Church during the stormy period of the rebellion. He continued to preside over the Southern church until 1868. He then edited the True Presbyterian, until called to Central University, and in its presidential chair finds the station for which his talents and training eminently fit him.

Mr. H. Harrison, a native of Harrodsburg, was unanimously called to succeed Mr. Logan, and after a few years resigned to accept a call to a large and prosperous congregation in Knoxville, Tennessee.

Dr. Montgomery again served the church a brief period and was followed by the call of the present pastor, J. J. Chisholm. That his congregation is satisfied with him is shown by a unimous protest against his resignation, lately offered, testifies unequivocally.

The foregoing is a history of both Presbyterian churches to the date of division, and of the First church to the present date.

The Presbyterians of Mercer also have nice houses of worship and thriving, active churches at New Providence, Salvisa, Kirkwood, Mount Pleasant, and Mud Meeting House. The last church is occupied in common by both branches of Presbyterians and served alternately by the pastors of both the Assembly and Southern churches. These people have held a prayer meeting for sixty years weekly without a single omission.

This is the common history of both the First and Second Presbyterian churches of Harrodsburg, in fact, the history of Presbyterianism in Mercer county for near the first half century of its existence.

The first house of worship of this church was a log cabin erected in 1784 on the land of Capt. Idur Haggin, now owned by Mr. True, and was called Cane Run for a stream that runs near by. It is about three miles east of Harrodsburg and can be seen from the cars, being identified by the old burying ground. In two years the congregation built on the same site a neat frame church, in which Father Rice and Mr. Robinson preached. In 1816 the church concluded, on account of Harrodsburg's centrality, to worship in town. First they occupied the old stone Court House, as did all preachers of any denomination that came. In 1818 a building in partnership with the trustees of the town—a school house during the week days, a church on Sunday—was built on the old Fort Hill. This before it was finished was razed by a violent storm. A sermon was preached by Dr. Cleland on "The King said unto Nathan, the prophet, see now, I dwell in a house of cedar, but the ark of God dwelleth within curtains," so aroused the people that they proceeded at once to build a comfortable brick church on South Main street, which was dedicated November 26th, 1920. This was enlarged in 1853 by subscriptions, but chiefly by the princely liberality of William Thompson, then an elder in this church, now a resident of Palatka, Florida. It was dedicated in 1854 by Dr. E. P. Humphrey, then professor in the Danville Theological Seminary. This house was used as a hospital for wounded Union soldiers from the battle of Perryville. When the congregation divided by an amicable settlement this property was sold publicly in 1872 and was bought by the Southern Presbyterian church. By general subscription of the members and the special liberality of Mr. Isaac Pearson, Dr. James H. Moore and Mr. Thomas C. Coleman in the centennial of its existence, this church was externally and internally repaired, changed and beautified in a style equal to any inland church in the state; the ladies of the church assuming the expense of furniture, etc., amounting to near $2,000; the whole cost of this work was about $6,000. The second Presbyterian church, adhering to the old General Assembly, occupies a building on Poplar street. The church has been built, burned and rebuilt since the division of '71, and is now up to the standard of artistic taste. It has always been kept in active and healthful condition and has had a succession of useful pastors, and in any interval between these, supplies itself from the ministerial force of Centre College.

Rev. Messrs. Torrance, Henderson and McKee are the succession of ministers that I remember.

CHAPTER XXXVII

Churches of Mercer County, Continued—Methodist—Episcopal—Northern Methodist—Baptist—Reformers or Christian Church—St. Philip's Episcopal Church—Churches of Colored People.

(Knowing that the history of the churches would be more valued than any chapter of this serial, I had secured full notes from Mr. Polk, of the Methodist church; President Williams, of the Reformed, and permission from Mr. Chisholm, of the Presbyterian church, to use his Centennial for this issue and had prepared carefully whatever I could collect concerning the other churches, but an unusual pressure of advertisements and other matter made it necessary for the Democrat's convenience for me to condense these chapters, which will be given in full in book form to be published hereafter.—Authoress).

The Methodist Episcopal Church was the next regular organization in Harrodsburg, and for many years Danville and Harrodsburg were one station on the conference record.

The pioneer preachers of this church, ever self-denying, active and missionary in its spirit and policy, were the Rev. William Holman, local preacher; Mr. Deike, as circuit rider, his co-adjuter, and Mr. Adams, presiding elder.

This church began its career as did the Presbyterian, and indeed all other churches, in the Court House, the upper story of which it soon and long filled with fascinated crowds.

The present Baptist church was soon after built for general uses—the Methodists, perhaps, by larger subscription securing a stated use of it semi-monthly. The present commodious, convenient edifice on Chiles street was dedicated in '41, and has its cozy parsonage close by.

The policy of this church which changes its pastor so often, renders it impossible in the limits of this serial to do justice to the long line of worthy and devoted men who have occupied this pulpit in more than a half century. The names of Taylor, Adams, James and Perry occur as presiding elders.

Akers, Stemper, Jameson, Stevenson, Deering, Hinkle, Huston, Ralston, Lynch, Letton, Buckner and Merritt, form at least a part of the long line, and none will deem it invidious to mention the name of the late Bishop Kavanaugh as towering head and shoulders above them all—Saul, the son Kesh, above the Israelites.

Mr. Redd served this church with peculiar acceptance last year, but the tendrils broken by his removal must soon attach themselves to a person of the marked geniality of his successor, Mr. Henderson.

One of the most memorable periods in this church's history was when Maffit, the national Methodist revivalist, held from its pulpit, this town, spell bound for six weeks by the marvelous sweetness of his songs and the elegance of his elocution.

The Centennial Methodist Church

occupied a conspicuous position on Main street, fronting below it the site from which was burned Capt. Samuel Daviess' family residence. It was a handsome edifice and it did seem a pity that this silent monitor, ever pointing the toiling world below to a higher, purer life to which it might aspire, should be removed. This church was built in part from the immense Centennial fund the Methodists collected during the anniversary year, and partly by private subscription.

It was reared more as an expression of loyalty to the government than from religious necessity; for the separation between Northern and Southern

Methodism had been peacefully made by the Methodist National Conference, and settled by geographical lines long before the war burst.

The Northern Methodist Extension Society held a lien on this property for money loaned for its erection. When L. D. Cardwell secured it, he converted the church into an Opera House, which was described among the public and private buildings of the town, and it is now used by him for commercial purposes.

The Christian or Reformed Church.

By courtesy of Rev. W. T. Corn I learn that this church has in this county a membership of about 1,200, and five resident preachers.

It has organized churches at the following points: Cane Run, Salvisa, Cornishville, Ebenezer, Berea, Liberty and Antioch. The church building of this denomination in Harrodsburg is on Main street, opposite the Commercial House. It is a commodious building with a gallery in the rear and lecture room and baptistry in the basement and is comfortably furnished.

This church is a religious body, the coalescence of the followers of Barton W. Stone, who with a considerable body of followers made a departure from the Presbyterian faith in the early part of this century, and of the Reformers of the Baptist church, who adopted the now widespread views of Alexander Campbell.

The concession of the right of every member of this church to preach, at first brought very uncertain sounds from their pulpits. But the establishment of the supremacy of the Bible over all human opinions as the foundation of faith and practice, worked its legitimate fruit of purification, and it has receded to the plane and practice of the most evangelic Christianity.

The directorship of the chief Female School and ownership of Bacon College gave this church preponderent influence at one time in this county, and time has brought us all down to the common rock bottom of real merit.

Baptist Church

We know that the Baptists were among the pioneer churches, and preachers who came to Mercer county. I regret that I could not procure a history worthy of it from its members. I lived under the eaves of Shawnee Run meeting house and remember when it was the most popular gathering place in Mercer county, and its longtime minister, John Rice, the most apostolical looking man of his generation. He probably received into the congregation over which he presided more members than any other man in the state. I do not remember the date of the building of the Baptist church in Harrodsburg. It was built by subscription for general use and called the Republican church. Its construction was the best in town and on the same plan much used now in the architecture of city churches. The entrance was from the front each side of the pulpit; the floor rose gradually so as to give each hearer a clear view of the speaker, the pews facing the pulpit and the front doors. It had pointed windows which lighted above as well as below the galleries which extended around three sides of the house, and on occasions of interest would be packed to their utmost capacity. This church since it has passed into the hands of the Baptists has undergone complete change, while one cannot but regret the lost style of the old building we can compliment the energy and liberality that has had a succession of able pastors, Vaughn, Harvey, Lorimer and Tupper, and is now served by Mr. Mullins.

The Baptists have beside at Harrodsburg, churches at Shawnee Run, Mt. Moriah, Unity, Lyceum, Benton, Bruner's Chapel and Deep Creek.

St. Philip's Episcopal Church.

The foundation and growth of this church has been watched by sympathetic natures with interest, and all were bound to admire this brave little congregation's struggles to hold its ground in which no seed of this church had been originally sown.

The building is considered by architectural connoiseurs a gem. It had the first stained glass windows used in this town, though now the indispensible completion of all of our lately constructed church. Those of the Episcopal church were the gift of the late Ben C. Trapnel, in memoriam of his late father and mother who were devoted members of this church.

This congregation was organized into a parish in 1858 by the Rev. M. F. Maury, rector of Trinity Church, Danville. It was then placed in care of Rev. Mr. West, General Agent of the Diocesan Missions. Mr. Venable followed, and with unflagging energy went about the collection of a church fund which finally took shape in the present building.

The corner stone of this church was laid by Rev. Bishop Smith in '60, and was opened for Divine service in the autumn of '61. Having been finally relieved of debt by the special liberality of the late Ben C. Trapnal, of this place, and of Mr. John Robinson, of Christ's Church, it was dedicated by Right Rev. G. D. Cummins, 29th of October, 1872. Since then the following rectors have had charge of the church: Reverends J. H. Bowlin, R. C. Talbot, E. W. Gilliam, W. F. B. Jackson, J. Gibson, D. P. Goodloe, A. Buchanon. Mr. Venable resuming his connection, was followed for a brief time by Mr. Stanberry, of Lexington, and he by Rev. Mr. Sutton, who resigned in '84, leaving the church temporally and spiritually in prosperous condition.

Lately the services of Rev. Mr. DeLearsay have been secured, who brings the character of deep piety and most scholarly attainments.

The Catholic Church

This church has always been extremely missionary in its spirit and it would be hard to find a mountain so lofty, a valley so lowly that the footsteps of a Catholic priest had not trod it. While at school at Nazareth I met Mr. Baddon, one of the first priests that had ever come to these western wilds. He told me, what I have since found corroborated by history, that a large number of Catholics had been in the first influx of populations in Mercer county. He had spent considerable time here in ministering to this wilderness flock before he went to the northwest. He was very venerable looking then and very courteous and intelligent. The first public religious services of the Catholic church ever held in Harrodsburg were held in the ball room of the Harrodsburg Springs by the Rev. Mr. Ryan, of the St. Rose Literary Society. The church then bought of Dr. Graham the property that now stands in the corner of the intersection of Chiles street and Perryville pike. The lot is a fine open one. The house affords a cozy home for resident priest and an extension of the building is fitted up and used as a chapel. On this lot is one of those wonderful cave stores of water that supplies the needs of scores of families.

Colored People's Churches

There are three churches belonging to this class of our citizens in Harrodsburg, and also others at several points in the county. The Baptist on Water street is quite roomy, has its yard and baptistry and is well furnished with pews, carpet, organ and chandeliers. It has a Sabbath School and supports its pastor. The Methodist church, South, is also on Water street on the east side of town. It is a very nice building, in good repair and well furnished and has hard by a comfortable house for the minister, who according to Methodist habits is changed at will by conference. The Northern Methodist church was rather the outgrowth of the imitation of white precedent than from any necessity for its existence. It is small and prematurely dilapidated, but has lately fallen into the hands of a devout woman who has resolutely dedicated it to the cause of education and religion.

CHAPTER XXXVIII

Men of Mercer Who Served in Various Local Offices—Governors—Lieutenant Governors—U. S. Senators—Foreign Ministers—State Senators—Members of House of Representatives—Judge—Circuit Judges—Clerks of the Circuit Courts — Commonwealth and County Attorneys and Commissioners.

I have given brief sketches of the lives of eminent military and civil officers who came here and resided as citizens; also of such as were reared here, and went to other places to fill posts of honor and usefulness. I give a list of those who continued with us, without remarks, merely for convenient reference to students of history, but do not attempt to record the time of their election.

Governors

Governors Greenup, Owsley and Letcher, had been citizens of Mercer county. Gabriel Slaughter from '16 to '20; John Adair from '20 to '24; Beriah Magoffin, elected in '59, resigned in '62.

Lieutenant-Governors.

Gabriel Slaughter elected in '16, became Governor by death of Governor Madison. Robert B. McAfee from '24 to '28; John B. Thompson elected in '53; he was elected U. S. Senator, and resigned as Lieutenant Governor; James Harlan was Secretary of State in Letcher's administration, and Nat. Gaither under Magoffin.

U. S. Senators

John Brown, John Adair and J. B. Thompson.

Foreign Ministers

T. P. Moore, to Republic of Colombia, South America, under General Jackson's administration; R. B. McAfee, Ecuador and Bolivia; R. P. Letcher to Mexico, 1849.

Members of the Legislature

of Virginia from Mercer county, Ky., were, in 1787 Mercer's first representatives, William McDowell and John Jouett.

From Mercer county, Thomas Allin and Alexander Robertson were members of the Virginia Legislature which ratified the present constitution of the United States. John Brown and James Harrod are found on another list, both of whom were then citizens of Mercer county.

The names of men residing in Mercer county all along the list of delegates who sat in the nine conventions that met in Danville, Samuel McDowell always president; Greenup, Speed, Willis Green, Harry Innis, Muter, Kennedy, John Brown and Jouett were there, but the members who signed the first constitution of Kentucky here Peter Brown, John Adair, Thomas Allin and Samuel Taylor. Under the first constitution senators were chosen by electors, and William McDowell, of Mercer, was one. Senators of the United States who have been sent by election of the Legislature since, were Brown, who had been but was probably not a resident of Mercer at the date of his election, and General Adair and John B. Thompson.

Mercer has furnished the following list of

Representatives to Congress:

Christopher Greenup, from 1792 to 1797; Thomas Davis, 1797 to 1803. Thence in broken succession, Adair, Letcher, T. P. Moore, Willis Green,

Kincaid, James Harlan, Milton Durham, Joshua Bell, John B. Thompson and Phil B. Thompson, were Mercer men sent to represent this district in Congress.

List State Senators

from Mercer county from first election under first constitution to present date: James Taylor, John Jouett, Jacob Frowman, Robert Mosby, Christopher Greenup, Harry Innis, Samuel McDowell, William McDowell, Robert Mosby, Gabriel Slaughter, Abram Chapline, John L. Bridges, Jere Briscoe, Robert McAfee, Sam McCoun, Samuel Daviess, John B. Thompson, Sr., J. A. Tomlinson, William Daviess, B. Magoffin, W .A. Hooe, James D. Hardin, J. Q. Chenoweth, D. L. Moore.

Members of the Legislature

Samuel Taylor, 1792, '93', '98; John Jouett, '92, '93; Jacob Frowman, '92, '93; Robert Mosby, '92; John Adair, '93, '94, '95, '98, 1800, '1, '3, '17; John Harrison, '93; Thomas T. Davis, '95, '92, '97; Thomas Barbee, '95, '96; Samuel Duval, '98; Christopher Greenup, '98; Gabriel Slaughter, '99, 1800; Jeremiah Briscoe, '99; ——— Ewing, '99; George Thompson, '99, 1804, '5, '6, '9; Jos. H. Daviess, 1800; General James Ray, 1801, '2, '3, '9, '10, '11, '12, '14, '15, '18; John L. Bridges, 1801, '3; William McDowell, 1802; William Sterling, 1804; Philip Trapnel, 1805, '6; General Robert B. McAfee, '10, '11, '12, '13, '14, '15, '20, '30, '32; George C. Cowan, '13; Samuel McCoun, —; James G. Birney, '15; John B. Thompson, '17, '35; Ed Worthington, '18; Thomas P. Moore, '19, '20; George C. Thompson, '20, '21, '40; John G. Allin, '21, '22, '25, '26; David G. Cowan, '21, '22; Samuel Daviess, '22, '24; William Robertson, '24; William Wade, '24, '25, '26; Joseph Haskins, '25, '26, '31, '33, '43, '44; Thomas Hale, —; T. T. Haggan, —; Joel P. Williams, '27; Robert C. Harrison, '28; Elias Tompkins, '28, '30; J. A. Tomlinson, '28, '29, '30; Charles Burton, —; Madison Worthington, '29; William Bohon, '31; Fred Lowlin, '32, '34, '35, '36; James Morgan, '33, '34; J. N. Bybee, '36; James Taylor, '37; Lud C. Cornish, '38, '39, '41; William Daviess, '38, '39, '48; Elijah Gabbard, '40, '53, '55, '61, '65; E. B. Owsley, '41; Joseph B. Renfro, —; J. J. Sweeney, '42; W. A. Hooe, '43, '49; John Lapsley, '45; Peter Jordan, '46; Ben C. Allin, '47; James Alexander, '50; Willis T. Chapline, '51, '53; Charles C. Smedley, '55, '57; Ben C. Trapnal, '57, '59; Corydon S. Abell, '59, '61; W. G. Conder, '65, '67; Beriah Magoffin, '67, '69; J. J. McAfee, '69, '73; Dr. Thomas Reed, '73, '74; Dr. John Powell, '75, '76; J. Charles Thompson, '77, '78; J. M. Duncan, '79, '80, '81, '82; J. W. Powell, '81, '82, '83, '84; Capt. P. B. Thompson, 85.

Mercer county furnished speakers for the Senate in the persons of Lieutenant Governors Slaughter, McAfee and Thompson. Her speakers in the House of Representatives were Adair, George C. Thompson, George Robertson, Robert P. Letcher, Guynn Page.

List of Circuit Court Judges

These offices were first appointive and lasted during good behavior. Judges Kelly and John C. Bridges held them under this tenure.

With the adoption of the second constitution nearly all offices became elective and are limited to a certain term of years; the parties being eligible to re-election. George W. Kavanaugh served two terms with an interval between, Judge Newman being the interlocutor. John C. Wickliffe following Kavanaugh's second term and Judge Charles Hardin, the present occupant of the bench.

County Judges were an institution of the second constitution, their duties having been previously exercised by a bench of magistrates called County Court; the oldest magistrate I think presiding and I think of this bench the successions of sheriffs was by some rule chosen.

County Judges

Capt. S. Daviess and Chris Chinn each I think served two terms and with Judge Edwards and Judge Wilson have filled the time since the court was an institution.

Clerks of the County.

The Allins, Major Thomas Allin and Phil T. Allin, his son, were circuit clerks while the office was appointive as also his oldest son, Thomas Allin, was county clerk before and after the office was made elective. Richard Board for a term of years has been circuit clerk and D. C. Abell held a clerkship for a number of years.

Commonwealth's Attorneys.

Our county has also furnished the circuit court a number of attorneys. The three John B. Thompsons held it not in straight succession, but at intervals. Phil B. Thompson, Sr., also was Commonwealth's Attorney from Mercer. The other incumbents, Schooling, Shuck and Noble, were from other counties.

Police Judges

I cannot give in succession but as they occur to my mind. Judge O. S. Poston, Col. C. E. Bowman, Haldon Grimes, William E. Keller, James Harlan, Thomas Hardin, John Kyle, Thomas Cardwell and the present occupant of the bench, John Hughes.

County Commissioners

We have had but three county commissioners, Judge C. S. Poston, Sanford McBrayer, John B. T. Daviess and now E. H. Gaither.

A list of professional and business men of Harrodsburg was brought in too late for publication in this issue and must, unfortunately, be omitted.—Ed. Democrat.

Old Graham Springs

CHAPTER XXXIX

Growth of Trade and Manufacturers in Mercer County—First Wool Carding Establishment—Robertson's Cotton Factory—Horse Mills—Water Mills, Steam Mills of Today—New Enterprises.

This, which should be one of the most interesting chapters of the history of Mercer county, must, by absence of facts, be one of the most meagre. Harrodsburg was the center of our county and the point from which it had its first growth; and picturesque as is its situation, it is cause of wonder that our practical forefathers should have selected so impracticable a position when they had the whole land before them, with all its rivers and other natural advantages of which they might have availed themselves in locating. For years and years to make on the farm what would purchase enough of groceries and store goods for the family, and for the merchant to sell enough goods to buy us wood, cheap supplies of provender and provisions from the country was about the whole commercial aim of country and town.

After a while some more speculative and enterprising spirits took up the flat boat system, in which (as such crafts never stemmed the current) they of course drifted southward; and then the boats were left with their cargoes at the El Dorado, and the steersman and his hands had to walk back some fifteen hundred miles. I have known men who have repeatedly performed this feat; and many amongst us can recall the tall, gaunt figure of Capt. Jack Cardwell, always on our streets "town meeting days" until within the past few years. This pilgrimage from New Orleans was a kind of annual recreation of his; and on one return trip it is said he walked seventy miles from about Russellville to Harrodsburg by sunset; and that finding when he reached home a physician was needed, walked back to Harrodsburg for him, thus adding about eight miles or ten to his day's journey.

This flat boat trade to New Orleans did not prove a bonanza to our farmers, but gave some outlet to the surplus products of farms; but men's fortunes were wrecked on them as on Cunards of today. I knew a speculator of this kind who lost in such a voyage the land on which Crab Orchard stands, a fine Mercer farm, a score of slaves, and still damaged badly some of his securities. He was to the sunset of his life one of the poorest men I have ever known. The work of his own two hands was was inadequate to the support of a large family, and the retrieval of his fortunes, and he died according to the sage's enunciation, "the noblest work of God," an honest man.

The increase of trade in Mercer continued for many years to be just the increased wants of professional and mechanical citizens filled by a farming community growing larger every year.

With the coming of steam boats to our western waters, our brave hearts made superhuman exertions, through horse power attached to wagons, to avail themselves of these improved commercial facilities; and that unwieldy, unsightly land barge, the road wagon, with its swaying, white-covered bows, was all along the roads between trade points such as Louisville, Lexington and Maysville.

The Cotton Factory.

Dr. Robertson's cotton factory was one of the earliest and most extensive manufacturing ventures made in Mercer county. It was located in Harrodsburg, as was everything of the kind in early days. Most adults of our town now remember the large, many storied brick building that stood at the entrance of the Chinn lawn, which property Dr. Robertson owned and improved. Dr. Robertson was of Scotch descent, educated and energetic, and successful in his profession, but by a sanguine temperament led into schemes far ahead of his times, to the detriment of his fortune, which was vast for that day. Calculating the then almost impassable cliffs of Kentucky river would give him a monopoly of raw cotton south of that barrier, he made extensive and expensive arrangements for business; did excellent work, and paid high wages for labor, importing his manager from England or the East, I do not remember which. The turnpike, made twenty years after, giving easy access to the markets north of the Kentucky river would have shattered all of these plausible calculations; but long ere this, the invention of some new machinery in Old or New England, at once undermined the usefulness of existing works, and wrecked the fortunes of many who had invested their whole capital in such ventures.

Dr. Robertson kept a factory for a while, on a smaller scale, on the farm now owned by Mr. Redwetz, a mile east of Harrodsburg, which was of very great convenience in supplying spun cotton to the manufacturers of domestics in the country. The old factory was used for a long time as a carriage repository for Mr. Seller's work, but was finally taken down and incorporated in other buildings; and thus was removed an interesting milestone of Mercer progress.

The first factories of any kind that I remember, were the

Wool Carding Machines

of Messrs. Fairman and Woods. They were not partners, but living one at the base of the Old Fort Hill, the other on his old homestead, now the property of his grandson and namesake, Archie Woods; and of which Litsey avenue is a part. This machinery was moved by horsepower and I think worked on a tread-mill.

Where our people got their bread stuffs in these days I cannot remember, but from handmills, I know, in pioneer days, for history records the use of such mills at both Harrod's and McAfee stations.

The next advance was to the use of horse mills, where one used his own, or the miller's horses, in grinding and paid him toll accordingly. I presume these mills were profitable, for I remember a woman who always looked to the possession of a horse mill as a sure provision that she needed to have for the "rainy day" or widowhood.

Water mills were presently built, not enough in number for years to supercede the horse mills. I remember a lawsuit kept up for a long time between two neighbors, the dam of the mill having backed up the water so as to destroy the usefulness of a cave spring and dairy.

Steam Mills,

for both lumber and grist are now common through the county, many of them, however, being only steam attachments that are adaptable to the mills to be used in dry seasons when the water power fails. The first

Steam Mill

built in Harrodsburg, and probably in the county, was that of Merrill Williams, where Chiles street bridges the town creek. It has changes hands a good ma~~es. and is now the property of Mr. H. C. Williams, has patent attachme: :anufacturers flour for exportation.

Marimon & Son

came to Harrodsburg many years ago and located on the corner long occupied by Marimon & Robards, and now by Marimon & Son. At first they owned and operated a wool factory including spinning and weaving. They also manufactured machinery for similar establishments; and there are now doubtless mills running in the West the machinery of which passed through Louisville and St. Louis from our village.

By a good providence in changing their location they chose a spot not a stone's throw from there the Southwestern depot was afterward located; and they have in the completeness of their works and capacity of their houses, every possible facility for the manufacture of wool and wheat for commercial purposes.

Carriage Factories

Somewhere, I should think, in the thirties Sellers & Company established a successful shop in Harrodsburg, turning out all their work in good style. Firms in this business have been numerous; John Q. Marimon surviving them all, whose work rolling all around and so often decorated with blue ribbons, needed no praise. By the death of Mr. Marimon this factory has passed into the hands of George Bohon & Company, whose motto is "Excelsior," and who will wear it justly if untiring persistent energy compasses its aims.

Mr. Ben Mills' Gun Shop

has been for a long time a noted point in our village. In the old days when Graham Springs brought such crowds to Harrodsburg, his shooting gallery was as attractive to the chevaliers of the South as ever was a lady's boudoir to a troubadour, and Mr. Mills' guns are doubtless now heirlooms in many houses of the land. His skill had the endorsement, too, of government appreciation. He was appointed to the superintendence of the Harper Ferry Armory. He was amongst the first jostled out of position by the concessions of North and South. He was at Harper's Ferry at the time of the raid of the celebrated John Brown. and being of decided Southern sympathies resigned and returned to his old home in Harrodsburg. Mr. Mills was a Canadian by birth, but is a wholly naturalized Kentuckian and still peerless in his work.

The introduction of steamboats on Kentucky river, especially after the locks and dams were made, lengthening the season of navigation, had a perceptible influence on the trade of our county. But the establishment of railroad communication by connection with the Cincinnati, New Orleans & Texas trunk line has removed the last commercial disability under which our town labored. The increased facilities for transportation have worked a wonderful change in the spirit of our people and new industries are springing up everywhere around us.

John B. Thompson's distillery was the next large manufactory built after the flouring mills, and for a while seemed to consume all the grain and labor of the county. The original plain, common building was burned after brief service, but was immediately replaced by a very commodious, complete and costly establishment. All machinery and fixtures necessary for convenient running, from telephone to tower, have been installed, and its productive capacity was very large. By a glut from over-production, and the operation of United States Revenue laws, this manufacturing was stopped, but the building is altogether too large, complete and convenient to railroad transportation to lie idle. Since this was written it has resumed work as a distillery.

Tobacco Factories

In the times of our county towns, we used always to have small establishmen where cigars were made and tobacco put up in simple, merchantable form. There are none now, but such an industry must naturally follow on such extensive cultivation of this crop as has been practiced this year.

Except flouring mills on every available stream, and one or two now disused distilleries, there have been no manufactories reported to me. The Shakers have always had fine flouring mills and there are some new industrial establishments which will be found under head of Burgin.

CHAPTER XL

Men of Mercer—Pioneers That In Other Places Were Prominent and Useful —Bowmar—Bowman—Dunn, Etc.—Citizens and Natives of Mercer That Had Military Service and Mention in Other Fields—Gen. Rosseau—Gen. Birney, Major Rue—Colonels Fry, Tompkins and Worthington — Captains Jones and Thompson.

Robert Bowmar,

with his wife and son, Herman, then 10 years of age, emigrated from Virginia in 1779 and settled at Bowman's Station in Mercer (See Collins' History of Kentucky, Vol. 2, p. 766). The family remained in Mercer for ten years, removing to Woodford in 1789, where some of its descendants still reside. Robert Bowmar was in the battle of Blue Licks, and was one of those fortunate ones who escaped alive. His son, Herman, in 1780, at the age of 11, made three trips to the Falls of the Ohio (now Louisville) for corn, riding one horse and leading another.

Herman Bowmar became a leading citizen of Woodford, held the office of magistrate, sheriff, and was twice returned to the State Senate.* He served in three campaigns against the Indians and was in the battle of Fallen Timbers, fought near Toledo, August 20, 1794, where Wayne crushed the Indians and put a stop to their incursions upon Kentucky. Major Bowmar was in that campaign, adjutant of Gen. Robert Todd's brigade. He died in 1855, aged 86. His grandson, Daniel M. Bowmar, is now editor of the Woodford Sun, at Versailles.

*See Collins', Vol. 2, p. 764.

Williamson Durr

was born the 25th of December in the then district of Kentucky, which by subdivision finally became Mercer and now is Boyle. His mother, Ellen Brewster, and his father, Samuel Dunn, were both of Scotch-Irish descent and of the most rigid type of Presbyterians.

Samuel Dunn fought in the bloody battle of Point Pleasant and afterwards in the Revolutionary war. He removed to Kentucky at its close in the autumn of the hard winter in 1780, and had thus his share in climatical suffering and the dangers of Indian warfare. Their home was near Crow's station in the vicinity of Danville. The day of Kentucky's admission into the Union, his son, Williamson Dunn, the subject of this sketch, was married in the house of the bride's grandfather, Col. William McKee, to Miriam Wilson. Her grandmother, a McKee, and an own cousin of Col. W. R. McKee, of Buena Vista fame and bloody fate, had been killed by the Indians.

Williamson Dunn, in advance of his day, was a practical emancipationist and left Kentucky for the free soil of Indiana, taking his inheritance of slaves with him, thereby freeing them. He was a man of remarkable physique, strength and courage and served by appointment of President Madison, an active and efficient officer in the Range, a very valuable wing of the Western Territorial army. By appointment of Gen. Harrison he was made a justice of the peace and afterward a judge of the Court of Common Pleas. He was a bold, firm, decisive man and these qualities in those days were so much needed that he was kept very steadily in important civil offices. He also served repeatedly in the legislature, but declined the opening offered him for the House of Representatives and Senate of the United States. He was not insensible to these honors, but being a very conscientious man, did not feel free to take any place inconsistent with the care and education of a numerous young family. He was subsequently made Registrar of the Land Office and held it until the popular enunciation of the doctrine of Gen. Jackson's school that "to the victor belongs the spoils" was received, and then he was removed as a partizan of Mr. Clay to give place to an appointee of the pregnant party. The rest of his life he spent in agricultural pursuits, engaging occasionally in politics, but giving more time, means and effort to religious enterprises. He gave the ground on which Hanover College, Indiana, stands for an Industrial College. That feature of the institution was found impracticable, but the college serves as an honor and beneficence to the state. There is a story told of one of his acts before he went to Indiana, characteristic of the man every ready to champion the weak and give to a good cause. As he drove into Danville one day he saw a young rough shamefully mistreating a feebler party; he sprang from his team, rescued and placed in safety the old man. Meanwhile the old man's assailant rained blows upon Mr. Dunn; he shook him off like a viper and remounted his wagon, but upon reflection sued the bruiser for assault and battery, received $200, which he handed over as a part of the foundation fund of the First Presbyterian church of Danville. He did not want salvage for his own injuries, but meant to punish the young rough where it would be the most felt—in the pocket.

Williamson Dunn died in '72, leaving a large and useful posterity, amongst whom are Gen. McKee Dunn, Assistant Advocate General during Mr. Lincoln's and some following administrations, who is yet prominent in the social and political circles of Washington City.

General L. Rosseau

was for awhile a citizen of Mercer county, and for awhile taught school in the Cane Run neighborhood.

Davis C. Birney,

Major General of United States volunteers, from Pensylvania, and his brother, William G. Birney, were sons of James G. Birney, the celebrated emancipationist, who married and resided in Mercer, partially rearing his family here.

Colonel John Fry

was mingled conspicuously in the civil and military affairs of this section during the rebellion, and is now a prominent lawyer of Louisville.

Major Carey H. Fry

was born near Danville, then in Mercer, educated at West Point, served in McKee's command in Mexico, and died a few years since in California.

Joseph Tompkins

was a Lieutenant Colonel in the Union army; after the war went South and died in New Orleans.

Colonel William Worthington

was a grandson of Governor Slaughter and was reared by his uncle, William Hord, in the town. He was shot by mistake by his own soldiers at Corinth, Mississippi.

Colonel Ebenezer Magoffin

was a junior brother of Governor Magoffin. His sufferings and heroism in the Confederate cause in Missouri, would probably make one of the most thrilling romances of the war, closing by his tragic death in Texas. John Magoffin and the wife of Judge Charles Hardin are two of his descendants that have returned to identify their fortunes with the people of their nativity.

Captain Stephen E. Jones

was born in Harrodsburg, and served in the Union army on the staff of General Nelson. He is now a prominent business man of Louisville.

Charles Thompson,

father of John Charles Thompson, was a native of Mercer county, but planting in Mississippi during the rebellion. He raised a company in Madison county of that state; was of the defenders of Island No. 10 in the Mississippi river. He was brave as any better than brave.

Major George Rue

At an early day in the history of our county there came to Mercer a colony from New Jersey and Pennsylvania, which became known here as the Dutch settlement, and was very distinctly marked by its superior farming and tidy, thrifty housewifery. Some of these folks, too, are understood to be amongst the numerous claimants of Anneke Jahn's estate, including the ground on which Trinity church, New York, is located. There is a tradition that these emigrants came already banded as a religious organization, or upon arrival organized into a Dutch Reformed church. Of this I find no written record and if it ever existed has long since blended into the Presbyterian church.

From Johnathan Rue and his wife, a Miss Bergen, the most beautiful matron of her day of this colony, Major George Rue was descended.

He he spent his childhood and received a substantial English education.

He volunteered when eighteen years of age and went to the Mexican war, and upon his return went to Ohio to live, where he has been engaged in farming and the manufacture of agricultural implements, except during the Rebellion while in the U. S. Army.

When the Civil war broke out he raised a battalion and joined the ninth Kentucky Regiment of Cavalry. With this regiment, and parts of one or two others, Major Rue was ordered by General Shackelford to intercept Morgan in his celebrated and disastrous raid in to Indiana and Ohio. This he accomplished successfully. This was no unimportant event in itself, and gave to our state, as well as to Mercer, a greater sensation than any event of the war save the attack on Sumpter and the surrender of Lee. Very many of the Mercer boys were in Morgan's command. Major Rue's report on that startling event was sent me too late to have the place it should have had in the chapter headed Loyal "Mercer." It would have made an interesting feature and since our great raider was to be captured we make a N. B. that his sword was surrendered to a Mercer county man.

Names of men who have attained civil station in other counties or states who were born or resided in Mercer: Ratliff Boone, Lieutenant Governor of Indiana; C. M. Cunningham, Judge of District Court of Louisville; James Buchanan, Professor of Mathematics, Centre College—Dean; Daniel Dunklin, Governor of Missouri; William Glover, member of Congress from Missouri; Guyn Page, from Louisville, Speaker of the House of Representatives 1850; Charles Smith, President Jackson College, Louisiana; T. B. Reed, United States Senator, Mississippi; William T. Wood, District Judge in Missouri, now of Lexington, Mo.; William Thompson, Judge of Superior Court of Mississippi; Phil B. Thompson, Sr., member of Congress, Daviess county, Ky.; Phil B. Thompson, Jr., Representative in Congress from this district from 1879 to 1885, now resident in Washington, D. C.; P. Watt Hardin, Attorney General of Kentucky; James H. Thompson, Hillsboro, ex-Judge of District Court of Ohio; Patrick W. Tompkins, M. C., from Missouri and now Judge Tompkins, of Montague, Texas.

Samuel T. Glover

Of none of the sons of Mercer county who have gone forth from her has she more right to be proud than of Mr. Glover, late of St. Louis, Missouri. He was born in Mercer in 1813 and in childhood was as merry as the singing brooks, his heart as warm and free as the blessed sunshine. Mr. Glover was educated at St. Joseph's or Centre College, and I believe studied law with Judge Boyle and for a term of years practiced his profession in Hannibal, Missouri, where he married Miss Buckner, a lady of unusual sweetness of disposition and excellence of character. After a short time he moved to St. Louis from which time his career was onward and upward. Mr. Glover's mind was purely legal and he probably never would have diverged for a moment from the paths of his profession had he not lived in the days when neutrality of thought or conduct were impossible to fearless, honest natures like his. The breaking out of the Rebellion stirred his soul to its lowest depts. He was intensely loyal to the Union, and at once engaged zealously in organizing for its defense. But no sooner was its supremacy established and the victorious began an unlawful coercion of conscience and disturbance of quiet citizen life by the requirement of a test oath, than he threw himself into the breach and challenged a trial of it on himself by refusing to take it. He took his case finally to the Supreme Court of the United States, which to his honor sustained the decision of the Supreme Court of Missouri, that Congress or no power could pass an ex post facto low touching any rights of any citizen. General Blain, head of this argument of Mr. Glover's in this case, was characterized by extensive and accurate learning, by marvelous power in the grasp of principles and irresistible force in application of them, by the highest order of forensic eloquence, by a noble courage, by a passionate devotion to the doctrines of liberty as declared in the magna charta and reproduced in the American constitution. Mr. Glover mingled little in general politics, never sparing himself if the nation or the interests of the state of his adoption were at stake, but lived in the bosom of his family in the enjoyment of the domestic happiness so consonant with his tender and affectionate nature. After all, the moral qualities of Sam Glover out-ranked his mental. His heart was larger than his great mind and ever beat responsive to the appeals of want or woe. He left his family high position and abundant wealth, and one of his sons, William, seems destined to keep alive his honorable name, being now a re-elected representative in Congress from Missouri.

Dr. James M. Bush

I believe as stated concerning James Bush, the artist, his brother was born in Mercer county. I know that James Bush resided many years in Harrodsburg and signalized himself by his tender care of his mother, a lifelong, patient invalid. He subsequently removed to Lexington and was adjunct to Dr. Dudley, finally becoming fully his peer in skill and fame.

Dr. Ben Bowman

Dr. Ben Bowman, who is understood to have been the originator of the practice of hypodermic injections, was the son of John Bowman, known as "California John," by way of distinction from other kinsmen of the same name. Dr. Bowman was commercially engaged while here, but moved to Lake Washington, practiced medicine successfully for some years and died there in the prime of life.

CHAPTER XLI

Mercer County Fair—Its Presidents and Prospects—Its Disbanding and Reorganization and Probable Future Localities—Benevolent Orders—Masons—Odd Fellows—Daughters of Rebecca—Benevolent Societies of Colored People—Prosperous and Useful Banks.

Mercer County Fair

as organized in April 1839, and continued its exhibitions to 1883. J. H. Grimes, J. W .Cardwell, William Daviess, J. Harlan and Jacob Chapline were appointed to draft a constitution, which was reported and adopted. Subscriptions were immediately taken and made so low that the privileges were available to the humblest means.

This fair was a decided success, attracted yearly great crowds and drew for exhibition the best stock in the state, and had a marked effect in the improvement of all kinds of domestic animals, and to a limited extent fostered the introduction of better implements and crops than had been previously used. The grounds on the left of the Frankfort turnpike, several miles from town, which were finally improved for the last fair, were very handsome, but the location was a compromise, as the directors hoped, with Salvisa. This fair disorganized, but combined with Lawrenceburg. Two years since Harrodsburg disbanded, but has reorganized again and will probably locate on the Government Grounds, or near Harrodsburg Junction. The fair was an event looked for eagerly by every household, and its resumed meetings will be hailed as a needful and welcome holiday, especially to the over-worked farming population. The women of our county had considerable stimulus also in the old fair, in prizes for various branches of domestic economy, and there probably can never be witnessed a more joyous phase of rural life, than that yearly scene in the good greenwood of our Mercer fair grounds. So many happy, prosperous families gather around their improvised boards, dispensing their generous hospitality alike to friends and strangers. The great want of the first organization was more arrangement for the development and fostering of mechanics and agriculture. An experiment station, however limited, is an indispensible feature to a first class agricultural fair. Stock rings are more attractive; but the stock industry must be based on intelligent farming.

Mr. William Snail, Mr. Add Walden, Dr. James H. Moore and Mr. J. L. Neal have chiefly borne the burden of the honors of the presidency of this association, and have to their executive ability fully endorsed their appointment.

The history of stock naturally comes up in connection with the fair; but Mercer's enterprise in that line ante-dates that organization.

In 1790, Capt. George Robards, having located his revolutionary land warrants in Kentucky, brought his mother's and his own young family to Mercer county. His wife's brother, Archibald Sampson, had been sent to England for education. When he came home he brought Magic, a handsome bay stallion, and Kitty Fisher, a "milk white steed," with him directly to this county. Mr. Sampson died soon after he came to this state. I do not know what became of the horses, but the tradition of their importation still lives in the family, and was kept alive in the minds of us "infans terrible" by the house girl whose duty it was to bring our elfin locks into dinner order. She would hold us fast by the arm saying, "Whoa, Kitty Fisher; whoa Magic," because we were as restless as these steeds which never lost

Battle of Perryville Monument

the motion they acquired in their long sea voyage to this country. Mercer has long been to the front in horses. I wish I could give a complete list of the winners that have been foaled and trained in Mercer, but I have failed to procure it. I know when war times made such possession uncertain, J. Chinn, Sr., sent old Blue Bonnet, Asteriod and Lightning across the river to Alexander. I know that Blondine, So-So, Fanny Witherspoon and Ban Fox were to our manor born, and have made Crit Davis' and Jack Chinn's stables famous on the turf and field. But I think we need more than these flyers, a draught stock, a combination of our own fine formed horses with large and strong Norman for our work and family carriages.

Cattle

The Shakers brought the first imported cattle to Mercer; Major Handy, I think, the next. Had Mercer county men have had half the pride that I have, I should not have to omit one item of so much interest as the name of the tnterprising first men in these adventures.

I have not been able to find who brought the first improved sheep. William Thompson, then of Cane Hurst, now of Florida, brought the first pure Berkshire hogs.

I remember well when the clarion notes of the first Shanghai waked Harrodsburg. Somebody from Bardstown sent Capt. Phil Thompson a pair of this foreign breed. Soon after we all had chickens that could pick corn off the table; and now the crow-shaped, every-other-day layer belongs to the curiosity shop, and bronze turkeys gobble and strut around us, and Pekin ducks quack, Hong Kong geese scream, and gorgeous pea fowls flaunt their brilliant plumage in our yards.

The Grange

This grand conception for the benefit of the farmers dates its existence from 1873. All over the United States at first it spread like wildfire, and had farmers "taken it at its flood" it would have lifted them on the tide to the heights of influence and power which belong to them numerically and democratically as a class. But with the indifference which belongs to them as a class, and the jealousies which scheming politicians contrived to introduce into the order, they failed to take the position open to them, and now must bide their time until increase of self-respect and intelligence prompt the agricultural classes to claim their just dues and places. There have been a number of lodges reorganized in Mercer county, and some continue vital. That of Harrodsburg, for the present, is dormant. Still Mercer is to the front in this as most other things. Our citizen, Mr. James L. Neal, is ever a diligent, active leading member. He is usually a delegate to the National meetings and is employed much of his time in the lecture field.

Benevolent Orders

Of the ancient and honorable order of "Free and Accepted Masons," I could get no certain date. I suppose they were early organized in this county, for they have for centuries been strong and respectable, and feeling the value of brotherhood, they naturally linked themselves in bands wherever they went. They have from the first had lodges in Danville and Harrodsburg, but records have not always been well kept and what the fire fiend has not destroyed has been scattered in the incident confusion. I remember when to see a Masonic march or burial was an event in a child's life. Our best men were chiefly Masons and the fidelity and generosity to brethren in distress was their chief defense against the anti-Masonic rage that followed Morgan's abduction, who threatened to reveal their secrets and sacred mysteries. I remember that the death of a seafaring man who had drifted deep into this western wilderness, leaving a widow and two orphan children, stirred to its depths the pity of Harrodsburg and how promptly the Masons threw the mantle of their care over her, and she, having had unusual mind and training in New England common schools, became the famous village school mistress and many acorns she has planted that have become tall oaks.

Odd Fellows

Talliaferro Shaeffer organized this lodge in Harrodsburg and it has met for years with but one single night omission. It has a lot of fine regalia presented by the gentleman whose name the lodge bears. For some years Mr. Thomas Curry, of our town, was a chief of this order, but I do not remember his title. He had in close prospect the founding of a large Orphans' Home in Harrodsburg, but with his death this prospect has faded out. There are four lodges in the county: Harrodsburg Salvisa, McAfee and Burgin. This lodge had a female branch here which was very active and accumulated a handsome sum towards the endowment of this school or home. I do not know whether they have disbanded or are temporarily quit. They were called Daughters of Rebecca.

Insurance

I do not know whether this branch of business claims a benevolent feature, though its working accomplishes something of kindred nature. But their advertisements and signs are their fugitive records. Our colored people have several very prosperous benevolent associations and I know no way old retainers can be so effectually helped as to keep them members of these societies, which provide for them when sick and bury them respectably when dead.

Banks

Like "the course of true love," these institutions have not had mainly "a smooth run."

The first bank that I remember in Harrodsburg was a branch of the old Commonwealth, chartered about 1821, I think. This was located on the first floor of Capt. Daviess' town mansion. The Captain, always sanguine, was entrusted with the financial prosperity this institution was to bring to Mercer and the regions around about. The story goes, that about noon the day preceding the set opening of the bank to receive deposits, a very honest, weary-looking old home-spun equipped citizen presented himself before the door, sitting one one horse and leading another well laden with saddle bags and poremanteau considerably worse for wear. He signified his intention of depositing the treasures contained in said ancient receptacles, and seemed much annoyed by his premature arrival. With prompt hospitality the Captain invited him and his beasts of burden to be his guests until the morrow and had the saddle bags locked in the bank until the next day, the fact well witnessed. The old man said as he was detained he wished he had kept out enough money for a trip over to Lexington.

Capt. Daviess said, "Never mind, sir, never mind, sir, will this do," tendering him a $20 bill. The pilgrim departed and never returned.

After awhile somebody from Washington county traced up one of the stolen horses to the Captain's stable; then the deposits were investigated and found to be carefully wrapped and packed brick, and I kept the saddle bags for so many years lying in the attic closet and they were burned when the old castle perished in the flames during the war. This was fraud No. 1 on the old Commonwealth's Bank. After a while it was robbed, and a white man and two negroes who left for parts unknown about that time, like scape-goats, carried off the stigma to Canada, as is the fashion of modern times. This bank went up unanimously with its fellows all over the state.

The Savings Bank

built and occupied the handsome house now owned and used by the First National. It had a rough and precarious passage through the war and finally, assigned as did also the McBrayer & Trapnal, a private banking institution. The losses by these institutions were numerous and some heavy. Why or wherefore they failed would perhaps make an interesting volume in the hands of some Dickens. They were unintentionally classed under the had of Benevolent Institutions. They certainly were managed in a most accommodating spirit and in mercy and emergency proved

"A friend indeed,
In time of need."

And time has proved there wtre no reserved fortunes in the settlements, our citizen, Mr. Trapnal, not only having lost his capital stock, but the whole earnings of his life, and also a family fortune that had crystalized in his hands. We have now two material institutions in Harrodsburg. The First National antedates the Mercer National and occupies the site of the Savings Bank. Its President is Abram Bonta; Cashier, H. C. Hohon, Sr., and has a complete corps of efficient clerks.

The Mercer National, recently based in the Commercial Hotel, is now occupying its new and elegant building which has risen from the ashes of the costly building swept off by the May fire. Dr. J. H. Moore is president of this bank and R. C. Nuckols is cashier. These institutions submit regularly through our local paper their status in capital conditions and capability, and if fire-proof buildings, efficient officers and ample capital are guarantees of success and prosperity these banks make a full manifest of these conditions of success.

FINIS.

INDEX

Introductory..Page 1

CHAPTER 1..Page 4
    Geography, Boundary Of Mercer County, Rocks, Minerals, Prehistoric Remains

CHAPTER 2..Page 8
    Soils, Timbers, Flora and Rivers of Mercer and Boyle Counties

CHAPTER 3..Page 13
    Earliest Days—Capt. James Harrod and Comrades Settle Harrod's Town—Fort Dwellers and Their Hardships—Clothes and Furniture of Forters—Pioneer Stations In Mercer

CHAPTER 4..Page 17
    George Rogers Clark And Gabriel Jones Bring Gunpowder From Virginia—First Women Arrive At Fort Harrod—Poage, Handicraftsman, And Wife (Ann McGinty) Arrive—Indian Raids—James Ray Saves Fort—Marriages, Births

CHAPTER 5..Page 23
    Hard Winter 1780-81—Conventions Seeking Separation From Virginia—Kentucky's Admission Into the Union—Municipal Affairs in Harrodsburg at the Close of Century—First Court in Kentucky.

CHAPTER 6..Page 27
    Eminent Men of Period—Capt. James Harrod—Gen. George Rogers Clark—Gen. Hugh Mercer—Daniel Boone.

CHAPTER 7..Page 32
    Eminent Men of Period, Continued . . . Simon Kenton—Gen. James Ray—Gen. Hugh McGary—Col. Silas Harlan—Capt. William Pogue—Hon. John Brown.

CHAPTER 8..Page 36
                          The McAfee Family

CHAPTER 9..Page 40
    Mode of Living in Early Days—Customs, Fashions, Manners—Furniture.

CHAPTER 10..Page 43
    Mode of Living Continued—Customs, Fashions, Manners—Food—Clothes.

CHAPTER 11..Page 48
    Aaron Burr's Conspiracy—Gen. James Wilkinson.

PART II

CHAPTER 12..Page 52
    Col. Joseph Hamilton Daviess

CHAPTER 13..Page 57
    War 1812—Men Of That Period—Gen. John Adair—Gen. Robert McAfee—Col. Gabriel Slaughter (Governor).

CHAPTER 14..Page 61
    Gen. John Adair (Governor)

CHAPTER 15..Page 66
    Civil Commotion After War 1812—Eminent Mercer Men—Judge John Boyle—Hon. George Robertson—Gov. William Owsley—James Haggin.

PART III

CHAPTER 16..Page 71
    Restoration of Old Court By Legislature—Lafayette's Visit To Kentucky as Nation's Guest—Emancipation—Colonization—Temperance—Cholera 1833.

CHAPTER 17..Page 75
    Elections—Celebration 1841 Of First Settlement Of Kentucky At Harrodsburg—Advance In Comfort in Living, Dress and Styles.

CHAPTER 18..Page 80
    Mexico War—Its Origin—Annexation of Texas—Kentuckians Enthusiastic Volunteers— Capt. Phil B. Thompson's Mercer Militia Accepted— Its Service and Return Sketch of its Officers.

CHAPTER 19..Page 83
    From 1850 to 1860—Formation of Boyle County Out of Mercer and Lincoln in 1842—Political Conditions—Abolition—Its Origin, Spread, Influence On War—Election—Gov. Beriah Magoffin, 1859.

PART IV

CHAPTER 20..Page 87
    Sketches of Prominent Men In Affairs Just Prior To War Between States—Gov. R. P. Letcher—Con. T. P. Moore.

CHAPTER 21..Page 90
    Biological Sketches Continued—John B. Thompson.

CHAPTER 22..Page 96
    Outbreak of War—Loyal Mercer—Camp Nelson First Recruiting Station in Kentucky—Organization of Several Regiments In Mercer and Boyle —Names of Officers—Remarks of Adjutant Gen. Lindsey on These Troops—Sketches of Officers.

CHAPTER 23..Page 100
Confederate Mercer. How Boys Went Off—Morgan's Raid—Adventures of Mercer Boys.

CHAPTER 24..Page 103
    More Adventures of Confederate Boys—Arrival of Ledbetter's Command —Gen. Braxton Bragg's Invasion and Brief Occupation of Conferedates —Gen. Don Carlos Buell, Commander Federal Forces.

CHAPTER 25..Page 106
    Battle of Perryville, Oct. 8, 1862—Hospitals in Harrodsburg—Incidents of Hospital Life—Guerillas and Regulators.

CHAPTER 26..Page 108
    "Our Brother In Black"—His Early Days and Advance in Living—Some Bought Freedom, Some Had It Given To Them—Effects of War—Freedom—Its Effects—Prospects of Race.

CHAPTER 27...Page 113
　　Towns of Mercer County—Harrodsburg—Location—Extension—First Buildings and Successive Styles of Private Buildings—Public Buildings—Old Court House—Jail, etc.

CHAPTER 28...Page 118
　　Harrodsburg, Continued—Public Private Buildings—Morgan Row—Greenville Springs—Chenoweth Hall—Opera House, etc.

CHAPTER 29...Page 122
　　Harrodsburg, Continued—Postoffice—Its Locations—Postmasters—Other Officers In County—Cemeteries.

CHAPTER 30...Page 126
Danville

CHAPTER 31...Page 130
　　Centre College—Origin and Presidents—Noted Men Of Boyle County.

CHAPTER 32...Page 134
　　Towns in Mercer—Pleasant Hill (Shakertown)—Lucto—Nevada—Bohontown—Cornishville—McAfee—Rose Hill—Dugansville.

CHAPTER 33...Page 138
Burgin

CHAPTER 34...Page 141
　　Schools and Colleges of Mercer—Mrs. Coomes' School In Fort—Schools of Early Times—Classical Academies for Boys—Bacon College—Kentucky University—Prof. James Newton Prather—Prof. Hogsett—Common Schools.

CHAPTER 35...Page 145
　　Female Schools in Mercer—Essex School—Misses Halcomb and Ben Ali—Methodist Academies—Greenville—Presbyterian Academy—Daughters College—Women of Mercer.

CHAPTER 36...Page 152
　　Churches In Mercer County—First Sermon in Fort—Cane Run Presbyterian—Baptist Churches—Roman Catholic.

CHAPTER 37...Page 155
　　Churches, Continued—Methodists, Northern and Southern—Episcopal—Reformers Or Christians—Colored Churches.

CHAPTER 38...Page 158
　　Men of Mercer Who Served as Governors, Lieut-Governors, U. S. Senators, Foreign Ministers, State Senators and Legislators.

CHAPTER 39...Page 160
　　Growth of Trade and Manufacturing in Mercer—Wool Carding—Cotton Factory—Horse and Water Mills—Steam Mills, etc.

CHAPTER 40...Page 164
　　Men of Mercer—Pioneers Who Became Prominent in Military Service and Other Fields.

CHAPTER 41...Page 168
　　Mercer County Fairs—Benevolent Orders—Masons, Odd Fellows—Societies of Colored People—Banks.

www.ingramcontent.com/pod-product-compliance
Lightning Source LLC
Chambersburg PA
CBHW052340230426
43664CB00041B/2577

Nurse Dorothea presents
Not Taking People and Things for Granted

Copyright © 2024 by Dow Creative Enterprises, LLC

All rights reserved

First Edition

ISBN 979-8-9905577-7-2

Printed by Lulu

Published by Dow Creative Enterprises®

Dow Creative Enterprises, LLC

PO Box 15357

Tucson, AZ 85708

Library of Congress Control Number: 2024914188

Dow Creative Enterprises® is a federally registered trademark with the United States Patent and Trademark Office.

Help Civilization Reach Its Potential® is a federally registered trademark with the United States Patent and Trademark Office.

Table of Contents

Title	Page Number
Dedication	vi
Part 1	1
Part 2	63
Part 3	107
Part 4	159
References	264
About the Illustrator	269
About the Author	271
Other Books by DCE	273

Dedication

The Nurse Dorothea book series is dedicated to Dorothea Dix. Her work in the 1800s helped people with mental illness live a more dignified life. She spent decades lobbying government officials to create state hospitals for the mentally ill. One person can make a difference.

Michael

Part 1

"Hi everyone. My name is Nurse Dorothea. Thank you for coming to the after-school club on mental health. I hope to provide you with some tools to manage your emotions and navigate life's challenges. Mental health is complicated because there are so many things that can affect it. This class was created to show that it is ok to talk about your mental health with others as well as give your ideas to improve everyone's mental health."

"We will be recording this session. People in the future will get to experience the same things you will today. Sometimes, I will speak to people watching this show or reading the future book about the class. This is an interactive class, and I want you all to ask questions as you have them. We will stop sometimes and discuss things with each other. If you are watching the show or reading the book, then I want YOU all to also discuss the questions and topics with those in the room. This book is an experience, and you will only get the full experience by talking with others. Please take breaks from the show as you need to since this will be a long discussion."

"If you are watching the show or reading this book alone, that is ok. Please take the time right now to get out a journal. I want those doing this class by themselves to write down responses to questions that I will ask so that you participate like all the others. Sometimes, we need to address some mental health issues alone, so it is ok to do this class by yourself. We are on a journey that is ultimately our own, but it is always nice to have people alongside us to help us in the bad times and share our joy in the good times."

"The main rule for the class is to respect others. If someone has a question, we are to be quiet and let them speak. Raise your hand if you have a question, and I will call on you. Respecting everyone is important since we can learn from everyone."

"Today's class will be about not taking people and/or things for granted. Some might say that this is part of polite society and not in the realm of mental health. Stop and think for a moment what you may have felt like in the past when you were taken for granted. I am confident you will say that it didn't feel good and may have distressed you. It may have disrupted your mental equilibrium, and it may have taken some time to return to your baseline before the incident. Therefore, taking people and things for granted affects your mental health, and since it can disrupt people's mental well-being, we should learn about the topic and think of ways to not let ourselves do this behavior."

"The dictionary at Cambridge.org states that to take something for granted means to never think about something because you believe it will always be available or stay exactly the same. It says that it is also not realizing or showing how grateful you are for what you get from them. In addition, the site says that it is to believe something to be the truth without even thinking about it."

"I'd like to recite a poem by Sara Jones about the subject. The poem is titled "The Unseen Treasure."

When beauty fades in love's own eyes,
And all seems dull, a worn disguise,
Do we then see what we've ignored?
A precious gem, no longer adored.
Once vibrant laughter, now a sigh,
Once eager touch, now a distant lie.
Oh, how we take for granted dear,
A love that once felt crystal clear.
But these illusions, we must shatter,
To mend the bond, to make it matter.
For in the depths of love's despair,
We find the strength to truly care."

"Another poem I'd like to recite is by Mark Anderson titled "The Forgotten Friend."

In laughter shared and secrets kept,
A friendship forged, so tightly wept.
But time moved on, and so did we,
Unaware of the rift that grew.
With absent words and missed embraces,
Our bond dissolved, replaced with spaces.
Oh, what a fool I was to stray,
To let our friendship fade away.
Now I sit, in solitude's air,
Regretting choices, unaware.
For in my blindness, I failed to see,
A friendship's worth, so precious and free."

"A third poem I'd like to read is by Lily Roberts titled "Fading Familiarity."

In the house I once called home,
Familiarity now turned to stone.
The laughter echoes, empty halls,
As an estranged love silently falls.
Once we danced to music's beat,
Now silence lingers, incomplete.
Oh, how I took your love for granted,
Until it vanished, seeds unplanted.
With every lost opportunity,
I yearn for warmth, for unity.
But time moves forward, never back,
And all that's left is what I lack."

"Now, I would like all of you in the room, those watching the show, and those reading the book to think about someone or something who you have taken for granted. Share with those around you or write in your journal. Please take some time to do that now."

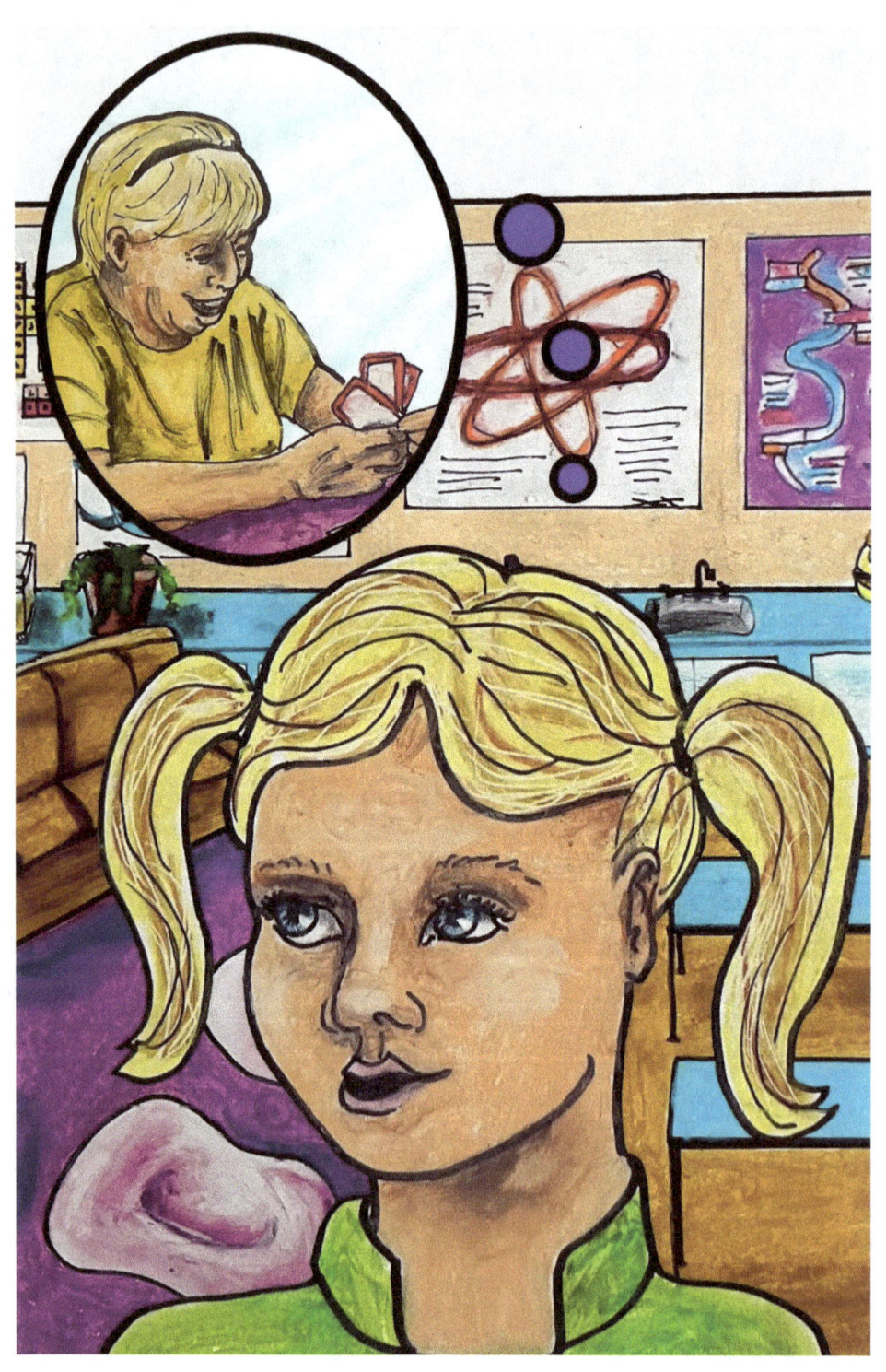

Frida raises her hand after everyone discusses the question, and Nurse Dorothea calls on her to talk. "I feel I have taken my aunt for granted. She always plays card games with me when we have family parties. We have a lot of fun and she doesn't want me to feel alone since I'm the youngest person at the parties. I've never told her how much I appreciate her. I need to thank her for thinking about my well-being."

"Great insight," says Nurse Dorothea, "It's important to identify places in life that we are lacking and ways we can improve. Now, you just need to act on that idea of showing her appreciation and telling her in words how thankful you are."

Amari raises his hand, and Nurse Dorothea calls on him to talk. "My dad taught me how to sail a small boat. There are two things. First, I never actually thanked my dad for teaching me this skill. It is a lot of fun to go out on the lake by myself and enjoy the peaceful water. Second, I've never given thanks to society for inventing the sailboat and giving people like me an opportunity to be independent and grow in my self-confidence. I want to find a way to give back to society and help the world even if it is a small contribution. I want to contribute."

"Very nice thoughts," says Nurse Dorothea, "It's important to give back to the world since we are given so many things."

Lian raises her hand, and Nurse Dorothea calls on her to talk. "I feel I have taken for granted our healthcare system like our system of vaccines. I know vaccines can protect me from developing a dangerous illness that would affect the quality of my life as well as possibly being life-threatening. So much work has gone into researching vaccines and how to make them. I think I have also taken for granted the doctors and nurses who have helped keep me healthy over the years. Maybe I'll get a job in the medical field to give back and show my appreciation."

"Great goal," says Nurse Dorothea, "Sometimes being grateful is taking a big action in life like devoting yourself to a certain career. Study hard, believe in yourself, surround yourself with a good support system and you can achieve your dreams."

Dimitry raises his hand, and Nurse Dorothea calls on him to talk. "I feel I have taken nature for granted. I love being outdoors and taking hikes. The world is a beautiful place and helps me feel happy. I guess I haven't known how to show appreciation to nature so maybe that's why I took it for granted."

"You are touching on a point about the purpose of the class. Maybe some of you have not known how to show appreciation for someone or something and need ideas for ways to not take things for granted. We're going to open the floor in the third part of the class for everyone to learn from everyone else about ways we might not take things for granted," says Nurse Dorothea.

Awira raises her hand, and Nurse Dorothea calls on her to talk. "I feel I have taken a lot of people for granted in my life by assuming they would always be there for me and support me. I feel bad. I hope this class helps me do better."

"Feeling bad when you become aware of taking other people for granted can be a normal emotion," says Nurse Dorothea, "It's important to learn to observe your emotions and not let them manage you. Let the emotion come and let it pass. Then, acknowledge you are in a class to help and will learn some things before you leave today about not taking others for granted."

"When people show appreciation to each other in words and deeds, they can develop healthier relationships. Sometimes, taking people for granted can start slowly and then turn into a large problem. Sometimes a person can take another for granted because the other person is a giver and is always giving, so it feels natural to just receive. If someone is a taker, they can start to take too much and even demand that they be given more. They might expect the giver to do most of the work in the relationship."

"When someone takes things for granted, they may develop improper resource management skills, and the resource or thing may not be available in the future. For example, if you take running water for granted, a person might use much more water than they require by taking long showers all the time or washing clothes in a full wash cycle, as if there were lots of clothes, instead of conserving resources. We will have a severe freshwater issue in the future due to over-pumping of aquifers or groundwater supplies. We must appreciate our fresh water and conserve it."

"When people take others for granted, relationships can eventually become broken. In close relationships like a marriage, the individuals might grow farther apart emotionally until they find no satisfaction in their relationship and want to exit the arrangement. When people are taken for granted at work, employees can leave and cause turnover which requires more resources to train new people."

"There might be signs that people can observe others doing or not doing that may show unappreciation or someone taking things for granted. The most common sign is that a person may take more than they give. A person should think critically about this though, since one person may give in a way that may not be what you wanted, but they are still giving— like working extra hours to provide more financial support for the family. Another sign that a person may show is being unwilling to return favors. A person may like to receive favors like getting financial assistance, being listened to when they are distressed about something, or getting help cleaning a house, but they may not offer any help in return."

"Another sign might be if a person never asks the other person about how their day was. This, though, could be a complicated sign since some people were raised by parents who never asked about activities of the day so they may just be mirroring their parents' behavior and not ask their new loved ones about their day. This may be a skill for some people to develop. Some things are simple, but even simple things need to be learned and practiced, like a toddler learning to walk and then run."

"If a person is always demanding the other person to say yes to their requests, then that may be a sign the person is being taken for granted. We are complex beings living in a complex world, so avoid continuous demands."

"If a person feels they are losing feelings of intimacy and closeness with their partner, it could be a sign that they are being taken for granted. Relationships are complicated and people should have constant communication to share info about themselves with each other so that each person understands where the other person is at emotionally, physically, and spiritually."

"If one person in the relationship asks their partner to do extra work often, then that might be a sign that they are being taken for granted. Yes, things need to be accomplished, but care and concern need to be performed in the relationship so that not too many demands are put on the person."

"Not being there for another person may be a sign you are taking someone for granted. When a person needs assistance and they ask for help, it is important to reach out and give the support they are requesting. If a person is growing up and their parent is not around to guide and mentor them, then that may be a sign that the parent is taking the child for granted. If a person is growing in skills in a company, and the supervisors spend little to no time to help strengthen their knowledge and abilities, then that might be a sign the supervisors are taking their employees for granted."

"If another person expects you to drop all of your plans to do what you want them to do, then that could be another sign of them taking you for granted. An example would be if you had plans to exercise one afternoon and then read a book afterward, and the other person wanted you to go shopping for clothes all afternoon. Even though we need to learn to adapt to others, we should respect each other's plans at the same time and find ways for everyone to do what they want and need to do."

"Another sign of taking someone for granted is taking credit for things the other person did. This can happen in the workplace with people trying to get ahead of the person, so they choose a path of taking credit for things they did not do to get a promotion. Give credit to whom credit is due."

"If a person is always late to appointments with a person, that could also be seen as taking that person for granted. It can show you do not respect the other person's time and are willing to let them wait for you. Remember, if you're not early for an appointment by about 10 minutes, then you're late, since things can happen like accidents that keep you from getting to a certain place on time."

"If you don't do things to help the other person feel supported, then that person could feel they are being taken for granted. Relationships take work, and part of that work is helping people feel supported by you. People need to feel appreciated. People need to feel that you are there to help them and support them when needed. Feeling supported by another person is especially important when the other person is in a time of crisis. People remember very strongly the people who did not support them when they needed a lot of help."

"If you demand that a person do a lot more than would be expected in a normal relationship, that also could be seen as taking the other person for granted. Some people can accommodate the other person by doing many things, and they are willing to do more than what is expected because they want the relationship to work. Just because a person is willing and able to do a lot for someone doesn't mean you should demand a lot from them."

"We have gone over a lot of material. I would like you to refresh yourselves. We'll start again shortly after our break. For those watching the show or reading the book, feel free to stop here and start the next part when you are ready."

Part 2

"Welcome back. Let's get right back into the material where we left off. If a person unfairly divides responsibilities between themselves and the other person, that could be a sign they are taking the person for granted. For example, if one person only volunteers to do laundry for the family while the other person is expected to do all the other house chores, that could be viewed as unfairly dividing household responsibilities. Every family will have a different division of responsibilities, so it may take time to find the best balance of the division of labor."

"When a person gives flattery that is deceptive, that could be a sign that they are starting or have already started to take you for granted. An example would be to tell someone that they do a great job with a household chore, but the person may not mean it. They may do this just to encourage the other person to do the chore so that they don't have to. Be sincere in your praise of others. Say true things as best as you know them to be true."

"When a person ignores another person's needs, that could be a sign they are taking the other person for granted. We should be considerate of other people's physical, emotional, spiritual, and cultural needs. Help others when you are able and do not neglect those close to you."

"If a person is rude to another person, then that could be a sign they are taking them for granted. Say what you mean, mean what you say and don't say it mean."

"If a person often cancels plans with someone, that could be a sign they are taking them for granted. If you promise to do something with someone, you should keep your promise. Try to only make promises you can keep. Being true to your word is important. If you do not keep your word, then people will lose trust in your promises which will frustrate you."

"When a person spends the other person's money without concern, that could be a sign of taking the other person for granted. We all must learn to be good financial stewards of what we are given or have access to. If a person spends like there is no limit, then they could be taking the other person for granted, assuming that they will always be there for them, and that they don't need to respect what is being given to them."

"Another sign of taking someone for granted is when you don't ask the other person questions. For example, if your partner asks you questions about how your day was, but you don't ask them about their day, then you might be taking them for granted."

"When a person does not compromise with another person, that could be a sign that they are taking the other person for granted. Life is complicated, and we need to find the middle ground when there is conflict. Negotiation is a skill that must be learned and practiced. Finding a solution that is a win-win for all sides is sometimes hard to do but is the most rewarding when everyone benefits from the decision."

"If you spend little quality time with someone, then that could be a sign you are taking them for granted. Make time in your life for those close to you. Create activities that help foster quality time to build and strengthen the relationship so that the relationship, or partnership in life grows. If the relationship is not growing, then it may be moving backward."

"You need to let others know about your life partner. When a person doesn't share information about their partner with others, that may show that they are taking their partner for granted. Don't try to hide your partner. Be proud of them and show them off to the world."

"If a person makes all the plans for the relationship without including the other person, then that could be a sign that they are taking the other person for granted. Life is a journey and is best when you share the decisions with your loved ones."

"Lying to the other person may be a sign you are taking them for granted. By not trusting the other person with the truth of a situation, you are not appreciating the judgment and insights which they could share with you."

"If you try to make the other person feel inadequate, then you are probably taking them for granted. People have value, and they have knowledge, skills, and abilities that you may not see clearly, so avoid making people feel inadequate. People have a purpose in life, and we may not see that purpose clearly. Stay humble and realize you may have more to learn about the other person."

"You have now been exposed to other ideas about how you might take other people for granted. Now, I would like all of you in the room, those watching the show and those reading the book, to think about someone whom you have probably been taking for granted and only realized it now after our discussion. Share with those around you or write in your journal. Please take some time to do that now."

After several minutes of talking, Amisha raises her hand and Nurse Dorothea calls on her to talk. "I think I have been taking my Aunt for granted. I spend very little time with her. I need to make time to talk with her and see her more often. I could even email her more."

"Thanks for sharing," says Nurse Dorothea.

"Life is short so we should avoid taking people and things for granted. We should value every moment. Every moment with someone is a chance to make a positive impact in that person's life to help them be the best version of themselves. Let us find ways to improve every relationship so that we can live a fulfilling life."

"When you take someone for granted, you could take away some happiness in your life."

"When you take others for granted, they may eventually become resentful and leave you and end the friendship. Losing friends is usually no fun and sometimes, we need as many friends as possible to get through a difficult time in life."

"Taking others for granted can cause feelings of regret. When you regret things, sometimes it takes years to forgive yourself for the wrong you may have done which causes internal discord. In some situations, people have lifelong regrets that they take to their deathbed. You should try to minimize the situations in your life that could cause regret, so that you live at peace with yourself and others. Another thing related to regret is that if the other person dies, then you may have regret for taking them for granted and not being able to show how appreciative you are that they were in your life."

"Living a life where you take others for granted means missed opportunities for making happy memories. Happy memories can sustain us in difficult times. Happy memories can help keep a relationship together when there is trouble. Happy memories can help inspire others to live a good life. Happy memories can help motivate us to do and to be our best."

"We have gone over a lot of material. I would like you to refresh yourselves. We'll start again shortly after our break. For those watching the show or reading the book, feel free to stop here and start the next part when you are ready."

Part 3

"Welcome back. We are going to continue our discussion on things you think should not be taken for granted. Open your mind and be creative. Almost anything or anyone can be taken for granted if we are not careful. By sharing with each other, it will help give us insight into our own behavior. Maybe someone's idea will help us think more critically about our own life."

Gustavo raises his hand and Nurse Dorothea calls on him to talk. "I think I have taken some of my friends for granted. Sometimes, I have canceled plans and just thought they wouldn't mind because they'll always be there. Other times, I have expected them to drop their plans for my plans. I have been a little selfish."

"Thank you for sharing, Gustavo. Letting yourself be vulnerable to others is an important step in gaining insight," says Nurse Dorothea.

Ji Ho raises his hand and Nurse Dorothea calls on him to talk. "I think I have taken my family for granted. Sometimes, I don't do what my parents ask me to do. They ask me questions about my day every day, but I don't always ask them questions."

"We can all improve on our relationships, and it is good that you can identify an area where you can improve. Also, parents may feel they are doing something wrong with their parenting if the child always has short answers. We should try to not make our parents feel bad," says Nurse Dorothea.

Juniper raises her hand and Nurse Dorothea calls on her to talk. "I think I may take my good health for granted. Sometimes, I eat junk food all day long and don't think there will be any consequences, but I guess if I do that a lot, then I could start having health problems."

"Maintaining good health is work, and we must strive to live healthy lives so that we will have the strength to help those around us," says Nurse Dorothea.

Wyatt raises his hand and Nurse Dorothea calls on him to talk. "I think I may take time for granted. We have one life to live, and sometimes I think my time on Earth will be unending. I need to value what time I'm given and spend quality time with those important to me."

"Time is a resource that should be used wisely. Have you ever tried to count how many weeks may be left in your life? You can do that by assuming you might live to be 100 years old. Then, subtract your age from 100 and multiply that number by 52. Do that some time, and it may help you see life as a resource to care for," says Nurse Dorothea.

Fatima raises her hand and Nurse Dorothea calls on her to talk. "I think I may take opportunities for granted. I have been given some opportunities in life to write for the school paper, and I did not take it seriously. Every opportunity can help me gain knowledge and skills to make me more able to do future jobs."

"Seeing opportunities in life as something precious is something we all must learn. It is great that you are mentioning that at your age. Some people are given few opportunities in life to thrive. We need to appreciate the chance we are given to thrive. In modern society, we can take having fresh water for granted since other parts of the world do not have easy access to this resource," says Nurse Dorothea.

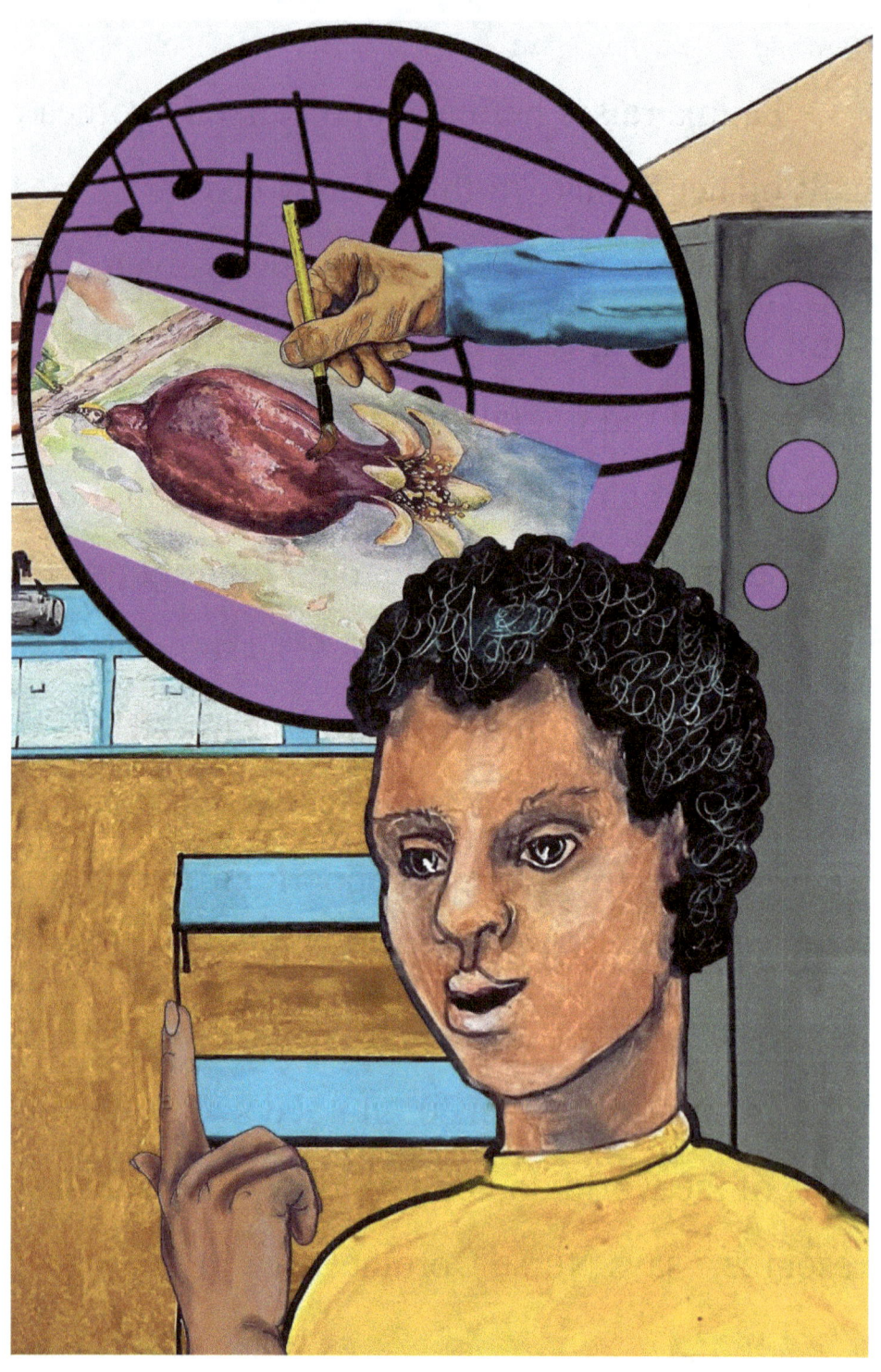

Ekon raises his hand and Nurse Dorothea calls on him to talk. "I think I have taken my talents for granted. I love to paint but don't do it often and don't share my paintings with others. Gifts that we are given should be shared with others to increase their happiness."

"We all seem to have some gift from the Universe and using that gift to the utmost is important to help live a fulfilled life," says Nurse Dorothea.

Antonio raises his hand and Nurse Dorothea calls on him to talk. "I think I take my appearance for granted. I don't always brush my hair nicely in the morning before starting my day. A person's appearance is important because it is the start of the first impression some people will have of you when they first meet you. I need to care for myself."

"Good point, Antonio," says Nurse Dorothea.

Maria raises her hand and Nurse Dorothea calls on her to talk. "I think I may take my achievements for granted. My achievements should help me push more, but sometimes I just think about what I have done in the past and think I don't need to do more things. Doing something important is a good thing, but maybe we shouldn't rest on our past achievements since we are always facing the future."

"Great thinking," says Nurse Dorothea, "You are bringing up an idea that not many people seem to consider. Achievements can help someone's sense of pride in themselves and their self-confidence, but we are truly on a journey always facing the future, so we should ask ourselves, 'What will we do next?' Maria, I like that line so much, I'm going to share it with others. We are always facing the future."

Pia raises her hand and Nurse Dorothea calls on her to talk. "I think I take my ability to remember happy memories for granted. Our brain is special and its ability to bring back memories for us that make us feel good is something we need to thank the Universe for. I haven't really done that, so I'd like to now, 'Thank you Universe.' "

"Being grateful for what makes us human is important. Thanks for leading by example," says Nurse Dorothea.

Levi raises his hand and Nurse Dorothea calls on him to talk. "I think I take life in general for granted. It is truly amazing how complicated things are, and yet they still work. Sometimes, I get frustrated with life when things don't go my way, but I need to remember there is a bigger picture, and maybe I'm not supposed to always get my way."

"Good insight," says Nurse Dorothea, "Life is beautiful. Let us allow amazement for things to fill our thoughts, and let us be grateful for what we see around us. Also, be grateful for what you have and try to not always want more things in your life."

Yulianna raises her hand and Nurse Dorothea calls on her to talk. "I think I may take love for granted. Being loved by others is a special feeling and I need to show those who love me more thankfulness for them being in my life."

"When we have loved ones in our lives, we should do extra things for them to show we care and love them back," says Nurse Dorothea.

Kalani raises her hand and Nurse Dorothea calls on her to talk. "I think I might take the future for granted. The future is there to give us new days to start fresh and new opportunities to grow as a person. The future is there to make new friends and share time with old friends. The future is a place where we can find our better selves. The future is important, and I would like to find a way to be appreciative of it."

"Maybe using coping skills to deal with any anxiety you may have of the future is a way to say thanks, although it is hard for some to greet the future with open arms due to past trauma," says Nurse Dorothea.

Kenji raises his hand and Nurse Dorothea calls on him to talk. "I think I take food for granted. A lot of work goes into growing it and bringing it to my table. I need to be more grateful."

"Some people say a blessing of thanks to their spiritual higher authority before eating every meal, so maybe you could try that. You can also try mindful eating," says Nurse Dorothea.

Azamat raises his hand and Nurse Dorothea calls on him to talk. "I think I may take my pets for granted. They seem to love me so much with not much expected in return except for food, water, and some petting. I should scrub them on the belly more often since they really like that."

"Pets are usually members of the family because of the love most people have for them, so doing things that they like is important," says Nurse Dorothea.

Diwa raises her hand and Nurse Dorothea calls on her to talk. "I think I may take my shelter for granted. We live in a place where there are not a lot of natural disasters, so we don't have the annual threat of losing everything. I do feel sad for those who lose their homes in earthquakes, wildfires, and other things. I need to be more grateful for my house and that I have a place to call home."

"It is great to have a place you can call home. Protect it and take care of your place," says Nurse Dorothea.

Connor raises his hand and Nurse Dorothea calls on him to talk. "I think I may take clean water for granted. I love to drink water and drink a lot every day. Maybe I could visit the water treatment facility in our city to be more appreciative of the hard work that goes into giving us this resource."

"Great idea! Seeing what other people do for you can help you be appreciative," says Nurse Dorothea.

Juniper raises her hand and Nurse Dorothea calls on her to talk. "I think I take for granted that the Earth rotates and gives us day and night. Having a time of the day we can devote to sleep and then a time in the morning to wake up and start fresh is great. Maybe I could do things to help out the Earth to show my appreciation."

"Helping the Earth is important since it protects us and helps provide an environment for life," says Nurse Dorothea.

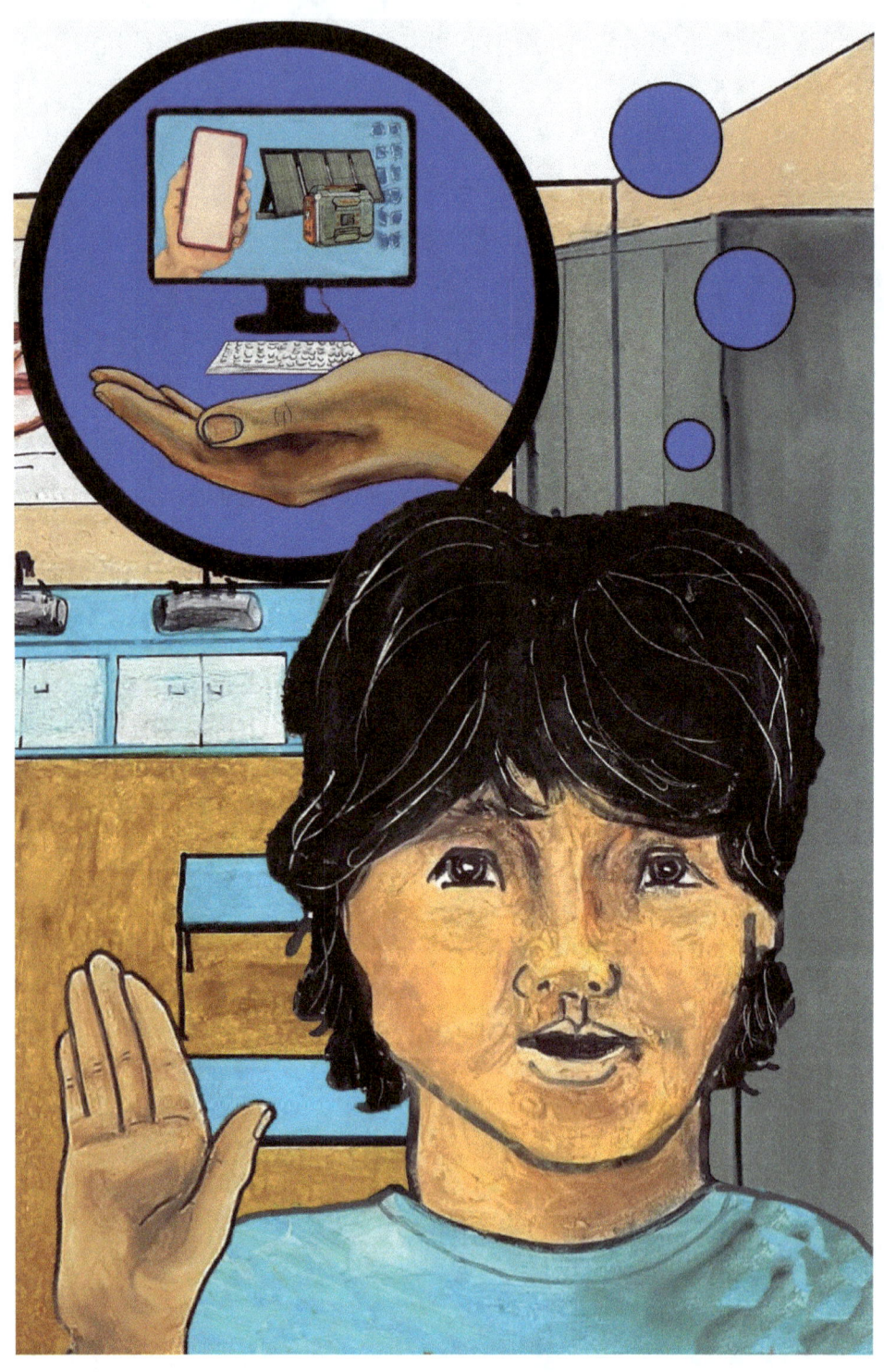

Ji Ho raises his hand and Nurse Dorothea calls on him to talk. "I think I may take technology for granted. I expect computers to always get faster and faster. I get very frustrated with technology whenever there is a glitch. I need to be more patient with technology."

"Technology is a great thing that lets us do many great things, so having patience is probably a good thing," says Nurse Dorothea.

Pia raises her hand and Nurse Dorothea calls on her to talk. "I think I may take reading and writing for granted. I have heard that there are some places in the world that do not allow certain groups of people to learn to read and write. This skill should be a basic human right, but we should also be grateful that it even exists."

"Some people have died for an equal education, so seeing education as a precious resource to be protected is also important," says Nurse Dorothea.

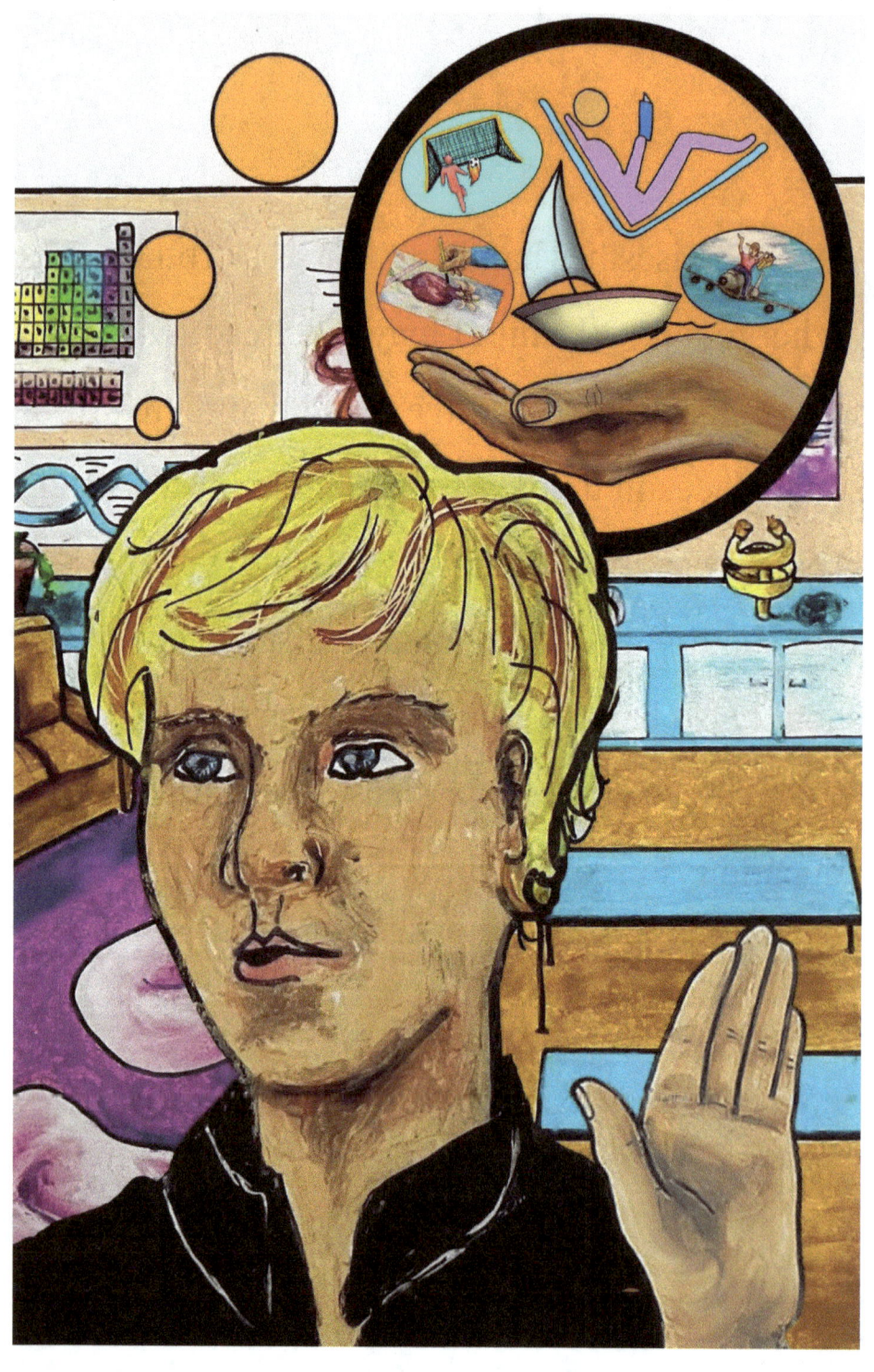

Dmitry raises his hand and Nurse Dorothea calls on him to talk. "I think I may take my hobbies for granted. I guess it's a great thing that I can even have hobbies instead of having to work and then sleep all the time. Hobbies bring joy to my life."

"We should find hobbies that keep our mind and bodies strong which can help make us perform better at work and in personal relationships," says Nurse Dorothea.

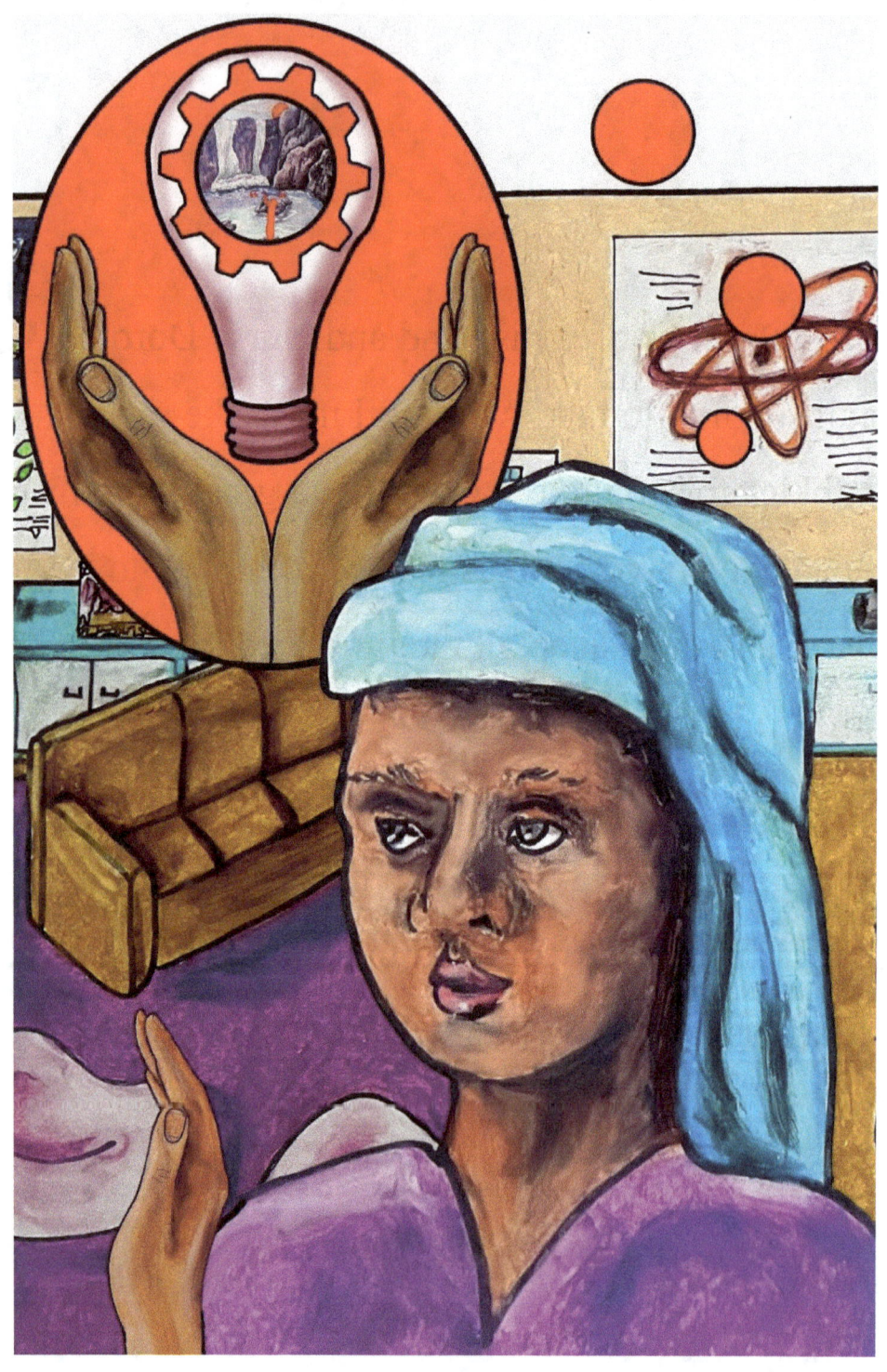

Yulianna raises her hand and Nurse Dorothea calls on her to talk. "I think finding your purpose in life can be taken for granted. When I discovered what I feel to be my purpose in life, which is becoming an explorer of nature and discovering new species, it gave me the energy to do many other things in life. Finding purpose touches so many parts of a person's life that I need to be grateful for finding it."

"Thanks for sharing your experience," says Nurse Dorothea.

Gustavo raises his hand and Nurse Dorothea calls on him to talk. "I think I take it for granted whenever I get a smart idea. We are a product of our culture so new ideas we may get are built upon many other people's ideas that came before us. I need to be more grateful for all the people who blazed a trail in front of me to help me get to where I need to be mentally."

"Culture helps us so much. You're right, we need to be more grateful for the people who came before us to help us get to where we are now," says Nurse Dorothea.

Maria raises her hand and Nurse Dorothea calls on her to talk. "I think I don't appreciate the creative spark within me enough. I need to nurture it so that it can blossom and help me create more amazing things."

"Creativity is fun, and we should nurture it," says Nurse Dorothea.

"We have gone over a lot of material. I would like you to refresh yourselves. We'll start again shortly after our break. For those watching the show or reading the book, feel free to stop here and start the next part when you are ready."

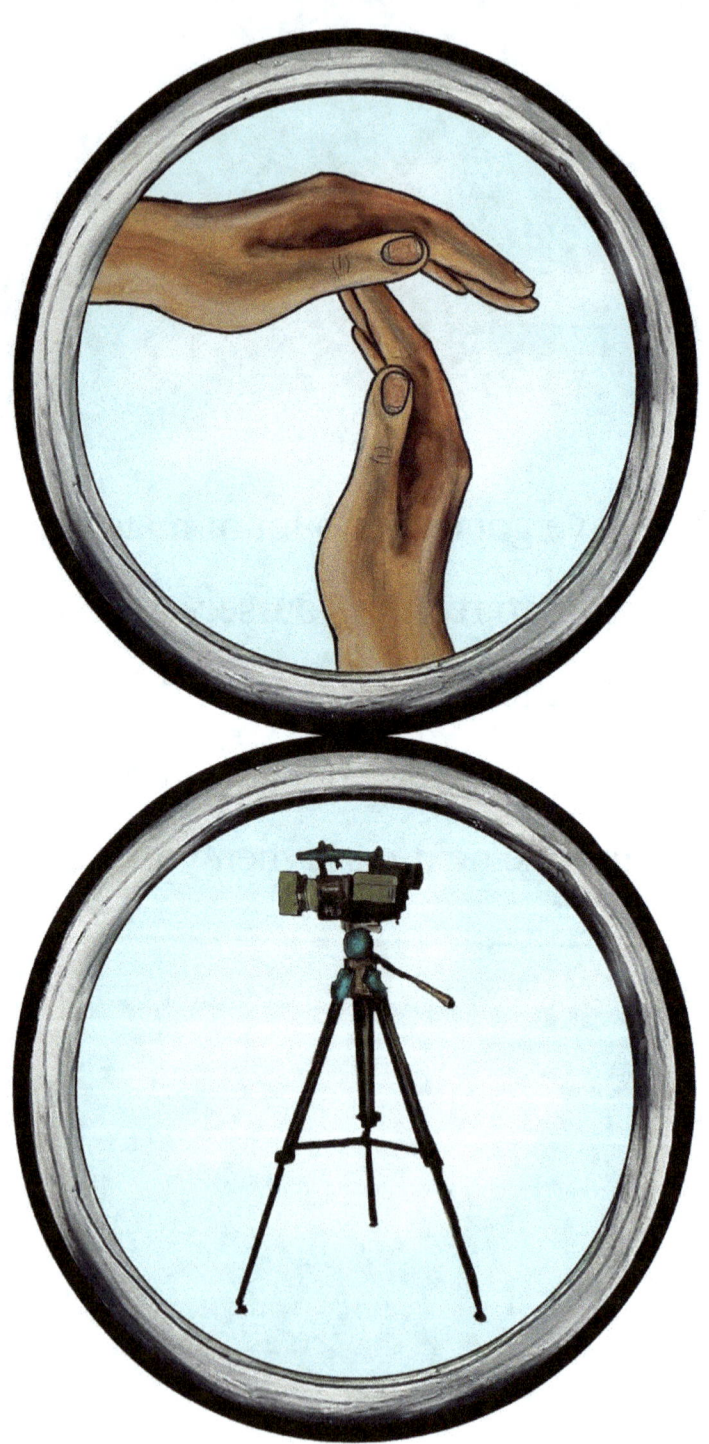

Part 4

"Welcome back. I know that being taken for granted might feel like you are being rejected. Some people feel like they are puppets with someone else trying to control their movements or even their thoughts. Other people may feel like their efforts are wasted and they may feel lonely. I would like us to brainstorm together to think of ways that would help us prevent taking other people and things for granted."

Diwa raises her hand and Nurse Dorothea calls on her to talk. "I think doing something simple like practicing gratitude for others and what they do could help. We should say thank you a lot to show our appreciation."

"Great idea!" says Nurse Dorothea.

Kenji raises his hand and Nurse Dorothea calls on him to talk. "I think if we slow down in life, then maybe we can stop and recognize the importance of the things in our life. There is an old saying that my grandfather says, 'You need to stop and smell the flowers.' I think slowing down will help us observe the things in front of us and around us. I don't think we need to always travel slowly, but sometimes it could be beneficial."

"I like it! Stopping to smell the flowers can be a good thing," says Nurse Dorothea.

Frida raises her hand and Nurse Dorothea calls on her to talk. "I think slowing down with some things to try to understand them better is important. We should try to understand the people around us and the things that enter our lives."

"This reminds me of an old religious saying, 'Seek to understand more than to be understood'," says Nurse Dorothea.

Antonio raises his hand and Nurse Dorothea calls on him to talk. "I think having a gratitude journal could be a good idea. Maybe we could write things at the end of the day that cause any type of feeling of thankfulness. Also, we could write things that should have caused feelings of thankfulness to help us in our journey."

"A journal of gratitude to help remind you of things you have been and should be thankful for is a great idea!" says Nurse Dorothea.

Lian raises her hand and Nurse Dorothea calls on her to talk. "Maybe we should stop expecting others to do things for us. We should be appreciative for any little thing done for us and not feel entitled for many things to be done for us."

"You're correct that a feeling of entitlement can get in the way of gratitude which can lead to taking things for granted. Great input!" says Nurse Dorothea.

Awira raises her hand and Nurse Dorothea calls on her to talk. "If we are more frugal with our money and try to live within our means, then maybe we will not take things for granted in our society. We will also be able to buy more things that are important to us instead of possibly spending recklessly."

"Most of us will have to balance our budget every month or we will get into financial trouble. Thanks for sharing," says Nurse Dorothea.

Ekon raises his hand and Nurse Dorothea calls on him to talk. "If we stop focusing on ourselves, then maybe we won't take people and things for granted. There is a big wide world in front of us and we need to care of it."

"Thanks for thinking big. We need to care for the world we live in," says Nurse Dorothea.

Lian raises her hand and Nurse Dorothea calls on her to talk. "We should take time for others."

"You're right. To appreciate someone means you are making time for them and spending quality time to grow your relationship with them. It is important for people to feel they are a high priority compared to a hobby. Make time for your loved ones. It can be hard to develop and maintain a good work-life balance, but you can do it," says Nurse Dorothea.

Kalani raises her hand and Nurse Dorothea calls on her to talk. "Staying in the moment and practicing mindfulness could possibly help you to not take others for granted. This might happen since you may become more aware of your feelings which may include taking others for granted and having a lack of appreciation."

"I love mindfulness and think everyone should practice it," says Nurse Dorothea.

Connor raises his hand and Nurse Dorothea calls on him to talk. "Everyone and everything has value. We should think about that and tell them what they mean to us. It is more than complimenting them. It is about telling them how valuable they are in your life."

"I love it! Great idea!" says Nurse Dorothea.

Levi raises his hand and Nurse Dorothea calls on him to talk. "I think it is important to set clear personal boundaries and to respect other people's boundaries. Some people have physical boundaries that they don't want others to get too close. There are also conversational boundaries beyond which some people do not want to engage with others. Discover boundaries and try to respect them all."

"That makes a lot of sense," says Nurse Dorothea.

Fatima raises her hand and Nurse Dorothea calls on her to talk. "We should speak up and be assertive. We should let others speak up and share their thoughts. Communication is necessary for a proper functioning society."

"Great point!" says Nurse Dorothea.

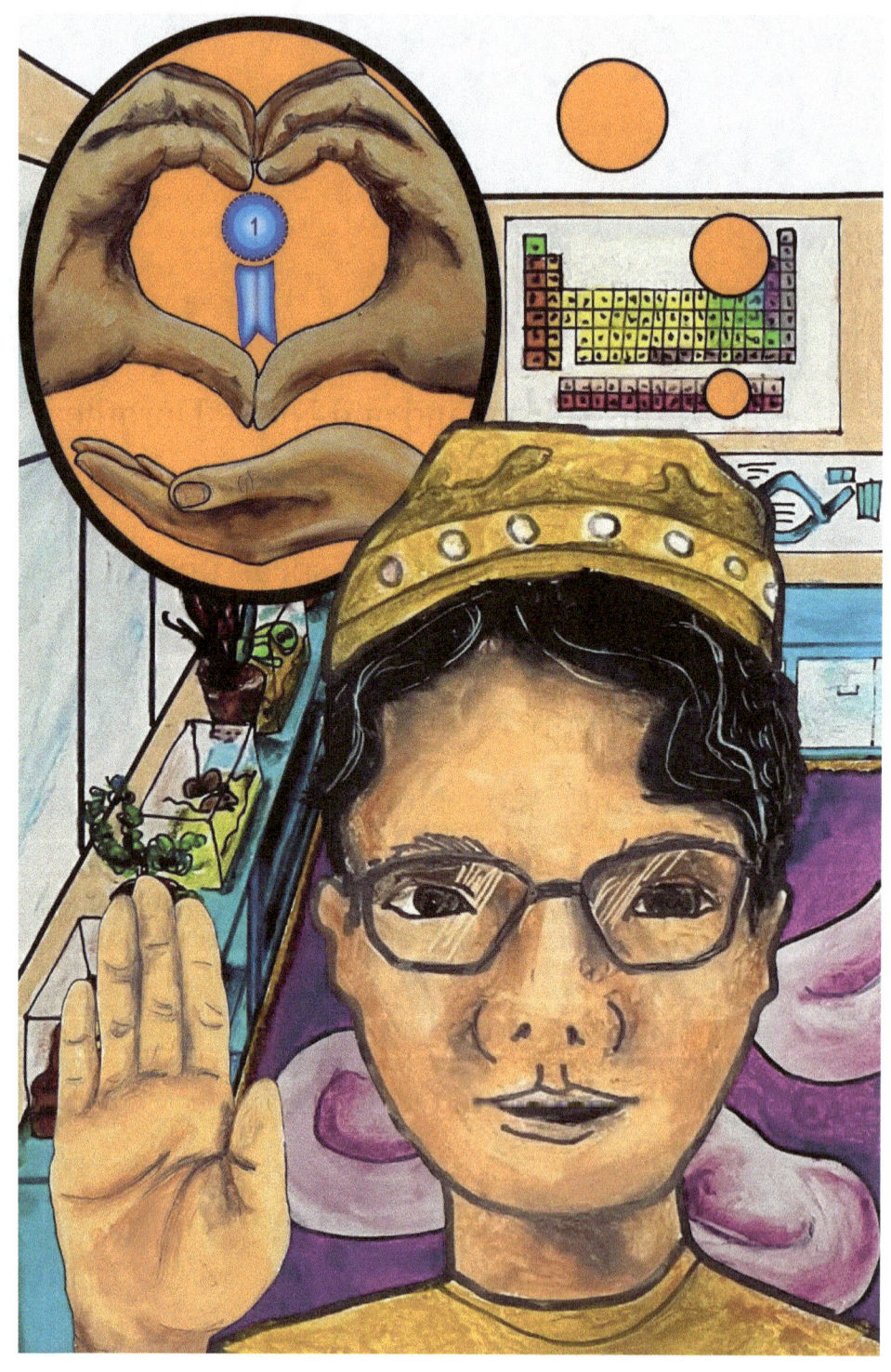

Azamat raises his hand and Nurse Dorothea calls on him to talk. "We should reward the gratefulness that others display. Rewarded behavior may occur more frequently according to psychology, so we should reward those that thank ourselves and others."

"That's great for bringing in a field of study that can help us understand people. To understand our world, we must understand how things work," says Nurse Dorothea.

Juniper raises her hand and Nurse Dorothea calls on her to talk. "I want to improve communication. Communication is a skill, and I try to write and speak more fluently with each passing year. I'm not there yet, but I'm on a journey of excellence, and I hope to be a role model in efficient communication. If we speak well, then we can properly show our appreciation to others through relevant words."

"Words are important, and they are a gift from society. Let us be thankful for this gift," says Nurse Dorothea.

Wyatt raises his hand and Nurse Dorothea calls on him to talk. "I think we should avoid overcommitting ourselves to people and things. If we overcommit, we will have less time to give to our loved ones and that may make them feel less important than how our heart feels. Commitment is a resource in life and if we overuse it, other things in life may go into disrepair."

"Great thinking!" says Nurse Dorothea.

Amari raises his hand and Nurse Dorothea calls on him to talk. "We should return favors to people. If we always take time and things from others, then we give the strong appearance that we are not appreciative of their things and their time. By returning favors, we show they matter."

"I love it!" says Nurse Dorothea.

Amisha raises her hand and Nurse Dorothea calls on her to talk. "A person should work on themselves and help themselves grow in all the realms of life. If we take care of ourselves, then we may need people a little less since we are properly nurtured. Sometimes, we are own best advocates and helpers."

"Nurturing and growing ourselves like a plant. Interesting idea!" says Nurse Dorothea.

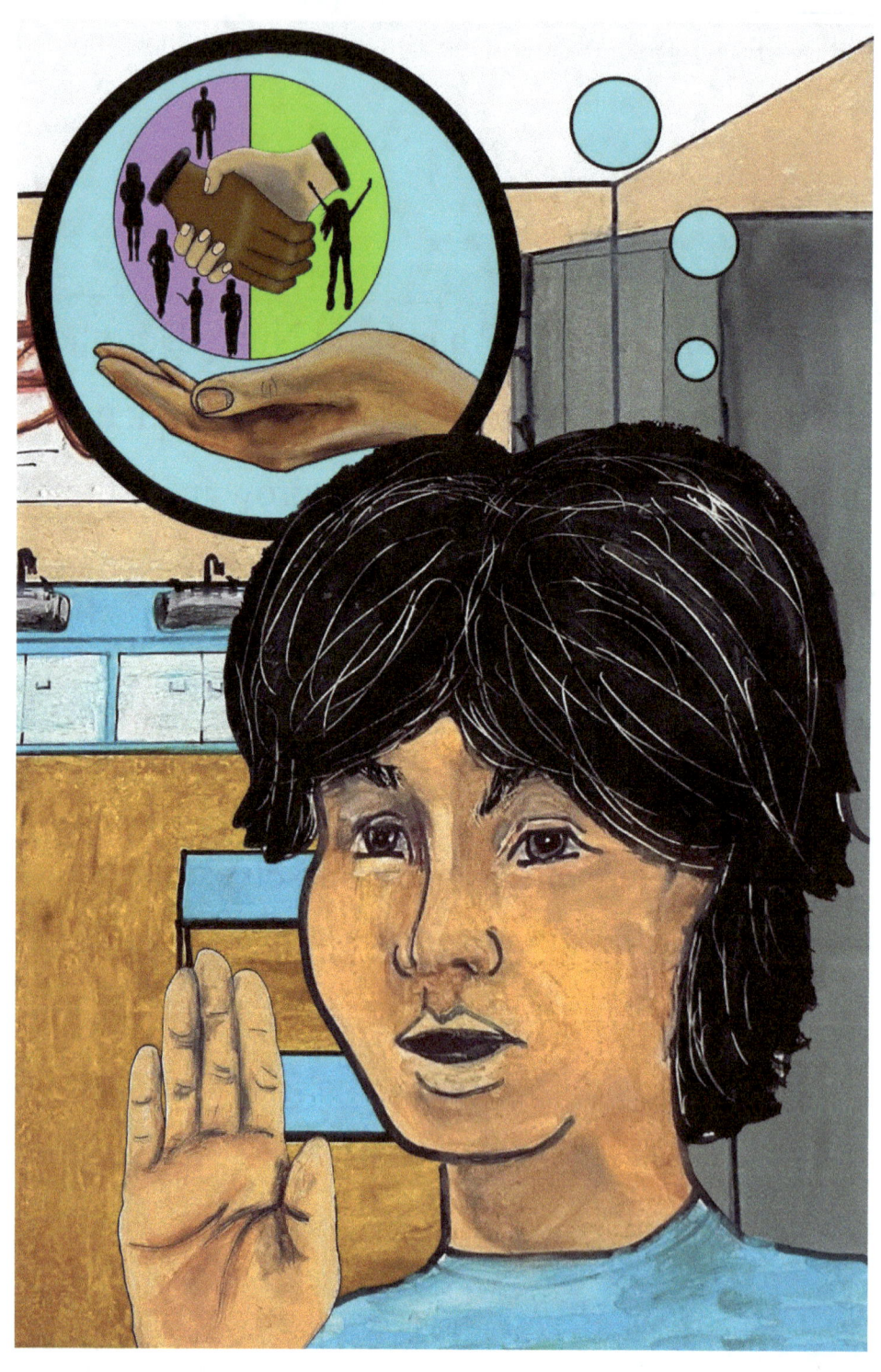

Ji Ho raises his hand and Nurse Dorothea calls on him to talk. "Respect others and respect yourself."

"We can all learn from each other so respecting each other is key," says Nurse Dorothea.

Pia raises her hand and Nurse Dorothea calls on her to talk. "My parents have taught me to be a good example, so role modeling gratitude for others could help others not take me for granted."

"Sometimes, you have to be the change you want to see in the world," says Nurse Dorothea.

Dmitry raises his hand and Nurse Dorothea calls on him to talk. "To combine some ideas, I think communication and boundaries are important. I think we should learn to clearly communicate our boundaries to others. Maybe a person might do things to take us for granted because they don't know what we need."

"Learning that others don't know us completely is part of life, and our journey includes sharing things about ourselves with others," says Nurse Dorothea.

Yuliana raises her hand and Nurse Dorothea calls on her to talk. "I think we should show appreciation through actions more than words. People will feel it more and possibly even be able to touch our show of appreciation."

"Tangible pieces of appreciation are important. Most of us have received gifts to open and touch, and I think we can all say that makes us feel good to get something that someone has put thought and care into," says Nurse Dorothea.

Kenji raises his hand and Nurse Dorothea calls on him to talk. "I think we should learn to say 'no' when it is needed."

"This also touches on the idea of communication and setting clear boundaries. Saying the word 'no' can be hard for some people and it should be practiced whenever appropriate," says Nurse Dorothea.

Diwa raises her hand and Nurse Dorothea calls on her to talk. "We need to practice kindness. Being kind helps others as well as ourselves."

"You're correct. Being kind seems to give us a feeling of goodness and goodwill. Being kind can transform others and ourselves," says Nurse Dorothea.

Maria raises her hand and Nurse Dorothea calls on her to talk. "I want to learn to reframe negative thoughts. Maybe, sometimes when I think people are taking me for granted, they really are not, so I need to be able to reframe the thoughts and situation into a different reality which may be closer to true reality."

"Good point! Finding true reality can be elusive though, since some of the stars we see in the sky have already died, but we get to still enjoy their light," says Nurse Dorothea.

Gustavo raises his hand and Nurse Dorothea calls on him to talk. "Maybe if someone is in a relationship where one person feels they are being taken for granted, they should both go see a couples counselor or family counselor so that their issues can be jointly resolved."

"Great point! Sometimes we need an outside observer to help navigate us through difficult emotions," says Nurse Dorothea.

Frida raises her hand and Nurse Dorothea calls on her to talk. "I like to give compliments to my friends. I think saying nice things to people will help keepme from taking them for granted."

"Complimenting others is free and should be done generously," says Nurse Dorothea.

Antonio raises his hand and Nurse Dorothea calls on him to talk. "Partners should spend time rekindling love."

"Love can be like a flame, and if the winds are too strong, then sometimes love may flicker gently. Love should be protected like a candle in the wind. Don't take your partner's love for granted," says Nurse Dorothea.

Awira raises her hand and Nurse Dorothea calls on her to talk. "Maybe sometimes, people in a family could take over the chores of others so that they can learn the struggles or frustrations that the others may have to deal with every day."

"Great idea! We should all do that," says Nurse Dorothea.

Ekon raises his hand and Nurse Dorothea calls on him to talk. "Maybe people could read stories from the past about how bad relationships can become, so that they gain appreciation for each other and what they have together."

"Great thinking! Comparing one situation to another can help people reframe things and give insight into their situation," says Nurse Dorothea.

Lian raises her hand and Nurse Dorothea calls on her to talk. "How about giving gifts to each other?"

"Great idea! Maybe for our last club meeting of the year, we will exchange gifts," says Nurse Dorothea.

Kalani raises her hand and Nurse Dorothea calls on her to talk. "I think by doing fun things together, it may help prevent us from taking each other for granted."

"That's great that you are being ambiguous with your idea and not saying it will definitely prevent you from taking others for granted. Maybe one of you will do a research project in the future to determine if there is a strong correlation between these two factors. For example, if someone does one fun thing a week with another person, will they show behavior that does not take the other person for granted?" says Nurse Dorothea.

Connor raises his hand and Nurse Dorothea calls on him to talk. "I think we should be thankful for every day that we are given."

"Gratitude is a key to help not take things like life for granted," says Nurse Dorothea.

Levi raises his hand and Nurse Dorothea calls on him to talk. "I think we should avoid fighting."

"Good point! It would be best to live in a world where we choose the win-win option for everyone. It can be hard to find and see, but if you can find it and do it, then it is worth it," says Nurse Dorothea.

Fatima raises her hand and Nurse Dorothea calls on her to talk. "I plan to say, 'I love you' often to the people I love."

"Some people were not raised to do that so it may be against the culture they were brought up in, so don't judge someone negatively just because they may not say it often. You be you, and let others be themselves and hopefully, we find the best common ground," says Nurse Dorothea.

Azamat raises his hand and Nurse Dorothea calls on him to talk. "I want to cherish the moments I am a part of. This life is amazing!"

"Some people have been through some difficult times, so it may be hard for them to see life as amazing. Try not to judge these people negatively either. You be you, and let others be themselves," says Nurse Dorothea.

Juniper raises her hand and Nurse Dorothea calls on her to talk. "I want to try to not worry about things that are not in my control. Doing this could take time and energy away from other important things so I should manage the things in my little world."

"Some would say that this idea you are discussing is managing what is in your sphere of influence. Influence what you can in a positive way, and let other things in other systems do what they are supposed to do," says Nurse Dorothea.

Wyatt raises his hand and Nurse Dorothea calls on him to talk. "We should avoid complaining about things we don't have. We should focus on being positive about the things we do have and work for things we would like to have."

"Again, we are bringing up the idea of being grateful for the things that we are given," says Nurse Dorothea.

Amari raises his hand and Nurse Dorothea calls on him to talk. "Maybe we take things for granted because we are not happy so what if we do something every day that makes us happy."

"Great idea! Self-care is important," says Nurse Dorothea.

Amisha raises her hand and Nurse Dorothea calls on her to talk. "If we try to see the good in a situation or person, maybe we won't take the situation or person for granted."

"Good idea!" says Nurse Dorothea.

Dmitry raises his hand and Nurse Dorothea calls on him to talk. "What if we live everyday as our last. Would we take others for granted?"

"Great idea and great research project!" says Nurse Dorothea.

Ekon raises his hand and Nurse Dorothea calls on him to talk. "Maybe being happy you are alive is important to not taking others for granted."

"Remember again, that some people have been through some difficult situations and they are not happy to be alive so to ask them to think like this would not be fair. If you can do it, then you should, and if it is hard to do, then maybe you could surround yourself with others that have the joy of life," says Nurse Dorothea.

Juniper raises her hand and Nurse Dorothea calls on her to talk. "I think if we find ourselves taking others for granted, we could try coping skills like deep breathing."

"Great point! Coping skills can help with more than just anxiety and depression," says Nurse Dorothea.

Kenji raises his hand and Nurse Dorothea calls on him to talk. "Maybe by finding the joy in the ordinary things of life, we can insulate our mind from starting to take things for granted."

"This is a hard one, but can be done," says Nurse Dorothea.

Awira raises her hand and Nurse Dorothea calls on her to talk. "Maybe we should look for magic in life. If we see things as special, then maybe we won't take them for granted."

"Einstein once said, 'You can see everything as a miracle or nothing as a miracle.' Living life in the miracle of life is a special place to live and we should find a way to get there," says Nurse Dorothea.

"I'd like to share some quotes to inspire you to not take things and people for granted."

"Don't let yesterday take up too much of today," by Will Rogers.

"Gratitude turns what we have into enough," by Anonymous.

"We often take for granted the very things that most deserve our gratitude," by Cynthia Ozick."

"The secret to happiness is not found in seeking more, but in developing the capacity to enjoy less," by Socrates.

"The things you take for granted, someone else is praying for," by Anonymous.

"Gratitude makes sense of our past, brings peace for today, and creates a vision for tomorrow," by Melody Beattie.

"Appreciate what you have before it turns into what you had," by Anonymous.

"Enjoy the little things; one day, you may look back and realize they were the big things," by Robert Brault.

"It's a funny thing about life, once you begin to take note of the things you are grateful for, you begin to lose sight of what you lack," by Germany Kent.

"And the last quote I'd like to share is:"

"When you arise in the morning, think of what a precious privilege it is to be alive – to breathe, to think, to enjoy, to love," by Marcus Aurelius.

"I want to thank you for attending today's presentation. I hope you learned a lot and will share this information with others. Don't only focus on your own mental health journey, but also help others on their journey to good mental health."

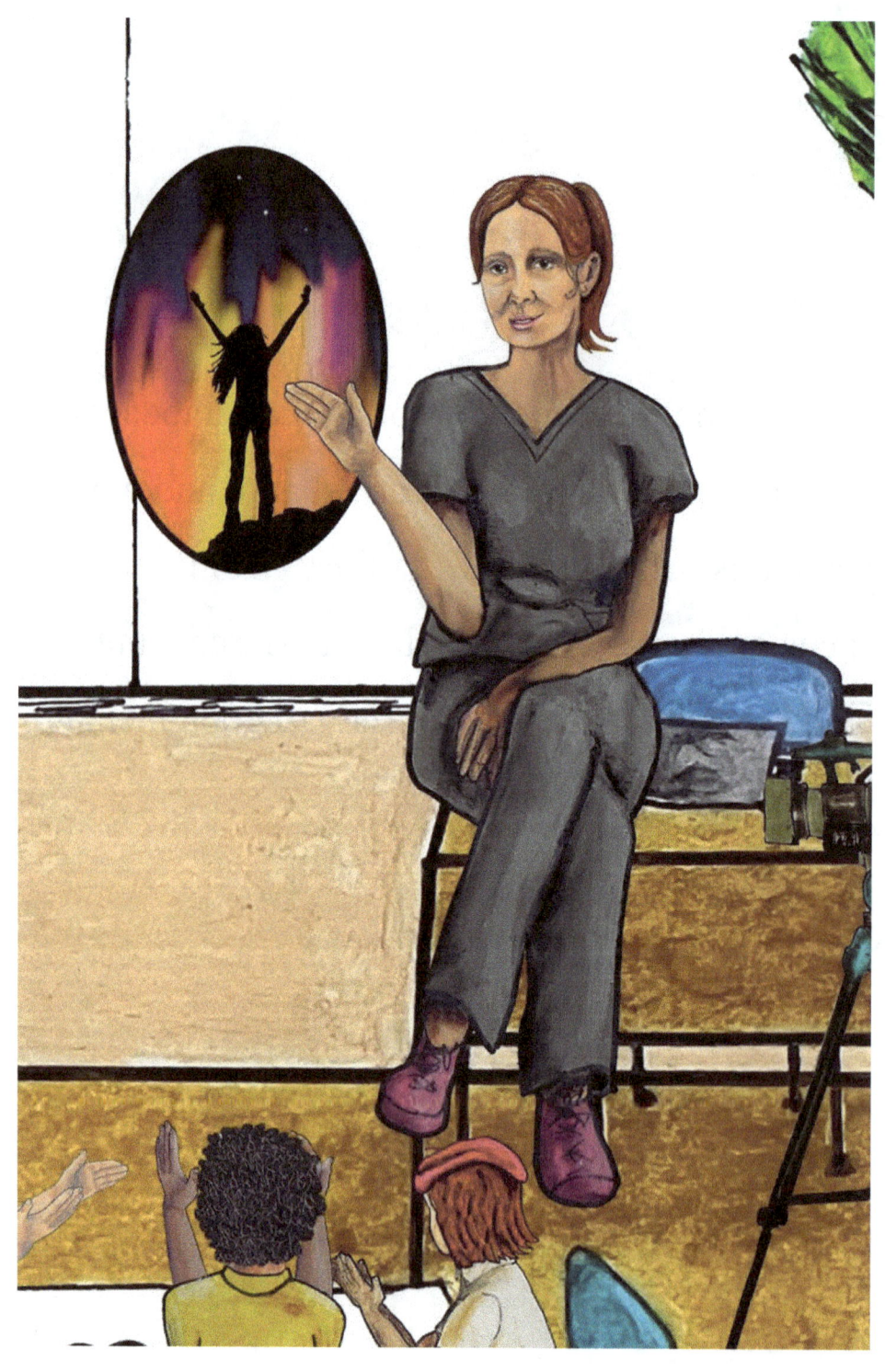

The class starts to clap, and many students say, "Thank you, Nurse Dorothea." Some come up to the nurse after the class is dismissed and give her a big hug telling her how much she helped them.

References

Anderson, J. (2023). How to Not Take Someone for Granted. Retrieved from: https://www.josephwriteranderson.com/blog/how-to-not-take-someone-for-granted

AzCaptions. (2023). 33 Quotes About Not Taking Things For Granted! Retrieved from: https://azcaptions.com/quotes-about-not-taking-things-for-granted/

Cambridge.org. (2024). Take something for granted. Retrieved from: https://dictionary.cambridge.org/us/dictionary/english/take-for-granted

Davenport, B. (2023). Are You Being Taken For

Granted In Your Relationship? 17 Ways To Put A Stop To It. Retrieved from: https://liveboldandbloom.com/11/relationships/taken-for-granted

Donvito, T. (2024). 14 Subtle Signs You're Being Taken for Granted-and What to Do About It." Retrieved from: https://www.rd.com/list/signs-youre-being-taken-for-granted/

Healey, J. (2018). Don't Take Life for Granted: 5 Notes to Inspire Pure Gratitude. Retrieved from: https://healingbrave.com/blogs/all/dont-take-life-for-granted

Huijer, H. (2023). 5 Ways to Not Take Things for Granted (and Why This Matters!). Retrieved from: https://www.trackinghappiness.com/how-to-not-take-things-for-granted/

Morin, A. (2023). 7 Things to Do When You Are Feeling Unappreciated. Retrieved from: https://www.verywellmind.com/7-things-to-do-if-you-feel-unappreciated-5081881

PoemVerse. (n.d.). Poems About Taking Someone for Granted: A Reflection on Lost Love. Retrieved from: https://poemverse.org/poems-about-taking-someone-for-granted/

Saha, W. (2023). Cherish Every Moment: The Importance of Not Taking Life For Granted. Retrieved from: https://www.selfmasterytips.com/not-taking-life-for-granted/

Tiodar, A. (2023). 27 Things We Take For Granted (This Will Make You Appreciate Life). Retrieved from: https://subconsciousservant.com/things-we-take-for-granted/

Weiss, S. (2016). Hot To Avoid Taking Your Partner For Granted. Retrieved from: https://www.bustle.com/articles/186473-how-to-avoid-taking-your-partner-for-granted-because-the-excitement-doesnt-

have-to-fade

About the Illustrator

Lindsay acquired her BFA from Columbus College of Art and Design. She was a self-employed metal artist beginning in 1985 and was part of the American Arts and crafts movement of the late 80's and early 90's with an art piece on permanent collection at the White House and the governor's mansion in Ohio. The majority of the works she sold then were done in metal, either soldered or welded. During that time, she spent 5 years serving on the board of Ohio Designer Craftsmen and networked part of her business through them. She sold many of her works through art galleries across the USA and Japan. She did many individual commissions and was also commissioned to do giftware design through Bath and Body Works, i.e., the Limited, in the year 2000.

In 2008, Lindsay went back to college to acquire another degree so she could try her hand at teaching high school art. She acquired a M.Ed. from U of A. She taught art at 6 different schools in AZ before retiring in 2022. In her last 4 years, she taught: Art 1, Advanced Art, AP Art, Ceramics, Advanced Ceramics, and Photography I, II, III, and IV (which was also producing the school's yearbook). Several of her students were recipients of HAA Art scholarships. During her first year of teaching at public schools, she taught Graphic Design. All this time, she enjoyed making art with her students and building her illustration, drawing, and painting skills.

During those teaching years she still accomplished a few commissions of steel sculptures. It started with the first commission from Norton Abrasives of creating the company's mascot. It was a larger-than-life French bulldog named Cooper. Cooper resides at the company's US headquarters in Brownsville TX. The mascot had long lines during one trade show of people wanting to take selfies with it. It was a hit and resulted in a personal commission for a couple in Los Angeles of another bulldog named Sebastian.

When Lindsay retired in 2022, she worked with an old friend in Ohio who is an author and performer on a children's book. All the illustrations in the book including the cover were created by Lindsay. The book is for 0-8 year old children and is called "Sleep Little Raven".

Lindsay has kept a blog since 2008 showing the progress of her works at www.curlycu.com.

In Lindsay's words:
"Making art is like breathing; it is a must for my own survival and sanity."

About the Author

Michael is married to Perla in Tucson, AZ. Michael served in the US Air Force between 2002 and 2010 as an Electronic Warfare Officer on the EC-130H Compass Call and deployed 6 times in the Global War on Terror. Michael then served 8 years as an Army Wounded Warrior Advocate. Michael used his GI bill to go to nursing school and works as an RN at an inpatient psychiatric hospital in Tucson, AZ. Michael enjoys listening to Beethoven and reading a lot of news.

Michael's college education:

B.A. in Psychology from Auburn University,

B.S. in Biology from the University of Alabama at Birmingham,

M.S. in Management from Troy University,

Master in Health Administration from the University of Phoenix,

M.S. from the University of Arizona through the accelerated Master's Entry to the Profession of Nursing program

Other Books by Dow Creative Enterprises®

Visit www.DowCreativeEnterprises.com for more information

www.ingramcontent.com/pod-product-compliance
Lightning Source LLC
Chambersburg PA
CBHW050731240426
43664CB00054B/2383